"I hope for nothing. I fear nothing. I am free."
—*Nikos Kazantzakis*

Michael Paradise at the grave of Nikos Kazantzakis

In memory of Michael. Your dream did come true.
May your memory be eternal, agapé mou.

Michael Paradise, 1927–2016

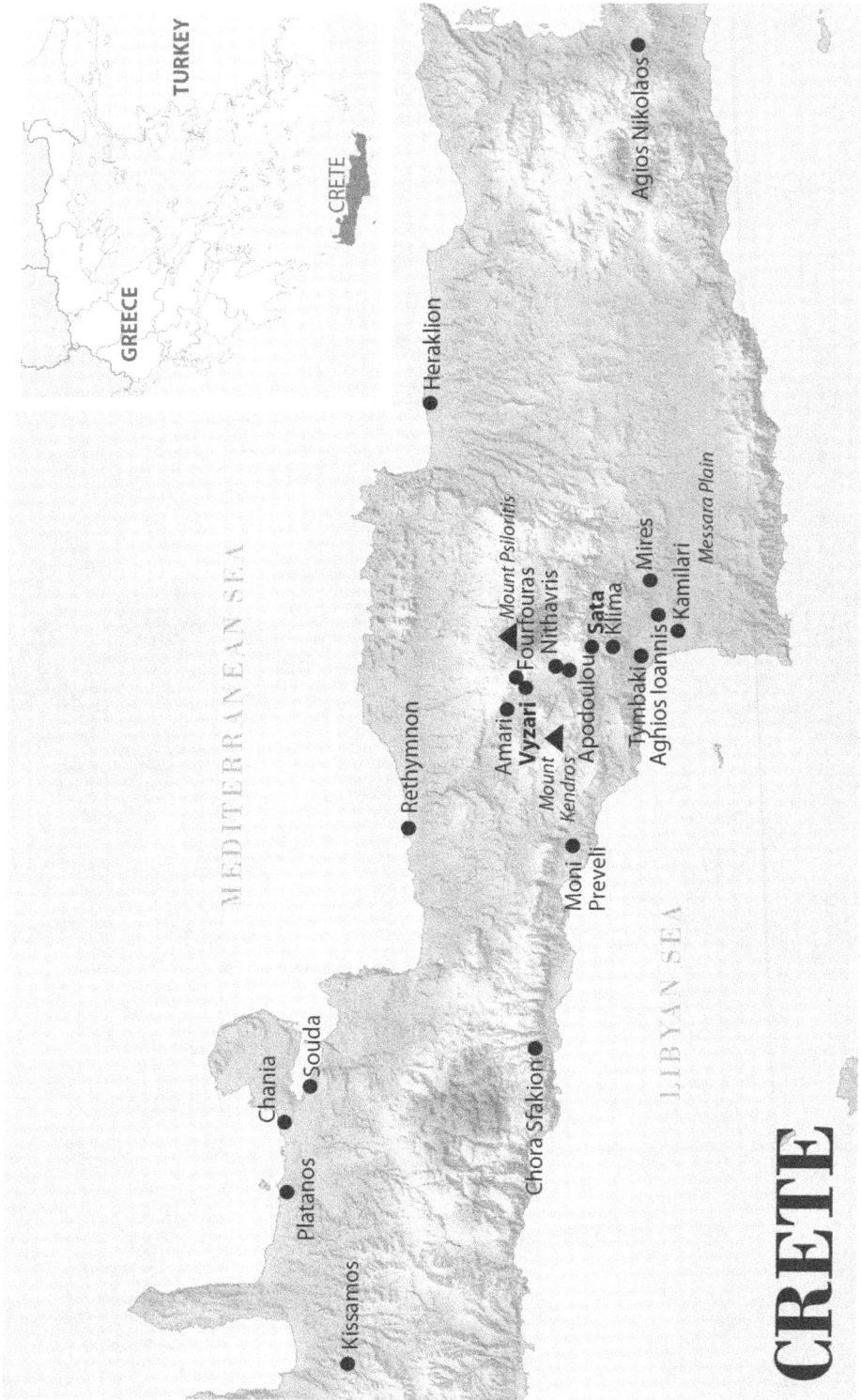

GREECE

CRETE

MEDITERRANEAN SEA

Heraklion

Agios Nikolaos

Rethymnon

Mount Psiloritis

Amari

Vyzari

Mount
Kendros

Fourfouras

Nithavris

Apodoulou

Sata
Klima

Mires

Kamilari

Messara Plain

Tymbaki

Aghios Ioannis

Moni
Preveli

Chania

Souda

Platanos

Chora Sfakion

Kissamos

LIBYAN SEA

CRETE

When War Came to PARADISE

BY MICHAEL PARADISE

APPRECIATION

To my kind and beautiful wife, Ann,
who faithfully read and reread each story and provided
critical assistance in proofreading and editing them.

Were they alive, I would have loved to thank my mother,
Maria Paradisanou, for the grand lady and great mother she was,
and my father Manolis Paradisanos, my Uncles Kostas and Yiannis
Paradisanos, and the dear Sphinx-like Colonel Tom Dunbabin
for the opportunities they provided for me when I was a teenager.
I was a lucky man to have had such mentors.

Published by Prairiesummer Books, Frederick, S.D.

Book design by Heidi Marttila-Losure

Cover photo credits:
Photo of Vyzari by Terry Moyemont
Photo of German paratroopers from Arthur Conry via Wikipedia

ISBN-10: 0-9848907-1-8

ISBN-13: 978-0-9848907-1-2

Printed in the United States of America

CONTENTS

PART FOUR: Consequences

INTRODUCTION

I n an earth-shattering war that pits giant powers against giant powers, historians and writers tend to concentrate on the actions of the Giants. Small nations caught in those wars are paid scant attention, if any; but the sufferings of their people are as great as or greater than the miseries endured by those who experience the depredations of war in the countries of the major powers.

In this memoir I revisit my boyhood on a fabled island in one of the smallest nations involved in the Second World War: Greece. But I am certain that my experiences reflect the contributions, sacrifices and hardships of the people in any one of those small countries.

I was born and reared in the mountains of Crete, the largest of the Greek islands. With the islands around it, Crete is the southernmost European land. The island is the fabled realm of the ancient Minoans, and of the alleged Labyrinth, Minotaur and the first humans to fly, Dédelos and his son Íkaros.

I grew up in the unsettling and grievously bitter atmosphere of the almost nefarious, dysfunctional marriage of my parents, in a little village tucked away in a corner of the incongruously beautiful Amári Valley. While in my teens I became an active observer of the events of World War II Europe. Then, when the Germans conquered Crete, I joined the covert British intelligence group that had secretly slipped onto the island by submarine to spy on and organize resistance to the German Nazi forces.

When I was 15 years old, I was apprehended by the Gestapo and evaded execution by escaping. I was 16 when I witnessed the SS interrogating my mother, and 18 when, with the Cretan partisans and British agents, I celebrated the fall of the Nazis.

Following the liberation of Crete, I received two citations from the British Government for activities during the war: One for assisting Allied forces, after the Battle of Crete, to "escape from or avoid capture by the enemy, and a second for services rendered to the war effort as a member of the Allied intelligence network (Advance Force 133) that "contributed to the liberation of Europe."

After the war I completed my high school studies, which I had been forced to abandon for almost five years due to the war. I then entered the Greek Air Force Academy and was trained as a pilot at Randolph Air Force Base in San Antonio, Texas. Returning to Greece, I served as an assistant to the Minister of Reconstruction, one of the members of the country's governing Cabinet.

At the invitation of relatives in Sioux City, Iowa, I came to America to study engineering. Following the launch of the Soviet Union's *Sputnik* satellite, however, America went into overdrive in an effort to reach the moon before Russia. The aeronautical industry raided schools for capable mathematicians, and many schools lost their math teachers to industry. Thus I found myself, although a foreign student, teaching mathematics in a small Nebraska high school. (While there, I met my wife, Ann Ramos of Mitchell, South Dakota. We were married in 1957 and had three children: Maria, George, and Andrew.)

To my surprise, I fell in love with teaching and continued to do so. I served as a high school teacher and principal, college and university mathematics professor, college president, university chancellor, and executive director of an international college consortium based in the National Center for Higher Education in Washington, D.C.

This book is not an autobiography. I simply wish to recount the major events in my life before coming to America, as I remember them. They are enriched by an intimate knowledge of the then-prevailing socioeconomic, political, and other conditions and trends, as well as by what I have been told, read, or researched. This is especially so in the reconstruction of event details and in developing dialogue.

Emotions in personal and family relationships, as well as in politics, always run high on the island. From my numerous trips to Crete, I have realized that even though most of the events I describe herein occurred some seventy years ago, the associated emotions live on in the island's elders and in their progeny as intensely as ever, if not more so. In order to prevent any embarrassment or animosity, I have at times changed the names of some persons, villages, or locations of events.

In recollecting events after all those years, the memory often plays games with us. So, in writing this book, I have been careful to double-check my recollections. Still, after more than seventy years, what happened and what had been said had to be reconstructed. I used my deep familiarity with the people, circumstances, and political and social conditions to be as close to the actual happenings as possible.

In recreating this portrait of people caught in the machinations of powerful, controlling, and destructive outside forces, I hope to inspire in the reader a deeper understanding and compassion for the millions of dwellers in our world's small countries who continue to suffer greatly at the hands of giants—including our own.

PART ONE

TORTURE

The Gestapo at the Door
A bit of trouble

It must be well after midnight when a sharp crack from the splintered wooden door-latch awakens me. Through the now open kitchen door a few uniformed men with their side-arms drawn burst into the room. Coming to a sitting position, I face the front end of their guns. Recognizing their uniforms, I realize they are Gestapo officers.

It is the winter of 1942-43. I'm a fifteen-year-old teenager living at our farmhouse in the hamlet of Sáta, a tiny settlement of subsistence farmers, in Amári, a remote central mountainous area on the island of Crete. My village of Vyzári lies north from there, about four-plus hours on foot, depending on my donkey's load and how well it negotiates the rough donkey path on the difficult and onerous terrain.

It was close to the middle of the Second World War, in late May 1941, when after a hard and nasty ten-day battle, the German Nazis forces took over the Island of Crete—my island. They had defeated the British Anzac (Australian and New Zealander) expeditionary forces sent there by Churchill, the war-time British prime minister, to defend the island. That defeat ushered in one of the darkest periods in the well over 6,000 years of recorded history of that tortured land.

Soon, the adult men in our family joined the British intelligence group spying on the Nazi occupiers and supporting the mountain partisans fighting the Germans. As the oldest remaining male left in our family, I had to move to Sáta in order to cultivate our fields for needed grain for the bread of our family—my mother and my four younger siblings.

It is close to the tail-end of the planting season, and I'm bunking on the kitchen's large πεζούλα (pezúla). In the mountain villages on the island, the only heat in our homes during the cool rain season comes from the fireplace, so the kitchen becomes the most popular room in the house from late fall to early spring. Being the only member of our family in our farmhouse, I use the kitchen for my bedroom as well, with the wood fire burning most of the night.

The house had been built centuries ago by the Ottoman Turks, with the kitchen in its center. The form of the kitchen's floor looks roughly like an isosceles triangle. The east wall of the room forms the base of the triangle, while where the north and south walls meet form the vertex angle of the triangle, and that corner houses the fireplace.

A pezúla, always attached to a wall, takes the place of a bench for sitting or sleeping. The villagers are still served by only donkey paths; they have no way to bring large furniture to their settlements, even if they could afford it. They partly solve that problem by building pezúlas when they build their houses. Our farmhouse kitchen has two pezúlas, each starting next to the fireplace and attached to the north and south walls. A narrow pezúla, just for seating, is attached to the south wall, while the one attached to the north wall is much wider and can easily accommodate two sleeping adults.

When I sleep, I put an old blanket on it and then cover myself with another blanket—no pillow. I'm sleeping there when the unwelcome guests arrive. By habit, I keep lit the λύχνος (lýhnos)—a small tin-made contraption with a wick and fueled by olive oil. It serves as a sort of weak lamp—and it is weak.

The house had been built on sloping land, without first leveling the ground. In order to access the kitchen, the Germans have to negotiate a few steps from the narrow street to enter the front room of the house.

We always keep that door unlocked, and the doors to the rooms don't have locks—just wooden latches. Besides having an extra high ceiling, the front room has the παραθύρα (parathýra), a huge, unframed and never covered window. One standing by the parathýra, and gazing out, has the command of the whole area toward the southwest, all the way to the sea—the part of the Mediterranean Sea called the Libyan Sea. It is the best view from the hamlet.

Since the house rests on sloping ground, the other rooms have been built higher than the front room. A series of built-in pezúlas, like sort of a stadium's bleachers, lead from the front room to the rest of the rooms. In the front room the Germans face two doors. The east one leads to the quarters of a tailor and his family, who are temporarily staying in our house.

They ignore that door, and they directly advance to the north door— the kitchen's door. Even though it's unlocked, they break it. They do so for effect, I think later; their side arms were drawn for the same reason. They likely hoped those antics would scare me.

Later the spy ring operatives speculate that the Gestapo must have been informed by a traitor that the doors aren't locked, that I'm a kid, alone, and I'm sleeping. The informer must also have told them in what part of the house the family of a tailor is sleeping and that the tailor holds no interest to them.

The first advancing officer marches to my bunk, reaches out with his strong arm, grabs me by my old T-shirt with his powerful hand, hauls me off the bunk, and steadies me against one of the large wooden posts supporting the heavy clay roof. I'm short and just a skin-and-bones teen-ager, so it's an easy task for a mightily-built man.

Besides the T-shirt, I wear a pair of flimsy under-shorts. I instinc-tively lunge down for my short-pants lying on the clay floor, but before I'm able to reach them, the same brusque officer kicks me down and then shoves me back against the massive wooden pole—no pants. With seemingly pure hate in his face, he addresses me in fluent Greek.

"Where is your father?"

"I don't know."

He follows that by a generous hit against my face.

"Where is your Uncle Kóstas?"

"I don't know."

Another generous slap.

"Where is your Uncle Yiánnis?"

The same slap again.

"I don't know."

Slap.

"Where is the asýrmatos (wireless radio)?"

"I don't know."

Slap, slap.

This questioning proceeds at a leisurely pace, on and on—slowly, methodically. At times, he lets me stand by the pole for what I think must be several minutes, but it probably is just two or three minutes at a time. While I stand there, he plays with his gun, pretending that he will shoot me.

He attempts to let me know that he can kill me at any time he chooses to do so. The lieutenant has pages of names, and he takes his time reading them and asking for their whereabouts. He also takes his time hitting me and then shouting at me after each "I don't know."

The officer has a mean slight smile on his face after he hits me. His mean smile may be for effect, but I later think he actually hates me. Initially he beats me on the face with the palm of his hand, then changes to the back of his hands, and later uses the butt of his pistol against my body.

At times I fall from the force of the blows. The officer kicks me, but not very hard, as I'm lying on the floor, and then he sets me up against the pole again and continues with the questioning. Later I feel that even though the hits and kicks are painful, they have been designed to scare me but not to kill me—they want the information first, I guess.

Since I come to expect these questions, I listen but then I readily answer, "I don't know." Then the officer asks, "Where is Souris?"

The question surprises me. "Souris?" I ask without thinking.

I had met Souris, a Greek-Egyptian agent, just a couple weeks before and I am surprised that the Gestapo knows his name. The inquisitor, apparently seeing something in my surprise, thinks that my reaction finally signals an opening. His face becomes relaxed and eager as he says with some expectation in his voice, "Yes, Nikos Souris." By that time I have recovered my senses. "I don't know," I reply, and his face registers his disappointment.

There isn't a clock in the house, but I later estimate that this interrogation lasts a lot longer than an hour. At some point I lose the ability to feel the punishment. I either don't feel it or I don't remember it afterwards. Yet, I have the presence of mind to occasionally chance some glances at the rest of the officers. My short stature, small-boned frame, and very lean body contribute to a more youthful appearance. Still, the Gestapo officers just stand by motionless, for such a long time, not voicing a single word while watching this brute do his work.

At the end of the list of names, the Gestapo officer makes sure I'm steadied against the pole and takes a stance a few feet from me. He points his pistol at me and tells me that he will count up to a number—now, I think it is ten but I don't really remember. "If you will not give me the information I want," he tells me, "I will shoot you." The officer starts counting, leaving what appear to me to be long pauses between the numbers, while eyeing me with a fierce expression. I notice again the hate in his eyes, as he is holding his sidearm ready to fire.

Watching him and gazing at the barrel of the pistol, I have no doubt that the officer is going to shoot me. I'm unafraid of dying. It seems strange to feel no fear, but I'm willing to die for the cause of the resistance against the occupiers. Looking at the bore of this barbarian's gun, even in my sad stupor, or because of it, I feel proud that he is going to kill me because he is unable to get the information he wants.

One of the things I had learned during my association with the British members of the clandestine military intelligence service on the island is to distinguish the ranks of the German officers. I have established that my tormentor is a lieutenant, while the officer of the highest rank among of the other officers is a major; so he is the commanding officer in this group. At some point, in the long pauses between numbers, as I'm standing by the pole with blood soaking up my flimsy underclothes, I happen to make more than fleeting eye-contact with the major.

Almost immediately the major addresses the lieutenant and the pistol comes down. I think I see in the inquisitor's eyes a fleeting moment of disappointment. Worn down and surprised, I fall on the floor from sheer exhaustion and fatigue—and, possibly, relief that I haven't been shot. Watching them from the floor, I see the major and my tormentor visiting for a few moments. Then, with a glee in his eyes and his mean smile back, the lieutenant tells me that they will be back to pick me up, and they all leave.

Shortly thereafter, one of the hamlet's senior women slips into the kitchen. By that time I have lifted myself up and I'm lying on the large pezúla. She looks at me and tears well up. "The German officer who seems to be in charge told me," she begins, "through the officer who speaks our language, to come to your house. I am instructed to mend you up as much as I can, clean, and get you dressed. Once that is done, I am to return to the square and report to them."

She peels off my bloody T-shirt and under-shorts, then begins to wash and rub my body with rakí, a strong local brew distilled from fermented grape stocks after most of the juice is extracted. The rakí and her careful but still firm rubbing hurt worse now than the pain from the beating.

While all this is going on, she briefs me on the situation. Her home is by the small square in the center of the hamlet, and theirs and the neighbors' barking dogs awakened her. When she ventured out, the Germans were coming into the square. They saw her, but they ignored her presence. The Germans congregated under and around the plátanos (a large plane tree) in the square. There were a few dozen soldiers and officers in the group.

Then almost all the officers and more than a dozen soldiers left, going in the direction of my house. The remaining two officers saw smoke coming from the chimney of her house, and realized that her kitchen would be warmer than the square, so both officers entered her house.

Having seen the officers going in the direction of my house, she was anxious to find out what is going on. She sensed the two officers in her kitchen were friendly.

Communicating by sign language, she asked them if she could go the stable and check on their oxen, as in the morning they will be cultivating. The officers, who seemed to know about the use of the oxen and the other details of how the villagers cultivate, indicated that she is free to move around the hamlet.

When she left the house, no one stopped her, and coming close to our house, she found that my house and the house of my neighbor (Manousákis), which are adjacent, had soldiers posted around them. Being free to roam around, she checked if the hamlet was encircled, and saw that it wasn't.

Then the Greek-speaking officer ordered her to come to my house. Coming to my house, she noticed the officers entering the Manousákis courtyard, and when she reached my house a German soldier was posted just outside the front door.

With the rubbing and massaging completed, my suffering from the beating is somewhat ebbing.

While she is dressing me up, I'm starting to feel alive, and another elderly lady walks in. She has news. "Besides you, they also have arrested Giórgis Tyrákis," she reports. "Giórgis with his hands tied has been brought to the square a few minutes ago. He appears to have been roughed up." And then, she adds, "I made a quick check. Your house and the Manousákis house aren't encircled, but there is a sentry on the street by your front door."

I have been surprised about Giórgis, as he hasn't been involved with the British spy ring nor with the antártes (the resistance partisans). He had eloped the year before with the beautiful teenage daughter of Manousákis. Since Giórgis' parents don't approve of that marriage, the couple lives at her parents' house, and he is staying close to his pregnant wife.

"Besides that sentry here, there are only two soldiers and an officer left," the newcomer goes on. Turning and facing the other woman, she continues, "They sit in your house drinking rakí and eating tiganites (fried batter) with your husband." Rakí has become the favored alcoholic drink of the German soldiers—they love it.

"Where are the others?" I ask.

"They left, going north toward Vathiakó, in a hurry right after bringing Giórgis to the square. I think the ones still here are waiting for you," she tells me. Vathiakó is another small hamlet, a few kilometers north of Sáta.

The fact that the German contingent is going north, toward the heart of the Amári area, bothers me. I suspect they might have the answers to some of the questions they had asked me. It now appears to me that Giórgis and I aren't the only targets of this Gestapo group. *This can't be a coincidence,* I think. Some informer must have apprised the Gestapo about the whereabouts of a number of the resistance leaders they had asked me about, who might be home this night. They have picked up Giórgis and me, and now they are going for more.

Just south of Sáta is a high hill, which I call the Sáta Hill. On the other side of that hill is the Messará Plain. The under-construction Tymbáki Air Force Base is in the middle of that plain and close to the shoreline. A few kilometers north from there lies the town of Míres where, I have been told, there is a Gestapo station. So, I surmise, the Gestapo team must be from Míres. Now, with this Gestapo team going north, I begin to be concerned, as I had known that the very first Gestapo raid to Sáta had come from an informant in the Messará Plain.

I feel especially worried about the village of Aghios Ioánnis (Saint John). Colonel Dunbabin, the senior military intelligence officer of the British spy group, my uncle Kóstas, the Cretan deputy to Dunbabin, and their main assistants are there this week. Even though they spend their time at Perdíki's Metóhi, a location away from the village and well camouflaged by nature, they would, two or three at a time, descend to the village for meals.

During my interrogation Dunbabin's name hadn't come up, but the names of Papadoyiánnis, my uncle Kóstas, and Aristédis Paradisanós had. Aristédis, a first cousin of my father, has been the asymartistís (wireless radio operator and cryptographer) of the spy ring's main base. Papadoyiánnis, a former governor of Crete and a prominent resistance leader now, has been in Aghios Ioánnis, his native village, during this week with his wife and young son.

When I put all this together in my mind, I feel that I must warn them. Since I am already thinking of trying to escape, I decide to try it immediately. "Go to the square to signal to the Germans that I am ready to be picked up," I tell the women. "But walk slowly." The women understand.

Sáta used to be an enclave of the Ottoman Turks, before the Ottoman Empire collapsed. When the Turks left, my paternal grandfather had purchased the properties of some of the well-to-do departing Turks. The house that came with those properties had become my grandparents' farmhouse. Before the war it had been the home of my two bachelor uncles, Kóstas and Yiánnis.

The main and oldest part of the house had been built with thick stone walls containing interlocking rooms, with no windows except the oversize parathýra in the front room—all of this for security reasons, during the Ottoman times. Even the kitchen doesn't have a single window. Light is provided only by a lýhnos, keeping the room in perpetual semidarkness.

Besides the now-broken door, there is a small opening at the corner of the room, where the north wall meets the wall forming the base of the triangle. That narrow opening provides access to the next room, which had been a quick and convenient sanctuary for the Turkish women, when men other than theirs had been present.

Later I reason out, with the help of my uncle Kóstas, that since the Germans hadn't checked the other rooms in the house, the informant must have told them exactly where they would find me, and that I'm the only person of interest to them in the house.

A narrow passageway from the kitchen leads into the stable via a back door. The stable, attached to the house, has three large rooms. The first room normally contains the chickens, goats, and sheep. A door leads to the next stable room, which is for the oxen and donkeys. That room has two additional doors. One leads to the aheróna—the áhera (straw) storage room—and a back door leads into the fields.

About two hundred yards from the house, the ground rises slightly. Since the hamlet isn't encircled by the Germans, I know that if I can make it to that rise, I will be safe. On the other side of the rise, a fairly steep field leads downward to a small creek, which cannot be seen from the hamlet. Once I'm over the crest of the rise my escape route isn't visible from the hamlet.

Using the interconnecting passages from the kitchen to the stables and then the back door of the second stable room, I walk out of the building. Part of the field I have to cross is visible from where the soldier is standing by our front door. There is no moon, but the sky isn't totally covered by clouds. In the semi-darkness of the night, I hope the sentry might be looking the other way, or if he sees me he wouldn't shoot as he hadn't been in the house and all the remaining villagers are free to move around. I decide to walk slowly.

回   回   回

Later, I find out that one of the ladies has stopped as she leaves our house, and by sign language is feigning that she needs some information from the sentry, thus distracting him from looking at my way. She tells me that she had asked (by sign language) the soldier if he wants some rakí to warm him up in the chill of the night—the soldier refused the offer.

My escape doesn't sit well with the officer who is in charge of the small group. Apparently, he must be a low-ranking one, possibly a non-commissioned officer, as he appears to be overtly frustrated and upset. After checking the house and realizing what has happened, he seems confused as to what to do next. The comment from one of the women had been that the officer, and his companions, had "too much raki, too early in the morning." Then, as they must have been instructed, they leave by foot, taking along the captive Giòrgis.

Before escaping, I take a few seconds to weigh my chances of reaching Aghios Ioánnis ahead of the Gestapo group.

Aghios Ioánnis is north of the hamlet, and between Sáta and the villages to the north stands a high, steep, and long hill. A few months before, a British war plane had hit that hill, and all of its crew members perished. On top of that hill the ruins of a Koulé, a fort built by the Ottoman Turks, silently remind us of past troubles. Turks had built the fort as a measure of safety for the Turkish population in that region during the frequent revolutions of the Cretans. The ridge of the hill is the highest and the most formidable one to ascend in the area. The Koulé Hill starts north of Sáta, a bit east of the Vathiakó hamlet. From Vathiakó the hill moves west and then turns south coming almost next to Rízikas, a hamlet straight west of Sáta.

Sáta is served by a donkey path going north or south, and it is out of the way of the main donkey "traffic." So one goes to Sáta if one has specific interest in that little settlement, which is nestled at the base of large high hills that enclose the hamlet from all directions, except from west-southwest.

The Germans had taken the only road going north, which goes through a narrow passage between the Koulé Hill and the foothills of Mount Psilorítis by the Vathiakó hamlet. In attempting to overtake the Germans I can't follow the same route as they. And going over the top of the Koulé Hill isn't an option. The only possibility for me is a small branch of the main north-south donkey road, going straight west from Sáta.

So, after reaching the gulley with the creek, I start running west on that road as fast as I can. I pass the hamlet of Rizikas, circle around the south end of the Koulé Hill, and on the other side of that hill I pick up another road.

My father told me later that some of the farmers feeding their oxen near Rízikas told him I had been "running like the wind." Others said I had been "like a scared rabbit." The latter was closer to the truth, I told him.

⊡   ⊡   ⊡

Life isn't easy for me. I work from daybreak to sunset every day, most of the year. Because I live all alone in our farm house, all the chores of daily life are mine. Day after day during the planting season, I cultivate the fields all alone, walking behind a plow pulled by two oxen. Following that I harvest crops and olives, this time with paid help. I walk up and down the never-ending steep hills, gullies and what I consider bottomless ravines. Since I now serve as a runner (courier) of the intelligence ring, I now occasionally move across those same hillsides, but at a run. That daily regimen has apparently hardened me for the physical punishment I can take and built up my endurance to move around fast and for long periods of time.

About two-thirds of the way from Sáta to Aghios Ioánnis, north of the Koulé Hill, stands the village of Apodoúlou (Apodúlu). It still is dark, when running uphill, just outside of the village, I hear the heavy steps of German boots on the road just above me. This heartens me, as I know now I have caught up with the Germans. But this also eliminates my chance of using the only donkey road. So, I take to the fields below and west of the village.

The German group passes through Apodoúlou without stopping. But instead of going directly to Aghios Ioánnis, they head to the nearby village of Níthavris. Níthavris has supplied several young and not-so-young men to the resistance. The Germans, however, don't find at home the man they are after. As a rule, a man who suspects that he might be a target of German raids usually sleeps outside his village, mostly in caves during the winter months and under trees in the summers. This must have been true this night. The Germans move out of Níthavris quickly and continue on for Aghios Ioánnis.

Their side-trip to Níthavris, however, gives me the break I need to reach Aghios Ioánnis first. As I find out later, luck has also helped me to be able to catch up with the German group at Apodoúlou. Even though I have run fast, the Germans took the short route, with close to a half-an-hour start on me, and they aren't moving slowly. On their way to Apodoúlou, I'm told, the Gestapo officers make a stop at Vathiakó. There, again, they are looking for a specific man, but they don't find him at home.

Luck also helps me in Aghios Ioánnis. By now, night has given way to early morning. Running into the village, the first person I see is Aristédis Paradisanós. Without my having a chance to say anything, he looks at me and realizes that something is seriously wrong. "The Gestapo is coming" comes out of my mouth as I breathe fast. Aristédis goes into action. He shouts at a group of operatives standing by his father's house to come closer to us. By that time I have calmed a bit, and I give them a short explanation for the reason I'm there.

Immediately, Aristedis asks an operative, Giórgis Maridákis, to take me out of the village. Other men let the people in the village know about the coming of the Gestapo, and others leave running to other villages to warn them about the possibility of a visit by the Gestapo. Meanwhile, Aristédis goes to wake up Papadoyiánnis, a brother of his mother. He is still asleep with his wife and little son, a mistake Papadoyiannis has made, and then Aristédis runs to the place the spying ring operatives are staying.

The operative, in whose care Aristédis had left me, takes me to Rové, a hill just above the village. There we lie down on the ground, among the tall vegetation, and wait for the Germans. From our vantage point we see Papadoyiánnis, his family, and a couple bodyguards leaving from the northwest edge of the village. Not long after, we notice the Germans entering the village from the opposite side—the southeast edge of Ághios Ioánnis. The Germans are well informed. Without hesitation they go straight to the house where the Papadoyiánnis family was staying.

The Germans leave Aghios Ioánnis going down the same road, in the direction that the Papadoyiánnis party had taken. Because of his child and wife, the Papadoyiánnis entourage is moving at a leisurely pace, giving them only a minute or so to get out of the view of the Gestapo group. And this only because of the alertness of one of his bodyguards, who hears the noise the Gestapo group is making with their boots marching on the rocky donkey-road.

Papadoyiánnis and his family had two close calls that day. If apprehended, he faces torture and execution, while his family could be sent to a work concentration camp in Germany.

CHAPTER 2

Pursued

Smiling luck

After the Gestapo men leave Aghios Ioánnis, I realize I can't stay there because the Germans may come back. Going back to Sáta isn't an option either, as I don't know how the detachment there has reacted to my escape. I also can't go home to Vyzári, because the Gestapo may have sent a group there too. Since the Germans went through Apodoúlou that morning without stopping, I surmise that, unlike other villages in the area, Apodoúlou doesn't interest them. I decide then to pay a visit to my uncle Stávros Psaroudákis in that village. His wife, Hrysánthi, is the eldest sister of my mother. I have come to like them, as well as the tiny library of my uncle—the only home library of serious books I have ever seen, in the mountain villages. That's where I read, for the first time, the Greek language edition of *Les Miserables*.

A few times in the past, walking back and forth from Vyzári and Sáta, I have shown up at their house, announcing that I'm staying overnight. This isn't unusual in the mountain villages of Crete, where there aren't any facilities for travelers to eat or stay overnight. Any man, as well as a couple—normally women don't travel long distances alone—coming to a village and needing to either food or a place to sleep is accommodated by the villagers, no matter how poor they are. The Cretans call this "philoxenía." In its literal sense it means friendly disposition toward strangers. But the same sense of selfless obligation of service to strangers is also extended to relatives and friends.

Aunt Hrysánthi nurtured me for about a week, until I had recovered the courage to venture back to Sáta. There, my friend, Nikolís Tyrákis, brother of Giórgis, has taken care of my oxen while I was gone, and life is going on, as if nothing has happened.

A few weeks pass. One night, Giórgis Tyrákis is able to escape from his Gestapo detention in Míres. He is headed for Sáta because of his pregnant wife. The Gestapo officers guess that's what he will do, and taking a group of soldiers, they go most of the way by military transports. Because Giórgis is on foot walking and running through the fields and hills, the Germans are able to get to the hamlet well before him, and they tightly encircle it. As Giórgis is about to enter the hamlet, he realizes that there is a trap. He attempts to escape again but he is injured.

The soldiers bring the injured Giórgis into the hamlet. The gunshots have awakened the whole little settlement, and Giórgis' wife breaks into shrill wailing when she realizes that the shots had been for her husband. She tries to approach him but she is rudely pushed back by the soldiers. When she is allowed to go close to him and sees how bloodied he is, she faints. The rest of the family's women break out in loud cries and a series of lamentations.

While all this is going on, officers and a few soldiers come to our farmhouse. The kitchen door is still broken and open. This time they carefully examine all the rooms, including the stables. Before leaving Sáta, they also make a detailed search of all the houses, stables, and other buildings of the hamlet. They apparently suspect that I might be hiding someplace there, but they are disappointed. By pure chance, I had gone to Vyzári the day before.

Giórgis is taken to Míres and then to a hospital in Iráklio. After that he is transferred to Αγυία (Aghyia), a notorious SS holding facility in the Haniá area—not a good sign. A person taken there is subjected to "intensive," and "systematic," no-holds-barred questioning and then execution or, rarely, taken by the SS to a work camp in Germany. Giorgis' pregnant wife doesn't stop hoping that her husband would survive the ordeal there. He doesn't.

⊡   ⊡   ⊡

The tragic irony of his death is that this Giórgis wasn't involved with the British intelligence or the partisans, even though he can't help but realize what has been going on in the little settlement. He doesn't know details about the current activities of either group. He does, however, have a first cousin, another Giórgis Tyrákis, who is also a friend of mine, and whose home is in Fourfourás. Currently, that Giórgis Tyrákis is deeply involved in the island's British intelligence operations. The informer turned in the wrong Giórgis Tyrákis, an innocent man.

When I'm told by intelligence operatives what had happened to Giórgis, I come to appreciate for the very first time how lucky I have been. I avoided death when the major saved me from the bloodthirsty Gestapo lieutenant, and I saved myself from "methodical" questioning and death by escaping, then I'm saved again by being in Vyzári, away from Sáta, when Giorgis is recaptured. "You are lucky," Nikolís Tyrákis, Giorgis' brother, tells me when I return to the hamlet.

The Gestapo's visits to our house continue. It appears that anytime a Gestapo unit goes through the little settlement, they stop at our house. I become careful during the daytime. All the folks, even children, become sort of sentinels for me, looking out for possible Germans soldier groups headed for the hamlet. Besides, in the daytime I'm working in the fields. Uncle Kostas, who now seems to be concerned about my safety, advises me to begin sleeping outside the village. After that, I sleep outside in the fields—a small cave in the winter, with an old blanket, and mostly under the olive trees in the summer. I sleep in, or near, locations where, using binoculars the British had given me, I can have a clear view of the hamlet in the mornings.

In the middle of a hot summer day, the Germans raid Sáta again. Since what they had done before hadn't worked out for them, they apparently decided to try trapping me during the daytime. Normally, the Gestapo comes from Míres, while the army comes from the Tymbáki Air

Base. The town of Tymbáki had been taken over by the Germans, after throwing all of its citizens out of their houses—and that's the reason the tailor is staying in our Sáta house.

The Sáta Hill separates Sáta from the Messará Plain. Sáta's elevation is a few hundred feet higher than that of the Messará Plain, which is only a few feet higher than the sea level. Close to Tymbáki, the Libyan Sea's waters caress the shoreline of the Plain. Because of the considerable difference in elevations, the side of the Sáta Hill facing the Plain is much longer than its side facing the hamlet—but scaling is difficult on either side.

Anyone coming to Sáta from Míres or Tymbáki, or any other point on the Messará Plain, can do so in only two ways—either scaling the south side of Sáta Hill or going around the west side of that hill, as the hill becomes short in meeting the sea. In both cases a mechanized transport could go only to Klíma, a village where the feet of the Sáta Hill meet the plain. From there on, only donkey roads exist. From Klíma, one must scale the Sáta Hill by using the zigzagging donkey road.

The Sáta Hill can be avoided by circling, on foot, around its west end and entering a long valley of olive tree groves that appears to gently rise from the shore all the way to Sáta.

Still, the shortest way from the Messará Plain to the hamlet requires going over the Sáta Hill. In doing so during the day, however, the Germans expose their arrival immediately upon crossing the crest of the Sáta Hill, thus giving the people in Sáta enough time to get prepared for them. So, this time, they choose to come from the valley of the thick olive tree groves. They also choose to do it at high noon in the summer. It is the best time for them, if they plan to come during daylight and unannounced. At noon of a hot summer day the villagers busy themselves with threshing the harvested grain and legume stalks.

All donkey paths to Sáta are full of loose rocks. Because of that, the noise of the boots of a large German detachment precedes them. And this time, they have brought what was estimated to be about 200 men. Today the German force spreads throughout the fields west-southwest of Sáta instead of using the donkey road. Their presence is protected by the olive tree groves. They apparently start early and are moving slowly, so they avoid making any significant noise. When they reach the hamlet, they form a line longer than the area covered by the houses of the hamlet. They wait there until all of their men are in place.

Then, they emerge from the olive groves, running. It takes only minutes to secure a ring around the small settlement. Two officers and a few soldiers march to our house. As the tailor reports, they search all rooms, including the stables, and then look at his room from the door but don't go inside. Following that, they methodically search all the other buildings of the hamlet.

Minutes before the Germans appear, I'm standing by the edge of the rise, the same rise that had helped me escape on that winter night. I'm visiting with Nikolís Tyrákis, next to his family's alóni, which is next to our own family's alóni. He is supervising the threshing of their crops, and we are talking about his progress. At some point, I ask to be excused, and I go down to the creek, at the bottom of the gully on the other side of the rise, to relieve myself—there are no toilets in Sáta. When I complete my job, I begin walking back up the hill.

Now, I notice Nikolís still standing where I had left him, on the top of the rise, but with his back toward me and his arms crossed behind him. He signals me with the motion of his hands not to come up. I understand that an immediate danger is present, and I melt back into the foliage of the creek. In the minute or so it takes for the soldiers to reach Nikolís' position, I disappear.

After they search our house and all the hamlet's buildings, the Germans gather the few village men, except small boys and old men, and herd them to Plátanos, a village more than an hour on foot from Sáta.

The next day the men are back. Nikolís tells me the same Gestapo officers who beat me up and took his brother waited for them in Plátanos. They examined one man at a time. They asked each man his name and carefully looked him over, spending much more time on the younger men. Then they allow them to return to Sáta.

After Nikolís' short report, he and I discuss the previous day's German visit to the hamlet. We both are puzzled by the swiftness, the speed and the apparent accuracy in fully covering the little settlement and the area around it in just a few minutes. The Germans must have rehearsed the maneuvers of that deployment.

"You know, Mihális," Nikolís comments, "it is funny that when they go into your house, they don't bother to ask the tailor about your whereabouts."

"I have been wondering about that also. Even when they had come to pick me up the first time, they came directly to the kitchen, not bothering the tailor."

"Also the second time, Mihális, when they recaptured my brother, and the rest of the times they have visited your house, they don't bother the tailor and his family."

"I know. The tailor has told me that, too. He also has noticed that, then and every time they have passed through Sáta, the Germans have taken their time in searching the whole house and even the stables, including the aheróna. Yet, each time they just have looked at their room from the doorway without going inside."

"That's kind of strange, Mihális. Don't you think so?"

"Yes. It appears that they are well informed. They must know that they have thrown the tailor and his family out of his house in Tymbáki and that he has had no interaction with the resistance. And, of course, he doesn't."

"So, Mihális, they seem to know that the tailor wouldn't be of any help to them."

"They apparently do."

"So, how do they get their information, Mihális?"

"I trust the tailor. I think the way the Gestapo treats the tailor's family's room is an attempt in raising our suspicion on him, instead of their real informer. You see, Nikolís, if someone from another part of the island looks at our situation, he will suspect that someone among us here is an informer. But that cannot be. If the tailor or someone else living here was informing the Gestapo, we would all have been dead by now and our houses and the whole hamlet would have been destroyed.

"Besides that, the Gestapo doesn't seem to have important details of our activities. They have zeroed only on me. It's also obvious that your brother has died without revealing what he had known about Sáta, while the tailor zealously protects his family and is running scared of both the Germans and us."

"I know, Mihális."

"While I was visiting Aghios Ioánnis, a few weeks ago, I was told that a group of patriots are researching the circumstances under which the various security leaks appear to be surfacing. It looks like that they have been zeroing in on the various wandering black-market peddlers."

"We have had a lot of them coming up here. Now only the Cypriot does, but even he comes rarely. He really must be missing his family in Cyprus, as he always seems to be so sad."

"Well, I hope they get the informer soon. I'm tired of sleeping outside, especially during the winter."

"Don't complain, Mihális. You have been the luckiest man around here. Look what happened yesterday. Luck did smile upon you, again!"

Nikolís does not mention that, this time, he had helped the "smiling luck."

A few days later, Uncle Kóstas, passing through, comments on that development. "Apparently the Gestapo has found out that you don't sleep in the hamlet anymore, and since they have missed you so many times, they must have been advised by their informer to use this tactic."

"Besides escaping, what have I done to deserve all this attention?" I ask. Uncle Kóstas smiles, like "I thought you would never ask that question," and he continues.

"It isn't your escape," he says. "It's what you did after that. For the Míres Gestapo station, Papadoyiánnis is the biggest prize around, and they had been sure they would catch him that day. And then you not only escape, but you also have the audacity of running ahead of them to warn him. So, you must have angered them, especially the major who had saved you from being shot by the lieutenant. But that isn't all. We suspect that the Gestapo thinks that since you had known where Papadoyiánis had been staying that night, then you must also know information about the resistance and the people they had asked you about."

When he leaves, he looks at me worryingly. "Continue being careful, Mihalákis."

Amári

The beautiful valley

I decide to go to Vyzári and visit with my mother before she hears about the new development from third parties. My friend Nikolís agrees to take care of my oxen, and I get on my donkey.

During the four-plus hours of the lonely ride on the slow-moving donkey, I reflect on my family's situation, our small village of Vyzári, the area around us, and the island itself.

Vyzári is one of forty villages and hamlets included in the mountainous and landlocked area, in the center of the island, called Amári. Amári is an éparchy, a small political administrative unit which, in turn, is part of a larger political unit called νομός (prefecture)—the Prefecture of Réthymno, whose political administrative seat is the city of Réthymno, on the north shore of the island and about 40 kilometers from Vyzári.

Crete has four such prefectures. To the west of Réthymno lies the Haniá Prefecture. Presently, the Germans have enthroned the top commandant of their forces on Fortress Crete, as the Nazis have baptized the island, in the city of Haniá, which used to be the political seat of the island. To the east of Réthymno lies the Iráklio Prefecture, whose seat is Iráklio—Crete's largest city. The Lasíthi Prefecture is the island's easternmost. Crete's population is about 400,000 souls.

Amári is blessed with a few small mountain valleys. The largest and the most beautiful one is the Amári Valley, which is sandwiched between Mt. Psiloritis on its east, and Mt. Kéndros on the west. Thus, entrance to the Valley from those directions by mechanized vehicles is impossible. At the same time, high and sharply steep hills at the Valley's north and south ends make approaching the Valley difficult.

My pristine small village of Vyzári is tucked away at the southeast corner of the Amári Valley. Uphill from Vyzári, less than twenty minutes by foot, the much larger village of Fourfourás has taken the lowest part of Mt. Psiloritis. Vyzári, even though small, is the medical and business center of the area. One creek meanders through the village, and another one skirts its north side, while two more creeks run close to the village on its south side—they are dangerous in the winter, but all of them, save one, are mostly dry in summers. The river Liyiótis, lying over a kilometer or so below the village, moves peacefully in its trip to the south shore of the island, where it meets the Libyan Sea.

According to my mother, I was born during the last week of March in 1927, but my father neglected to officially register my birth until sometime in 1928. I was the first-born of the five children of Manólis (Emmanuel) and Maria Paradisanós. While my mother, my four younger siblings and I live in Vyzári, my father works and stays in the cities, especially Réthymno and Iráklio. My uncles, Kóstas and Yiánnis, the two bachelor younger brothers of my father, live in the family's farmhouse in the hamlet of Sáta, a minuscule farming community, where they take care of the family's properties. I like my uncles, so, from grade school, anytime I had a chance to visit them, I did—especially during the hunting season, when their important friends from the Messará Plain and the cities, especially Iráklio, came hunting with my uncles.

In 1937, because of changes in education laws brought about by the fascist dictator Metaxás, my parents took me out of Vyzári's single-room school and enrolled me in a private school in Iráklio. When, in 1938, Uncle Yiánnis was recruited by an Iráklio bank, he moved to Iráklio, and I lived with him while I was attending school.

The Second World War started in Europe in 1939, when I was 12. At the beginning, it pitted the Allies (the democratic countries of Britain and France) against the Axis Powers (Nazis Germany and Fascist Italy). Quickly, the Germans took over the Low Countries and conquered France, while the Italians reached over the Adriatic Sea to easily annex Albania, a northern neighbor of Greece.

In 1940, my father's job base was relocated to Iráklio, and he moved the whole family there. My father seemed to be happy having all of us together; my mother was glad, as it was the first time she was in a place where she could pray and socialize with other Jehovah's Witnesses. My siblings and I loved to have our father home every night, and we all liked our schools.

Then the situation changed, and the change was sudden and dramatic. And it was the events of that change that eventually brought me to our family's farmhouse in Sáta and my unpleasant business with the Gestapo, the German police.

But let's take the events as they occurred.

PART TWO

 INVASION

War!

WWII starts

Germany had been the loser during the First World War (WWI). By the middle of the 1930s, however, under the leadership of Hitler, Germany has rearmed itself, and joined by Italy, under Mussolini, they become the most powerful military force in continental Europe. In time, Hitler began acting aggressively, seeking revenge for Germany's WWI humiliation. Eventually, the German army invaded Poland in 1939, and the old allies (England and France) declared war on Germany, and thus the Second World War (WWII) began.

The Germans stormed the Low Countries, defeated the combined French and British forces and conquered France. The British, fearing an invasion by the Germans, feverishly prepared their defenses, while Hitler was left unchecked in picking up allies among his neighboring countries by invading them or bullying them into submission.

Meanwhile, Greece declared its neutrality, and our family and the rest of the people around us felt secure. Sure, there were changes happening in Europe, but they were away from us. Our family and the rest of our citizens continued in our business and life, ignoring the conflict between England and Germany.

We didn't know that Hitler was moving to become the master of all Europe and eventually one of the most powerful men in the world. Mussolini, the Italian fascist dictator and Hitler's main European ally was going along with Hitler in hopes of benefiting from Hitler's plans.

To accomplish their plans and maintain their superiority in Europe, Hitler and Mussolini need plenty of oil for their factories and war machines. Europe has no oil, except in Rumania and in Russia (Caucasian oilfields). The Rumanian oil, however, is just a "drop in the bucket" compared with the huge quantities that the powerful Axis machine needs, and the Soviet Union commands the Caucasian oilfields for its own use.

Hitler's Germany used mostly synthetic oil, produced chemically—a time-consuming, expensive, and labor-intensive process, even though the Germans are using forced labor—men, women and children from the conquered countries that the SS (Hitler's overall and fanatical military police) has shipped to Germany. Because of that, Mussolini wants to reach the Middle East oilfields.

He attempted to do so from North Africa. But the Italian army in Libya (an Italian colony) was blocked by the British forces in Egypt (a British colony). Another way to get to the Middle East oilfields is through Turkey, a neighbor of the oil-producing areas. To go to Turkey, Mussolini's first choice was to go through Yugoslavia and Bulgaria, but Hitler doesn't approve the Yugoslavian route.

So in 1939, Mussolini reached across the Adriatic Sea and conquered Albania, setting his sights on Greece, a neighbor of Turkey.

The Greek-Italian War
David and Goliath

Greece was among several European countries that declared their neutrality, and our island was peaceful. Hitler, however, either invaded or pressured smaller countries to become Germany's allies or satellites. Mussolini felt that he must also move on.

At 3 a.m. on October 28, 1940, Emanuele Grazzi, the Italian ambassador to Greece, woke up Prime Minister Metaxás and handed him an ultimatum from Mussolini.

"A large number of Italian forces are posted at the Greek-Albanian border. Allow them to move to Turkey through your country or we will attack you at six o'clock in the morning," was the substance of Mussolini's ultimatum.

Metaxás consulted with King George II. The Greek government refused to accept the terms of Mussolini's message.[1]

As soon as Mussolini received Metaxás' reply, he ordered the Italian forces to invade Greece—not waiting till 6 a.m.

---

1 The Greeks still celebrate that refusal, on October 28 each year, as the OHI MERA—the NO DAY.

That day, just before daybreak, airplanes flew over Iráklio, showering the city with bombs. Soon the radio reported that during night the Italian army had invaded mainland Greece from Albania.

People were sleeping while the planes flew above the city letting their bombs go. The sirens came alive after the planes had already gone. Then, the sirens went crazy. They blew again and again without any planes showing up. And then more planes rained bombs upon us, with the sirens howling.

The unsuspecting population went into a tizzy. Panic was the order of the day—and the days that followed. The people, the city, and the island weren't prepared for war. We, the children in our family, hadn't quite settled in either the neighborhood or the schools before this pandemonium was unleashed upon us. The inadequacy of the warning system contributed to many false alarms that, in turn, made the people behave like yo-yos—going down to and coming up from the bomb shelters again and again and again.

And there are no shelters constructed exclusively for the purpose of protecting the population from bombing. The tallest buildings with basements were hurriedly designated as bomb shelters—even though there is hardly a building that has more than three floors. People ran into those buildings looking for the stairs leading to the basement. No such stairs have any railings, and the basements aren't adequately lighted, if at all.

In their rush to get down to the basements, people crowded in the concrete stairways—some falling off the stairs onto the basement floor below. More people were injured by running down to dark basements than by the explosions from the Italian bombs.

My mother and I were caught in such a scene on the second day of the raids. We were moving fast down the concrete stairs, she ahead of me, into the dark, unlighted basement. Suddenly, someone next to my mother was pushed by the people running next to him. He collided with my mother, sending her several feet down to the concrete floor of the basement. I ran after her. When I picked her up, she complained of pain on the right side of her rib cage, but she was okay otherwise. The pain lasted for a few weeks.

The next day she told me, "Mihalákis, I really don't know why I had been running down to that basement. The planes never showed up, and I almost had been killed, but thanks to God, I'm only injured. And why, really, should we run? Even if the planes come and bomb us, Jehovah would protect us. I will not go to a shelter again." And she didn't for the balance of the weeks that we stayed in the city.

Schools closed. The frequent shrieking and screeching of the sirens, the rush to the shelters and the overall war jitters of the adults affected the younger children. Since schools were closed, thousands of husbands started sending their wives and children to the villages. The exodus became so massive that it was difficult to find transportation for whole families to move out of the city.

At that point, Agapitós Tarlás, a contractor who is married to Vasilía, a distant cousin of my mother, approached my father. His house had been bombed by the Italian planes. Vasilía's home village, Aghía Paraskeví, is one of the Amári villages. Since my father works at the main transportation company on the island, Agapitós asked him for help in finding transportation for his wife and their two children to Vyzári—as no motorway goes to Aghía Paraskeví.

During the latter part of November, my father secured a truck. My mother and Vasilía rode in front with the driver, while all seven of us children rode in the open truck bed, with the furniture and provisions we took with us. It was a pleasant trip. Vasilía apprised her relatives in Aghia Paraskeví. A few weeks later, her relatives came to Vyzári with a bunch of donkeys and took them to Aghía Paraskeví.

Manólis and Agapitós didn't have to answer the general army mobilization because of their age. They stayed in Iráklio—my father because of his job and Agapitós for his business. Even though his house was bombed, Agapitós chose to stay. Because of the bombings, he looked forward to more business opportunities.

Still, neither of them, nor any of us, even suspected that this marked the beginning of a hellish life we would have to cope with for years.

The war affects all families. In our family, my father's two brothers, Kóstas and Yiánnis, answered the general mobilization call. My father lost his job and his investment in the Syngelákis Company when the government appropriated, for the armed forces, the buses and cars of the company. And, of course, my siblings and I left school, not knowing when we might go back.

Early that morning Mussolini and Hitler had a prearranged meeting. There is some supposition that the Deuce, as Mussolini is known, must have advised the Fuehrer, as Hitler is known, about his intention to invade Greece. But there are also reports that he surprised Hitler when meeting him that morning with the announcement. "The Italian armies are marching toward Athens," Mussolini began. "I will have coffee under the Acropolis by tomorrow noon," he added.

Mussolini forced Greece to enter the war—and Greece chose to enter it on the side of England. There are two significant points about that development. First, at that point, the Axis was winning the war, yet Greece chose to go with Britain. The other point is what followed between the Greek and Italian forces. To the amazement of the then-free world, the Greek army met the Italians and defeated them.

Before invading Greece, Mussolini started a war of nerves with the Greek government. This included amassing forces to the Greek-Albanian boundaries, Italian planes over Greek airspace, and Italian warships in Greek waters, culminating in the sinking by an Italian submarine of a Greek warship, the cruiser Ellie, during a religious celebration at the island of Tínos.

Because of the war of nerves and intelligence reports, the Greek government decided early on, under super-secrecy, to take two actions, apparently totally missed by the intelligence apparatus of the arrogant Deuce. The Greeks moved some forces closer to the Albanian border. Most importantly, the army leadership drew up plans for the first actions to take in case of invasion from Albania. Those plans included an extra-fast and seamless mobilization of the Greek army and securing the necessary troop transportation means. And those actions paid off later.

An apparent flaw in the Axis alliance is that Mussolini and, especially, Hitler act with some independence of one another. They reportedly make general plans together—which in essence are Hitler's plans—and they discuss possible future actions. Reportedly, however, early on Hitler avoided sharing his specific timetable for the implementation of those plans.

Hitler felt that Britain would be an easier target if its dependency on its Middle East and Pacific colonies for oil, men and supplies was more difficult or interrupted. Reportedly, Hitler and Mussolini discussed the possibility of getting Greece and Turkey to join their alliance. That would give them Crete, my island, which commands the sea traffic in the eastern Mediterranean Sea.

Mussolini, however, failing to get Middle East oil through Egypt, devised a plan of going through Greece and Turkey. Some feel that using the oil gambit was a pretext for attacking Greece. The route through northern Greece became famous during the Roman times, as it was used by the Roman armies to move their forces, slaves and supplies back and forth between Rome and its Middle East territories. Mussolini, who visualizes himself as a modern Roman emperor, salivates thinking of becoming master of that area.

Even though the two Axis leaders made plans for taking Greece, Hitler reportedly didn't like Mussolini's invasion of Greece. He had plans for attacking the Soviet Union (Russia) as early as possible in the spring of 1941, and the Balkan entanglement might have been a distraction for those plans. Russia is the largest country in Europe and an obstruction to Hitler's plan for unchallenged supremacy of Europe.

Turkey, even though it was a German ally during the First World War, is staying neutral. Both Greece and Turkey are poor and not prepared for war, so they both zealously protect their non-alignment. Still, Mussolini apparently believes that a small country like Greece, with eight million people, and with a tiny and poorly equipped army, would readily capitulate to Italy with a 20 million population and a huge and well-armed military force—and by taking Greece, Turkey would follow.

All able young men, and thousands not so young, who heard the call for mobilization on the radio dropped what they were doing and moved to the mobilization centers as quickly as they could without waiting for official mobilization notices. The older volunteers were rejected. Some reinforcements came to the front within hours. The largest town the Italians took, before enough reinforcements from the mobilization arrived at the front lines, was Igoumenítsa, a small harbor town on the Ionian Sea (south Adriatic Sea) in Ipiros (Epirus), the northwest province of Greece, which borders Albania.

After that, somehow, the Greek army was able to check the advance of the Italians, including a number of Albanian forces that had been recruited by the Italians. When the Albanians and Italian soldiers were forced to give up Igoumenitsa, they destroyed the town before leaving.

After the Greeks fully mobilized, they counterattacked.

They were able not only to firm the front line, but also to advance at some points. Within days, the Greek army found itself advancing on the whole front line. Within weeks, the Greeks threw the Italian and Albanian forces off Greek soil and back into Albania. From then on, the Greeks, week after week, continue moving deeper into Albania—slowly, but they are moving.

To understand the significance of this, one must realize the war situation at that point in time and place. Just months before, the German forces, in only a few days, went through the Low Countries, easily defeating the combined British and French forces and conquer France. After that, they took most of the smaller European nations, either by force or cowing them into submission.

Besides England, at that point, the only European countries that stand out of the Axis area and are not publicly aligned with Germany or Britain, are Spain, which is governed by Generalissimo Franco, a friend of Hitler; Portugal; Switzerland; the Soviet Union, which has an nonaggression pact with Germany; the Scandinavian countries; and the Balkan countries of Yugoslavia (leaning toward Germany), Greece, and Turkey.

At that point Britain is the only country standing against the Axis. True, General De Gaulle is attempting to coalesce some of the French forces in the African and Middle East French colonies, but at that time it is an iffy situation, at best, for him.

What the Greeks are doing in Albania is a huge surprise. A little country is able to check the might and arrogance of Hitler's major European ally. England has finally found a European ally that fights in earnest. It is a puny ally, but it delivers a devastating punch. It has been reported that Britain's wartime Prime Minister, Winston Churchill, in one of his radio talks to his people, stated, "The Greeks don't fight like heroes, heroes fight like the Greeks."

We, as distant observers of the fight, thought it was the sheer bravery of the Greek army accomplishing that feat. As a young teenager, I thoroughly believed it, and so did our villagers. This is only partially correct, however, no matter how brave the Greek soldiers are and how much they are motivated by the fact that they are defending their own country.

In reality, the victories of the Greek army can't continue without some unusual circumstances and conditions.

To begin with, Albania had proved to be easy prey for the Italian generals, so they grossly underestimated the will of the Greeks to fight in defending their own country. The Italians expected a quick punch and found a stalemate in only a few days. The Italian generals also expected to fight a traditional frontal war, but because of the wildest mountainous topography of the Balkan Peninsula and the timing (the harshest weather in that region of the Balkans for the last twenty winters), they found themselves fighting skirmish after skirmish. The tanks and planes of the Italians weren't of much help because of the topography and weather, while the Greek and Albanian mountain villagers use their donkeys and mules to move guns and supplies, and spy on the movements of the Italians.[2]

---

2 Some of those elements have been documented by George Blytas in his book, *The First Victory.*

Hitler Moves
The Huns arrive

Considering the might and size of the Axis forces, the Greeks' fight is in vain. A tiny country like Greece can't embarrass for long the powerful and arrogant Axis powers without being punished. And punish us, they do.

Hitler was indeed surprised by Mussolini's action against Greece. Reportedly, as we already have seen, the two Axis leaders discussed the need to bring Greece into the Axis sphere of influence. Crete, along with the Suez Canal, is vital to Hitler's long-range plans to close the door that allows the British to reach their Middle East colonies and dramatically shortens their sea distance from their Pacific Ocean colonies. However, because of his desire to get rid of the Soviet Union first, Hitler wasn't in a hurry to do so. Thus, there had been no firm decision as to when the Axis would move against Greece.

Hitler and the German generals knew that historically the brutal Russian winter could inflict grave and perilous damage to their campaign when they attack the Soviet Union. Consequently, they decided that, in order to inflict a knock-out punch to the Soviets, they had to capture the capital, Moscow, before the onset of the following Russian winter. Accomplishing that, they figured, would break the will of the Russians to further resist. Again, the lesson from history was that in order to be able to conquer Russia, they have to move as early as possible in the spring and march relentlessly forward until they reach Moscow. Hitler set the timetable for attacking in early spring of 1941.

The Fuehrer didn't like Mussolini invading Greece at the time he does, mainly because it could have tactical military implications when he attacked the Soviet Union. And he was proven right. The Albanian front first affected Hitler's diplomatic moves and, secondly, his plans for the Russian campaign.[3]

As the fighting continued in Albania, the British moved a few Anzac (Australian and New Zealander) forces and planes into Greece. The result was that Hitler began to worry about the south flank of his forces when they attacked Russia. The English forces were small, and the move was only to show that England appreciated what the Greeks were accomplishing. Their arrival, however, opened the door for more Allied forces in Europe.

Hitler had thought that he had thrown the English out of continental Europe, but now the British were back!

With British forces back in Europe and the Albanian front making headlines, Germany suffered three serious diplomatic setbacks. The setbacks involved German diplomatic moves, which the Fuehrer personally initiated, with Generalissimo Franco, dictator of Spain; General Petain, the puppet president of the part of France not physically occupied by the German forces; and the government of Yugoslavia.

Spain could provide Hitler with an ally, Generalissimo Franco, who is a tested military man, and with a substantive and hardened army fresh from the Spanish Civil War. Petain, on the other hand, could actively use his influence in swaying the French territories, especially in Africa and the Middle East, to keep their men and naval forces from joining the movement of General De Gaulle, the leader of the Free French.

Before attacking the Soviet Union, Hitler wanted Yugoslavia, the largest Balkan country, to join the Axis. For that purpose, he courted the uncle of King Peter, who was acting as the head of the royal family since

---

3 This is according to Blytas' research.

Peter was still too young. It basically was a done deal for Yugoslavia to go with Germany.

In previous months, Hitler had thought that he was winning all three initiatives. What happened in Albania and with the Anzac forces in Greece, however, showed a possible weak link in the Axis alliance. The longer the Italians were being chased by the Greeks in Albania, the more Franco and Petain demur. In the end Franco never joined the Axis, even though the Germans had helped him win the Spanish Civil War, and many of the French colonial forces went with De Gaulle. Then the Greek victories over the Italians emboldened the Yugoslavian army and the young King Peter. A palace coup followed. King Peter took over the government, and Yugoslavia went with the British.

As we have seen, in the Balkans, the only countries not aligned with Germany were Yugoslavia, Greece and Turkey. With the Italian invasion, Greece went with England. Now Yugoslavia chooses England. And, even though Hitler sent to Turkey, as ambassador, one of his top diplomats hoping to goad Turkey to join Germany as it did in WWI, Turkey demurred.

All this was frustrating for Hitler, who was used to getting his way. In addition, if the Greeks were successful in taking Albania, the Greek army and the Anzac forces couldn't be ignored any longer. Thus, the presence of the British in the Balkans and the successes of their Greek allies presented a real threat to the southern flank of the German forces as they prepared to move against the Soviet Union.

Hitler had had enough.

In an ill-timed decision, he postponed the Soviet Union invasion and moved into the Balkans in order to save the Italians in Albania, punish the Yugoslavs and Greeks, and, most importantly, secure the southern flank of his armies while they were invading the Soviet Union. Some military and political analysts felt that Hitler's negotiations with Petain, Franco, and Yugoslavia were the reason for that postponement, but the Greeks wouldn't hear of that—and justifiably so, as it was the Greek presence in Albania that prevented Hitler from getting his way this time.

Hitler's decision to change the time-frame for his campaign against the Soviet Union was a strong factor in the Germans getting bogged down in the Russian winter, just as they were almost within sight of Moscow. The Russians regrouped during the winter's stalemate. They received weapons and supplies from America, they firmed the war front, and eventually began to push the Germans back. And this marked the beginning of the fall of Hitler's Nazi Germany.

One wonders why leaders of nations make such grave mistakes. Hitler is known for overruling his generals in pure military decisions, but invading the Soviet Union was a brilliant idea. If Hitler had succeeded, Germany would have become the undisputed master of Europe, and England would have been forced to seek peace. Hitler could have ignored Greece and the Italians in Albania. Or, he could have moved against Greece long before the approaching spring, so he could have met his timetable for invading Russia—but he didn't. But, of course, there are a lot of ifs in all war cases.

The Yugoslavs weren't ready to face the German might, so the German army waltzed through the country in moving toward Greece. Meanwhile, the Germans also moved forces into Bulgaria, another northern neighbor of Greece and a German ally. From there, they and the Bulgarian army invaded Greece. During one of those battles, it was reported, a Greek unit put up such a brave resistance that when they were overcome, the German general saluted the surviving soldiers and allowed them to leave free. The Bulgarians were allowed to occupy Thrace, one of the northern Greek provinces.

The British recommended that the Greeks withdraw their forces from Albania, and with the British forces already in Greece, form a defensive line by Alyakmós River, close to Mount Olympus. Because of the topography, it was a favorable defensive location. General Papágos, the Commander-in-Chief of the Greek armed forces, however, refused to withdraw the Greek armies from Albania. Papágos' stubbornness cannot be rationally explained, and some pundits have various suspicions. The most benign theories are that he didn't want to allow the Italians to walk into Greece without direct help from the Germans, or that since the British proposed it, he rejected the idea because it wasn't his.

Following Papágos' refusal, the Greek army, fighting on three fronts, collapsed, and the British evacuated their forces to Crete. The Germans allowed the Italians to manage large parts of western Greece, including the Ionian islands, but the German forces became the real masters of our ancient land. Mussolini's dream of having coffee under the Acrópolis could then be realized, albeit with the German flag flying above him on top of the Acrópolis.[4]

---

4 A few years back, perusing a travel guide to Greece published by National Geographic, I noticed that it reports that the Italians had only a little and temporary problem with the Greek army. The inference the writer gives is that the Italians had conquered Greece. It could have been a surprise to me that the author, in writing about Greece, has failed to study WWII and the country's modern history, but I understood how such an ignorance could occur. Hitler's decision to take Greece nullified the gains that had been achieved by the hard-won victories of the Greeks in Albania.

This, in turn, contributed to reducing the Greek-Italian War to a very tiny footnote in the history of WWII and taking it out of the history textbooks.

The Battle of Crete

The barbarians are coming

With the fall of the Greek mainland, my parents worried about the safety of my uncles, Kóstas and Yiánnis. They both were members of the all-Cretan Fifth Army of the Greek forces fighting in Albania. There was also some anxiety among them and the villagers about the possibility that the Germans might also come to Crete; but when the British Anzac expeditionary forces were evacuated from the mainland to Crete, the villagers felt safe.

Hitler, however, had moved forces to Libya to help the Italians fight the British and hopefully break the resistance of the British in Egypt and thus reach the Middle East oil fields. He sent one of his best military leaders, General Rommel, to command the combined German and Italian forces there, with the charge of clearing out the British from Egypt.

After mainland Greece fell, there was a discussion among Hitler's advisors as what to do next in the Mediterranean Front, in order to help General Rommel by moving troops and supplies to North Africa. Two islands were thought to be most important for that purpose: Crete and Malta. Reportedly, the majority of Hitler's advisors chose Malta. But Hermann Goering, Hitler's Air Minister, convinced Hitler to choose Crete.

The Germans, however, had no adequate naval forces in the Mediterranean Sea, and Hitler didn't have enough confidence in the Italian navy, which was mostly bottled up in their bases by the British navy. Because of that, moving large forces on ships to attack Crete and having the necessary warships for support wasn't a viable option for the German military.

The German generals found themselves facing a conundrum. General Kurt Student, head of the paratroopers, most likely supported by Goering, came to their rescue by proposing that the attack on Crete could succeed by using his paratroopers. The paratrooper ranks were the cream of the German forces—and they all were volunteers. Only select men, who meet certain prescribed and strict physical, philosophical, and personality criteria, were inducted into the paratrooper ranks. Every one of them had to take an oath dedicating his life to the Fuehrer. Because of that, they were one of Hitler's most trusted and loved military units, just ahead of the terrible SS, his dreaded security forces.

The Germans started moving their paratroopers to an air base just outside Athens. In doing this, they attempted to move them secretly, so British intelligence wouldn't realize there would be an air attack on Crete. Because of that, the trains carrying paratroopers had their window-shades down. That was in vain, however, as the British had broken the code the German air force units used for communication, and they detected and followed the German preparations for attacking Crete.

On May 20, 1941, the German paratroopers attacked Crete. Since the all-Cretan Fifth Division of the Greek army has been taken off the island, Crete's defense fell upon the British expeditionary force. General Bernard Freyberg, a New Zealander and Churchill's personal pick, was in charge of the defense forces. Since the British had broken the German military air force communication code, Freyberg knew the date, time, and places the German forces would attack.

Because the break of the German code was such a vital secret for the British, however, Freyberg couldn't share that knowledge with his subordinates. For the same reason, no overt defensive preparations could be made at the specific locations the paratroopers are to fall. But Freyberg was confident that his forces would effectively deal with the paratroopers.

The paratroopers landed at three sites. The main body of the attackers fell at Máleme, the island's military airport a few miles west of Haniá. Also, near the airport was where the main body of the British forces is located. Smaller bodies of the attackers fell on the fringes of the city of Réthymno, about thirty miles east of Haniá, and at the airport area of the city of Iráklio, about eighty miles east of Haniá.

During the first few days, few paratroopers made it to the ground alive or uninjured. The defenders devastated them. Hundreds of the dead paratroopers lay in the water, in fields, and on trees in olive groves. At that point, the battle was going in favor of the defenders at Máleme, while the paratroopers in Réthymno and Iraklio had already been contained.

Even though Freyberg knew the particulars of the attack and had strong forces, he neglected to develop, on his own, plans for the coming battle. He felt that he had enough forces to defend the airport and, apparently, the initial successes of his forces lulled him into complacency. It is said that he failed to personally observe the battle lines at the airport. A report put him drinking tea at his headquarters at the most critical turn of the battle. Thus Freyberg failed to have his forces counterattack and eliminate the small beachhead of the remaining few attackers.

Meanwhile, General Student, who was still in Athens, became alarmed and sent in a lot more forces by crash-landing Junker 52s at the beachhead. Without air support, the defenders were bombed and strafed from continuous air raids, while a large number of paratroopers made it to the beachhead. The battle lasted ten days; at the end of it, the Germans had another victory.

While the invasion battles were going on, a large number of German airplanes bombed and strafed the cities and villages. Those actions against the villages seemed to be at random and mostly for the morale effect on the civilians. It seemed that the pilots hadn't given thought to which of the hundreds of Cretan villages to bomb—just bomb and strafe towns and villages. Because of the difficulty presented to the pilots by the rugged topography, most of the bombs miss their targets, and the ones that fall on the villages do little damage.

Two bombs were dropped on Vyzári, falling a little over one hundred yards north of the village. A friend, Giórgis Koufákis, and I were on the side of the Mount Psiloritis, watching the planes coming and going, then we saw the one dropping the bombs on our village—we actually saw only the cloud of dust and dirt resulting from the explosion of the bombs. A bomb that fell on Petrohóri, across the river from Vyzári, killed a cow—and that's all. This air activity seemed to be a way of intimidating the population. The villagers in Amári were shocked at first, but soon they started making jokes about the German planes and their apparently inept pilots.

Unintended Consequences
Bravery resulting in false conclusions

An event that took place during the ten-day assault came to haunt the mountain villagers of the island for the following four years.

The mountain villagers have been known through the eons of Crete's long history to be fanatical defenders of their freedom. Centuries of enslavement have taught them that you don't earn and keep your freedom unless you fight for it. So, with the first news of the paratroopers' invasion, men and women from the mountain villages descended to the areas where the paratroopers were being dropped.

Most were from mountain villages fairly close to the battlegrounds, but they also came from mountain villages in the interior of the island. One of the latter was a friend of mine, Giórgis Tzítzikas, from Ano Méros, a village on Mount Kéndros and close to Vyzári. He and some of his fellow villagers walked about thirty miles to partake in the battle against the paratroopers in the area around the city of Réthymno.[5]

They came to help the defenders, but they had a serious problem. Cretans always preferred a republic rather than a kingdom. Once when they had attempted to revolt against the king, they failed. From then on,

---

5 The historical museum in Iráklio (www.historical-museum.gr) has published a book (in Greek) on Giorgis' accomplishments during the war.

the Athens government directed the police to confiscate all guns and ammunition from the Cretans. The only weapons they were allowed to keep were shotguns. Some villagers were able to hide their rifles and pistols—most of them antiquated—but there were only a dear few in most villages.

So, these volunteer defenders were armed mostly with shotguns, a few with old rifles, a smattering of handguns, hunting knives, a lot of pitchforks, and even hatchets and axes.[6] They weren't the reinforcements General Freyberg wanted to have, but they were men and women who didn't know fear and were ready to die to keep their island free. To military and casual nonmilitary observers who didn't know the Cretan psyche, these groups of unorganized, unruly, untrained, and basically unarmed men, and women, would be laughable.

A number of paratroopers ended up on olive tree branches in the abundant groves throughout those areas of the island. The olive trees are ancient and huge. During the ten-day battle, some of those paratroopers became hopelessly entangled on olive tree branches and were thus fairly easy targets.

According to those surviving volunteer "defenders," the paratroopers falling on those trees were caught by surprise and found men and women waiting for them, under the trees and on the trees. Because of the "weapons" used, the wounds by which some of those paratroopers died weren't the typical wounds sustained in a regular battle.

At the end of the battle, that incident took on a life of its own in two ways. Most likely, the paratroopers who had been thus killed probably numbered a few dozen on each battlefield. But the men and women who participated in that effort, and have survived, boasted about their deeds and greatly exaggerated the results of their actions.

Because of the animosity of the Cretans toward the king and the Athens government, the German intelligence advised the generals that the Cretan civilians would likely be friendly to the German invading forces as they fight the British, or they would stand neutral as observers. But General Student found out that Cretan civilians, whom he had expected

---

6 Wes Davis describes this in his book *The Ariadne Objective*.

to be at least neutral to the arrival of his men, have participated in the defense of the island and that those civilians weren't city folk; they were villagers who had come down from the mountains to fight against his men.

General Student was shaken by the tremendous losses of his paratroopers and was in deep fear of facing Hitler's anger. So, apparently, it was easy or convenient for him, that when he saw the wounds on a few of his dead paratroopers, not to bother investigating how they occurred. Instead he jumped to the conclusion that those wounds were inflicted upon his men after they were captured and were still alive.

In his anger, General Student branded the Cretan mountain villagers as uncivilized beasts. The Teutonic minds of the generals coming to Crete after that accepted Student's explanation of the wounds and his characterization of the mountain Cretans as primitive brutes, and that mental perception of the mountain Cretans stayed with the top management of the German forces for the duration of the war.

While all this was going on in the western and central parts of Crete, a unit of the Italian army, under General Carta, came to Lassithi on the eastern part of the island. Finding no resistance, they settled there. The Germans allowed the Italians to occupy that part of the island.

CHAPTER 9

The Nightmare Begins

The Nazis show their true colors

In order to punish the mountain villagers, General Student instituted a systematic program of executing mountain men. And that program was continued by his successor, General Waldemar Andrae. An army unit marched into a mountain village, collected a number of men, took them to the village square, and executed them, while the rest of the villagers were forced to watch the execution, and then the unit marched out without giving an explanation.

This stopped eventually, but the notion that the Cretan mountain villagers are uncivilized wild beasts remained with the top echelon of the German command. And, because of that, throughout the occupation, when the Gestapo punished a village, their men encircled the village at night. In the morning, they moved the women and young children out of the village and then killed the male villagers by making it a game. They hunted the unarmed men in the streets of the village before shooting them down. So, the action of those villager volunteer defenders came to weigh heavily on the Cretan mountain population during the four-year Nazi occupation of the island.

That this perception of the mountain Cretans is so, until the end of the war, was shown in a 1944 episode. At that time, Major Patrick Leigh

Fermor of the clandestine British military intelligence service on the island was able to abduct General Kreipe, the divisional commandant of the German forces in eastern Crete. During their long, clandestine trek through the mountains, General Kreipe begged Leigh Fermor not to leave him alone with the Cretan mountain villagers who were members of the abduction team. He told Leigh Fermor that he didn't trust those men because the Cretan mountain villagers were uncivilized animals.

CHAPTER 10

A Movement Is Born

The Cretans show their own colors

In the midst of gloom and despair, my uncles Kóstas and Yiánnis arrived, on foot, in Vyzári. It was a joyous occasion, and our family couldn't help but feel fortunate. My two brave uncles escaped captivity and walked from Albania until they reached the coastline. A patriot fisherman took them, in his small boat, to the little harbor of Kíssamos in western Crete. Most of the alive and uninjured members of the Fifth Greek Army returned to Crete in a similar way. But they were much too late for defending their island.

Immediately after the reports of the first unexplained, unprovoked, and what appeared to be capricious and whimsical executions, Cretan leaders realized that to fight the new Barbarians, they have to do it themselves—forget the British. That is the reason that, while it took several months on mainland Greece and in other occupied countries to develop political organizations to coordinate and support active resistance to the German occupiers, in Crete it occurred within the first few weeks.

When the first word-of-mouth reports of the widespread and unexplained executions of villagers by the Germans reached Amari, Antónis Lítinas, an attorney, put together a group of men. That group organized as the Εθνική Οργάνοση Αμαρίου (National Organization of Amári) early in August 1941. It was known by the Greek acronym EOA. The group welcomed members from the Amári villages—anyone who was interested in being part of the methodical development of resistance to the occupiers was welcome—and my father and uncles joined. It had a loose agenda in reviewing the situation and examining ways to cope with it. It came to be that most all the members of that group were former followers of Venizélos, a liberal Cretan prime minister. There was also a sprinkling of conservatives. The few communists around and their sympathizers refused to participate.

Soon, Lítinas found out that similar organizations had sprung up in the Réthymno prefecture and in the other prefectures of the island, including Crete's three largest cities. Eventually, they are bound together to form the Εθνική Οργάνωσης Κρήτης (National Organization of Crete), or EOK, by its Greek acronym.

EOK's first priorities were the formation of resistance armies of andártes (partisans) and the repatriation of the Anzac soldiers left behind when the British evacuated the island.

The formation of partisan armies was accomplished first, because of John Pendlebury's work the year before. After the Italians attacked Greece, the British approached Pendlebury, a British archaeologist on Crete, to become an agent of Special Operations Executive (SOE) and bring him back to active service as a captain. The SOE, or Advance Force 133, was a secret organization the British used during the war for planting, in territories occupied by the Axis forces, special intelligence units dealing with espionage, facilitating resistance, and sabotage.

Pendlebury recruited three men and trained them in the art of resistance against occupying enemy forces. The three men were Antónis Grigorákis (Sátanás), Giórgis Petrákis (Petrakoyiórgis), and Manólis Badouvás. And those were the initial and main EOK leaders that the andártes (partisans) were coalescing around. Pendlebury, by the way, was captured by the Germans and executed.

Amari and the eparchies to its east and west provided most of the initial partisans, and its mountains Kéndros and Psiloritis offered the first safe liméria (camps) of the partisan armies in the island's center. Capetán Petrakoyiòrgis and Capetán Badouvás had the largest partisan armies, while the one under Antónis Grigorákis, who was an extraordinary man, captured the imagination and fancy of the Cretans because of his moniker Capetán Sátanás—Captain Sátan.

CHAPTER 11

The Anzac

Helping brave men

After the defeat of the Anzac defenders, an unruly and badly planned and poorly executed evacuation of the British forces followed from Hora Sfakion, a small fishing harbor on the south shore of the island. The British men had to cross from the north shore to the south shore of the island, through massive mountain terrain, while being bombed and strafed by the German planes. As a result, several hundred men were left behind on Crete.

Earlier, the Cretans had been angry with the British for promising to effectively defend the island and then failing to do so. But after the German forces' atrocities against innocent villagers, the mood totally changed. Cretans looked at the British for help and eventually salvation from the Teutonic yoke.

EOK's help to the trapped Anzac soldiers took longer to accomplish, as it was more complicated than the formation of the partisan armies. It was complicated, as the Anzac soldiers were in small groups of two to five men, wandering in the mountains of the island attempting to avoid Germans patrols. And then EOK had to somehow begin communicating with the British in Egypt to send vessels to take the Anzac back to Egypt, and that was the reason for EOK's efforts to send Morse code messages by light sources.

During the efforts of EOK to establish communication with the British SOE desk (office) in Cairo, the trapped Anzac men on the island moved little by little from the north toward the south shore of the island.

Not being familiar with the topography, the care by which the British moved to avoid detection extended their trip by weeks. The roughness of the land, hunger, and the search for food and night cover took their toll. There were reports of shepherds finding dead soldiers on the mountainsides. It was from hunger or from eating wild greens that weren't good for them.

The only relief that these men had was when they decided to approach a village. Almost all of them did that, especially after word spread among them about the helping hands of the villagers. The sooner they made that decision, the less hardship they suffered because they found only love and admiration. They were fed, directed to safe locations to spend the night, and given directions to the next safe village farther south.

The first involvement I had with the resistance against the German occupiers was the same that most mountain Cretans had. I assisted wandering British soldiers in avoiding capture by the German forces, eluding possible informers, and guiding them to secure, safe night locations for rest—mostly small caves, some distance from our village.

I also taught them how to recognize the local agricultural policeman, who is thought by some of the villagers to be a collaborator, or at least not trustful. I provided them with portions of our food—wild greens, boiled, and then sprinkled with olive oil by my mother—and gave them directions to the next safe place.

This didn't happen just occasionally. Anzac soldiers passed by our village in what seemed to be an unending slow stream. And I'm not the only one who did this in Vyzári. Other families were doing the same. Giving needed assistance simply depended on who is the first to see the soldiers as they timidly and tentatively approached the village.[7] In my case, I knew that my uncles and the other families in Sáta had developed a "safe haven" for the British soldiers, so I attempted as well as I could to direct them there.

It was an amazing thing that I, and the rest of the people in the villages, could somewhat effectively communicate with the soldiers. Not only did these men understand what we wanted to tell them, they also were able to follow what they were told to do. All communication is via crude sign language, and, as we find out later, most of them ended up at the destinations they were told to go. My experience with the people I deal with was that they readily understand me—or so I thought.

They seemed to understand information about a possible collaborator, the need for spending the night in a cave to which I had taken them, the fact that the cooked wild vegetable I gave them to eat is the only food we had, and how to move to the next safe village. I realized, of course, that by the time they reached Vyzári, they have communicated with villagers in other parts of the route they followed, and they have some experience with sign language.

Regardless of the general feelings of the Cretans toward the British government, taking care of the wandering British soldiers became one of the first concerns of the organized patriot groups associated with EOK. Through our efforts, clandestine centers were formed as close to the south coast as possible. The Anzac men either found them by luck or, most likely, were directed to those centers, where they had to wait until something like a miracle happens.

My uncles in Sáta, assisted by the rest of the men and women of the hamlet, organized one of the largest "safe havens" for the British in the Amári region. Additional clusters had been organized in other villages. When Anzac soldiers come through Vyzári, we guided them to go to one of these clusters, but many also found themselves protected in groups

---

7 The only families in our village that showed no interest in helping the Anzac soldiers were the ones who at the last year of occupation emerged to be members of EAM, the leftist resistance organization. "We didn't care to help the plutocrat Brits" is the remark I received after the war from one of them. I'm told this wasn't a unique occurrence, as it happened in other villages also.

by families in Ághios Ioánnis, Apodoúlou, Aghía Paraskeví, Kouroútes, Níthavris, as well as in the settlements of Rízikas and Vathiakó.

When the British clandestinely land officers on the island, they and Cretan leaders, such as Capetan Petrakoyiórgis, begin the repatriation of the Anzac.

My contribution to the resistance has been minor. But I can brag about helping the Australians and New Zealanders. I consider that effort to be my most satisfying contribution to the conflict.

Our Christmas Pig

And then we cried

The reason we only had wild vegetables to eat ourselves, and to give to the Anzac soldiers, was because Crete didn't produce enough grain and other food stuffs to sustain its population of 400,000—and when the Italians attacked Greece, all imports stopped.

Because my father's job was in the cities, my mother had taken over the management of our household and our properties. Since we had extensive groves of olive trees, and there were villagers with only a few olive trees, she paid with olive oil for most of the services we needed on our properties.

A number of villagers haven't enough or appropriate properties for the production of sufficient grain for their families. Because of that, they cultivate some of our properties and share with us whatever they produce. Mother negotiates with those villagers how much of the grain they produce they must give to us for using our fields. This is always a spoken agreement, and it works fine.

One poor farmer regularly cultivated our land, and this worked well, year after year, until 1940. During that summer my father made one of his irregular visits to Vyzári, from his job in the cities. He spent some time with this farmer, as they have been friends since childhood. That visit resulted in my father asking Mother to charge that farmer lesser amounts of wheat than she had charged him in previous years. Mother agreed to do so, and that fall he was the only villager who cultivated one of our fields.

In October that year, the Italians invaded Greece, and the whole family returned to Vyzári. During the 1940-41 winter months, since we only had a small amount of wheat, my mother, alarmed by the war with the Italians, advised my father to purchase more wheat—enough to last us at least a year. But every time she mentioned buying wheat, my father postponed doing so. Apparently, he hadn't been as alarmed as Mother.

The island imports grain because it is mountainous, with poor soil, and the villagers are subsistence farmers, producing small amounts of wheat and other grains for their own use. The grain farming season starts with planting at the onset of rain in about late fall and ends with harvesting of the grain by early June.

With the island's young men fighting in Albania, the 1940-41 planting season found the farm families short of men for the cultivation of their fields, affecting the grain production, and then the Germans invaded Greece in the spring of 1941 and then Crete in late May. Right after taking over the island, they proceeded to confiscate, for their own use, any and all grain and other food supplies remaining in the importing merchants' storage facilities.

So, when Father finally decided to purchase wheat, he found that wheat and any other grain or legumes weren't available in stores, and that some farmers who might have had extra grain were hoarding it.

The fall of Greece brought the collapse of the value of the Greek currency. The drachma lost its value, and inflation was rampant. This forced the villagers to start a barter market. To buy something you need, you must exchange something else of approximately the same value that the seller wants. If you don't have what the seller wants, the transaction doesn't occur.

Bread is, by far, the main staple of the island's diet. Because of that, wheat has always been one of the most important commodities on the island. Thus, when the barter economy was established, grain, especially wheat, became the main commodity in the island's economy. If one has wheat to spare, one can acquire anything else one needs that is available. It follows then that it wasn't strange that farmers with excess wheat might hoard it.

At the same time, the major product and export of the island, olive oil, lost its value, as international trade had been interrupted by the war and almost all village families produce olive oil.

It is because of these conditions that our poor farmer, who has a large family, refused to give us the wheat he and my mother have agreed upon. Mother suspected that the farmer knew that my father doesn't like confrontation, and since he and my father are close friends, my father wouldn't press him for the wheat. Mother, however, always operating in a proactive mode, wasn't going to let this slide.

She simply told my father that he asked her to lease the property to his friend for a lesser amount of wheat than he normally paid us, and now instead of thanking her, he was refusing to pay. For the first time, I saw mother let her anger against my father surface. I heard her saying, "How many times did I suggest to you to buy wheat and you postponed doing so? Now we are out of wheat and we cannot find any to buy. Your friend owes us this wheat, and you are not pressing him to give it to us. Are you going to deprive your children of bread?"

For the first time that I remember, Father found some backbone and actually pushed this fellow hard. But even so, his friend gave us just a small fraction of the agreed amount. And the grain wasn't wheat, as the agreement called for, but a less desirable mixture of wheat, barley and oats. Mother didn't like it a bit but decided not to press further.

By winter, some people in villages and many in the Greek cities went hungry. Yet, the situation in the villages wasn't as dire as in the cities, mostly the large ones. Word-of-mouth reports filtering in from Athens indicated that the Germans had forced city officials to run trucks in the city streets during the early morning hours, before the night curfew was lifted. The task of the trucks was to collect the dead bodies lying in the streets. They had been put there by friends or relatives during the night.

By early fall, we were out of bread. By the middle of fall, we were out of legumes also. We had nothing from our gardens, as my father didn't get any seed for vegetables and potatoes. My mother had nothing to cook. We ate roasted carobs from our trees, but that just didn't work for long.

Then, luckily, autumn rains arrived and brought wild greens in the fields. It was left up to my sister Ouranía, my brother Títos, and me to roam the fields and collect the edible wild greens that my mother cooks for the family. But we weren't the only ones collecting those weeds. Other families were doing so also. Every morning, we had to get up while it was still dark, get to the fields before the crack of dawn, and go as far from the village as we can. We liked to roam the high steep hills, ahead of other villagers, and ahead of the sheep and goats.

The edible weeds came in two types. Some weeds were best boiled and served with olive oil sprinkled upon them. Other weeds were best sautéed in olive oil with onions. We all preferred the sautéed ones, but they weren't as abundant, and it was much more difficult to find them. We put extra effort in finding our preferred ones, but everyone else hunted them also. More often than not we ate the boiled ones. All five of us children came to hate greens. I imagine our parents did, too, but they kept it to themselves.

At the end of the Lenten period, preceding Christmas, it is the custom for the families in our villages to butcher a hog. Each family acquires a baby pig sometime after the first of the year, and raises it during the year. On celebrating the birth of Christ, the evening before Christmas, or on Christmas morning, each family butchers their hog. Those hogs are huge and provide meat for the families for several weeks.

Sometime in January 1941, my father acquired a baby pig, by exchanging honey—his avocation was honeybees. We fed it lots of greens cooked with olive oil, and plenty of acorns and carobs from our trees. The pig grew to be huge. We looked at it, salivating. Come Christmas Eve, my father would butcher it. We would have as much meat as we could eat for several days, and then we would not care if we didn't have bread.

Meanwhile, it became obvious to me that both of my parents were stressed because of our situation. I feel that my father for the first time seemed to seriously worry about his children's health. So my parents finally decided to leave their passive behavior in accepting the situation as it was. Now they became active in doing something about bread. And this time they worked together—the last time it has happened, if I remember correctly.

They started experimenting making bread with acorns and carobs, both from our trees. They dried and roasted them in the oven. They milled them using a simple milling contraption we had. What came out wasn't as fine as wheat flour, but that didn't stop them. They worked on it as my mother had done with wheat flour. But no matter how they used their materials, either alone or mixing them in various proportions, they refused to become edible bread.

Out of desperation, my parents decided they could make and sell soap using olive oil and lye—they already were making such soap for our own family's needs, and they had plenty of lye. They thought that they could barter soap for grain. They began doing that. Father made a rough oval stamp from olive wood, and we used it to imprint each soap bar. This, he thought, would give the bars a professional look. Even so, the large soap bars looked rough and ungainly. Still, the soap was as effective as any other.

My parents reasoned that farmers who didn't have lye or a lot of olive oil, or who didn't know how to make soap, would be their customers. Vyzári and the surrounding villages are mountain villages, however, and the villagers either didn't have much wheat to spare or the ones that had some hoarded it for more pressing needs.

Besides that, the mountain people who had excess grain had already exchanged it for guns and ammunition on the weapons black market. My uncles in Sáta had grain, but they used it to support the Anzac soldiers there and, later, the nucleus of the British military intelligence group.

My parents spent some time talking and pondering how they could sell their soap. By now they had realized that they needed to look at a few areas that produced more grain than the mountain villages. They also reached the conclusion that such an area should be away from the mountains and the gun-loving mountain villagers. After considerable searching and agonizing, they came up with what they think could be a viable solution.

One of the sisters of my paternal grandmother is married to an affluent farmer in Kamilári, a village located at the fringes of the Messará Plain. That plain is the largest flat area on the island, and a number of fairly prosperous villages and towns dot the Plain and the areas around it. Father decided that's where we'd sell our soap. He also decreed that my brother Titos and I would be the salespeople. We would go to our great-aunt's house and use that as our base. Then we would go around Kamilári and nearby villages, if needed, to sell the soap for wheat.

In late December, Father loaded our donkey with soap and gave us directions on how to reach Kamilári. The roads had no directional signs, as with all the donkey paths in the island. But it helped that Sáta is that way and I had been there many times already. We estimated that it took us more than five hours to reach our great-aunt's house.

Phones had been outlawed by the Nazis, so our arrival was unannounced and unexpected. Still, our old great-aunt and her husband gave us an effusive welcome with all smiles. Their children, their youngest being several years older than I, seemed to love us right away. We found out then, and on subsequent trips, that those folks are the warmest, most loving relatives we have. They treated us as if we were very special. No matter how much we suffered on the long trip there, we felt glad we made it, then and every time thereafter.

"Go around the village and sell your soap? No way!" Our old aunt wouldn't hear of it, and her husband agreed—I sensed that he didn't dare not to. "You just stay with us for a few days, and we will sell the soap for you," she stated in a categorical enough tone to eliminate any objections. And they did. Later, I wondered if they really sold the soap or if they kept it for themselves, and if they did the same thing even in subsequent trips. It seemed to me that selling the soap had been done surprisingly fast and with ease.

We liked it there so much that we wanted to stay longer, but Christmas was coming. We knew that our parents waited to find out if we succeeded in selling the soap. We knew that on Christmas Eve our father would butcher the pig and we would eat as much meat as we wanted. Remembering Christmas pigs of past years, we already can almost taste the meat. We know that we would have meat from it most of the rest of the winter.

Two days before Christmas, we left Kamilári. Throughout the long trip we talked about how happy our parents will be that we have brought wheat home. But mostly we anticipated our pleasure in tasting the roasted pig's meat. When we reached the small spring, Tsimí Te Vrýsi, as the sun was going down, a handful of our fellow villagers were watering their goats and sheep on their way home for the night. They greeted us and congratulated us on our donkey's load. Some took longing glances at the sacks of wheat. We watered the donkey and ourselves.

We became part of their group. We liked having more company after the long hours with just the two of us and the slow-moving donkey. On the way to the village, our companions wanted to know what we had seen on our long trip and what sort of village Kamilári is and other details of the trip. None of them had ever taken a trip that far away from Vyzári.

A few minutes from the village, one member of the group made the announcement that our pig had been stolen.

We stopped. We exchanged glances and we started crying. We cried, sobbing loudly and without shame. It hurt. It hurt too much. Our dreams evaporated instantly. It hurt so much. We cried continuously until we reached home. Our parents heard the crying and came out of our courtyard to meet us on the street. It is the first and only time that I saw my father cry. We cried until we went to bed that evening and even the next couple of days.

Months later, my father joined Advance Force 133, the clandestine British intelligence network on the island. One of the Cretan operatives, a distant relative of the thieves, tells Father that his friend, the one who wouldn't give us the wheat that he owed us, conspired with his wife's relatives from her former village to steal our pig. It had been a matter of revenge for him.

The bread from the wheat Titos and I brought made it easier for all of us to eat the boiled wild greens.

CHAPTER 13

The First Contact

Hope returns

We were angry at the British government, but we felt a strong kinship with the stranded British soldiers. It didn't take long for the leaders of EOK's Cretan patriots to realize that in order to solve the problem of the stranded soldiers and to organize a competent and effective resistance front against the occupiers, we needed serious assistance. But for all practical reasons, such assistance could be provided only by the British in Egypt. Once the leaders of EOK made that decision, the question was, How do we get that help?

With so many soldiers left behind, the EOK leaders felt, and hoped, that British submarines might patrol the south shore of the island in hopes of establishing contact with their soldiers or Cretan patriots. Because of that possibility, patriots either individually or in groups descended to the island's south shore. Each such group claimed a position at areas that shielded them from German surveillance posts. These groups spent their nights sending, through light sources, Morse code messages toward the Libyan Sea.

One evening, a truck driver from Iráklio who knows my father brought to our house a guest and his two large and heavy bags. I knew the man from the time I attended school in Iráklio, as he and my father had been together often. Talking with my parents about the atrocities of the Germans, "I came," he told my father, "because I remembered what you told me about your house in Sáta. As you said, it's some distance from the shore but it faces the Libyan Sea." He continued by telling us that he could send Morse code messages, and it is because of that he was sent to our house by his colleagues in the Iráklio EOK leadership.

This friend of my father, whose name I don't remember, was among the many members of EOK from the cities, on the island's north shore, who came to the island's south shore with as powerful light sources as they could find and sent messages to the open sea. The next day, this fellow and my father loaded our donkey and left for Sáta. My father and his brothers spent night after night, for weeks, watching their guest sending light messages toward the Libyan Sea from our front room's large parathýra. Once in a while, my father brought batteries to be recharged at the local factory in Vyzári.

Unbeknownst to them, a large number of EOK operatives, either sent by their chapters or on their own, had descended to or close to the south shore of the island and, with light sources, were sending Morse code messages to the open Libyan Sea.

The SOE Desk (Office) for Force 133-Crete in Cairo noticed. In deciphering the various sources describing the Brits' first contacts with the Cretan patriots, it appeared that in late 1941 they selected the agent Jack Smith-Hughes, who had been in Crete before the war, to lead the effort and Ralph Stockbridge to operate the wireless radio. They put them in a submarine, whose captain was familiar with the Cretan waters. The men disembarked from the submarine long before daybreak. They stashed their dinghy in the little cove and walked up to the Preveli Monastery. It took some time for the monks, and then the abbot, to establish the credentials of their visitors. With shameless tears, the monks embraced their guests warmly.

In their contacts with EOK officials, Smith-Huses and Stockbridge realized the dire conditions of their stranded soldiers and their EOS office's immediate responsibility to arrange for their repatriation. Soon after that, in fall 1941, Colonel Woodhouse arrived on Crete to develop some sort of organization in repatriation of the stranded soldiers. He conferred with the island's three main partisan leaders: Capetán Badou-vás, Capetán Petrakoyiòrgis, and Capetán Sátanás. Because of the large safe haven for the Brit soldiers that my Uncle Kóstas had developed in Sáta, Petrakoyiórgis took him to Sáta for a visit with my uncle.[8]

The cove below the Préveli Monastery became one of the largest centers for the care of the roaming stranded British military men. It was hidden and safe, the seawater was deep enough for the English Navy motor launches, and it was large enough to easily accommodate large groups of men without crowding. The monks provided food, the river clean water, and the mountainous area safe sanitation.

A German patrol came to the area. The officer in charge asked the Abbot, Aghathángelos Lagouvárdos, if any wandering British soldiers had come to the monastery. The abbot tells the Gestapo man, "This is a place of worship and meditation. No instruments or men for destruction are welcome." The statement was simultaneously true and false. British soldiers were not in the monastery, but they were in the area. The officer left satisfied that there were no British soldiers around.

Even men of God can lie convincingly.

---

8   When the regular Anzac repatriation program started, the effort wasn't soon enough for those Anzac men left on Crete. How they felt and what they thought about the Battle of Crete and being left behind on the island, as well as their life during that time, is indicated in two books: *On the Run*, written by Seam Danner, an Australian, and Ian Frazier, a New Zealander, and *Anzac Fury*, written by Peter Thompson.

Advance Force 133

And now some serious business

Uncle Kóstas must have impressed Woodhouse to the degree that when, in the spring of 1942, Colonel Dunbabin came to establish and develop a full SOE chapter on Crete, Uncle Kóstas was asked to meet him at the location where he disembarked from the motor launch on the night he came from Egypt.

Crete is important to the British for the same reasons that the island is important to the Germans. The Brits lost the island, but they need to know how the Germans were using it in assisting the Axis forces under General Rommel in their fight with the British forces in North Africa and how the island hinders their relationship with their Mideast colonies.

But that isn't all. The Brits also feel that because of the strategic position of the island, if they make trouble for the Germans on Crete, the Germans will station more forces there than they would need otherwise instead of sending them to fight in North Africa under General Rommel. They want to use the threat of resistance by the Cretan population and their partisans. So, once they moved Dunbabin, it didn't take long for the Brits to move intelligence personnel onto the island.

Dunbabin became the overall supervisor of all the Force 133 activities on the island and was directly responsible for such activities in the Prefecture of Iráklio. The Iráklio Prefecture was quickly becoming the most important prefecture of the island. It's the largest, it has the most military bases, and includes Iráklio, by far the largest city in both population and overall importance as an economic center. In order to help Rommel in Libya, new bases were constructed, including a new airport, directly south from Iráklio, in Tymbáki, at the south part of the Messará Plain. And because of all this, the German general in charge of the prefecture was a semi-independent "divisional" commandant of that part of the island.

Besides Dunbabin, the Crete Desk of SOE in Cairo also sent agent Xan Fielding. Xan became responsible for the western part of Crete. That included the city of Haniá, which is the seat of the overall commandant of the garrison of Fortress Crete.

With the Cretans already upset at the barbaric behavior of the German forces, the formation of EOK in place, and the existing nuclei of partisan armies, Dunbabin had no trouble finding capable native recruits for the core of his organization. Dunbabin, an academician and archaeologist, is by nature a deliberate, careful, methodical, and unhurried worker. So, it took him a few weeks before he selected his basic group of co-workers. And, as it turned out, he and Patrick Leigh Fermor are the two agents that became the protagonists of the British clandestine operations on Crete.

The three Paradisanós brothers served under Dunbabin. My uncle Kóstas was among the very first of Dunbabin's recruits, his closest Cretan associate, and the official representative in the spy ring of the Greek government in-exile in Cairo. Uncle Yiánnis, who knows some German, followed Kóstas, but when his health took a bad turn, he was moved to a hospital in Cairo. My father joined them a few months later, as part of the security squad of their clandestine headquarters.

The young and bright Aristédis Paradisanós from Ághios Ioánnis, a first cousin of the three Paradisanós brothers, was also recruited by Dunbabin. He was moved to the Middle East, where he was trained as a wireless radio operator and in using encrypted codes. When he returned to Crete, he became the main wireless operator, coder, and decoder of Dunbabin's core managing group of the spy ring.

After Uncle Kóstas met Dunbabin at the shore on the night he disembarked from the boat on his arrival on Crete, he took him to Sáta and put the family's farmhouse at the Brit's disposal. Dunbabin, apparently, liked the location.

Still, careful as he was, he asked Uncle Kóstas to take him around the area. In the ensuing few weeks, the two of them moved around the Amári area and the areas adjoining it. After meeting and visiting with some village mayors and EOK leaders, Dunbabin became comfortable with the people in the mountain villages and felt reasonably secure in the Amári area. Thus, the Amári region became the main clandestine base for his intelligence organization. That stability gave him the time, with the help of EOK leaders in the area and the cities, especially Iráklio, to establish a firm organization on the island.

Dunbabin's base, after Sáta was compromised, was floating in various locations in Amári and in the adjoining areas in the Mylopótamos and Aghios Vasílios eparchies, especially the mountains of Psilorítis and Kéndros.[9]

The first time I meet Dunbabin was at the family's house in Sáta. Although there were a few other British agents around, Patrick Leigh Fermor wasn't among them. Unbeknownst to me, Leigh Fermor came to Crete later, in the west part of the island, in order to replace Xan Fielding, who returned to Egypt for a new assignment elsewhere in Europe—I believe France.

---

9 It appeared that during the almost four years of German rule, no one gave the Gestapo concrete information about the existence of the central core of the spy ring after one communist from the Iráklio prefecture compromised Sáta. This silence occurred, even though our area's leftist-leaning villagers weren't enamored with England, to put it mildly. Before the war, Great Britain was envied for its wealth by the poor populations of the globe, including Cretans, and scorned by some intellectuals because of its military prowess. It is not much unlike the way some people in the world presently look at America.

When I finally met Leigh Fermor for the first time, it was almost a year later in Aghios Ioánnis, in the house of my great-uncle Koronákis, the mayor of the village, when Uncle Kóstas introduced me to him.

When a British agent speaks Greek and is supposed to stay for some time in Crete, he is given a Greek code name. I met a good number of British agents and know some of their code names, but my association with them was short or passing.

Dunbabin and Leigh Fermor were the first ones whose Greek code names I learned—and that stayed with me. Colonel Dunbabin is known to us as Κύριος Γιάννης—Kýrios Yiánnis (Mister John). Leigh Fermor is known as Κύριος Μιχάλης—Kýrios Mihális (Mister Michael).[10] Both of them speak Greek fluently, and both have adopted the idiomatic Cretan Greek.

In civilian life, Colonel Dunbabin served as an archaeologist and a university (Oxford) professor. He must be in his early thirties, and he strikes me as a dour man. He is austere both in behavior and talk, never laughing, and he hardly ever smiles. I grow to like and respect him because I sense that he likes the common folk of the mountains, and he does his best to avoid hurting us by his own or his organization's actions.

Major Leigh Fermor, "Paddy" to his friends and close associates, is younger, in his middle twenties. In civilian life, he was a traveler, reporter, and writer. Paddy's personality is the glaring antithesis of that of Dunbabin. He is an extrovert, an exciting, and excitable man, a daring operative—a dangerous man. Handsome, dashing, and a romantic, Leigh Fermor courts danger and loves good times.

Even though I don't have a chance to know him as well as Dunbabin, I heard stories about his exploits on the island from the Cretan operatives who accompanied him, especially Giórgis Tyrákis from Fourfourás. Since he had spent some time in Germany before the war and had mastered the German language, he pretends to be a Cretan villager, mingling with Germans in the cities and their patrols in the villages, listening to their conversations.

---

10 It was only after the war that I learned their real names.

I am impressed by the methodical, cautious and conservative Dunbabin; he oozes calm and safety. On the other hand, I am overwhelmed in the presence of Leigh Fermor. His dynamism, the way he moves about, and his reported exploits are exciting and smell of danger and more danger. Every time that I see him, I know he is special. I have fallen in love with Leigh Fermor—I wish that when I grow up I will be like him. But I also know that, even though I have been introduced to him, he looks at me the way one looks at a skinny, poorly dressed young child—I also realize that, months later, the next time I'm in his presence he doesn't even remember that I had been introduced to him.

It is no surprise that, considering the two dramatically different personalities of those two leaders, Dunbabin and Leigh Fermor don't philosophically agree on how Advance Force 133 should operate on the island. Dunbabin moves in a way that his actions do not unnecessarily endanger the Cretan population. Leigh Fermor, on the other hand, moves and acts without much regard for the suffering of the population due to his actions.

After serving a few months, Uncle Kóstas was brought to active duty by the Greek government-in-exile in Cairo, which appointed him as the official representative of Greece to the management of the Force 133 section on Crete, and he was accepted by the British Middle East Command. Uncle Kóstas was brought into active duty as a lieutenant.[11]

One of the efforts of Dunbabin's spy ring centers was moving people from Crete to Egypt who need to leave the island for security reasons or to join the few Greek forces there. Part of Dunbabin's and Uncle Kóstas' responsibilities is the vetting of those people before they are allowed to move on.

---

11 By the end of the occupation, he reached the rank of major. After the war, I discuss this with Uncle Kóstas. He tells me that Dunbabin felt that since Greece and England were fighting Germany, both allies should be recognized for fighting that common enemy. That was also the reason, besides the native intelligence of Aristédis, my uncle tells me, that Dunbabin had Aristedis trained and then appointed as the central cryptographer and wireless radio operator of the core of the spy ring.

Going back and forth between Crete and Egypt is a difficult and dangerous affair. It is done by clandestine night runs of British submarines at times, but largely by speedy British navy motor launches. Each run is top secret. It is planned with extreme care, methodically and meticulously executed, and always at night. They take place almost always from one of the thousands of coves in the south shore of the island, and often close to the numerous German sentinels on vantage locations by the shoreline.

While all this is going on, the Germans are busy in their efforts to better the assets of the island in order to improve their services to their North African forces under General Rommel. One of those efforts is the development of modern facilities and the improvement of roads and airports.

And the Germans do this by using forced—slave—labor.

The Perils of Aggaría

Slavery

The Germans found that the existing airports on the island didn't adequately serve their needs in supporting General Rommel in Libya and in effectively damaging the to-and-from sea movement of the British with their Middle East colonies. Plus, the airports are on the north shore of the island, while Rommel and his armies are in Libya, which is straight south of Crete. To correct this, they are building a modern military airport in the Messará Plain. The location is at the edge of where the Plain meets the section of the Mediterranean Sea, locally known as the Libyan Sea.

It is somewhat close to Sáta, as only the Sáta Hill separates Sáta from the Messará Plain. This is convenient for the British agents. They simply scale the Sáta Hill from the hamlet's side, sit down at the top and use their special binoculars. From there, the airport construction site is less than four kilometers away, on the plain below.

The town of Tymbáki is adjacent to the airport's chosen location. The Germans condemned the whole town and ordered its citizens to leave their homes. Two of those families found refuge in Sáta, with the help of my uncles. The town's ousted mayor brought his family to Sáta, and so did the only tailor in Tymbáki, who now stays in our house.

To build an airport in a hurry, the Germans needed engineers, technicians, office workers and lots of laborers. They had their own engineers and some of the technicians. They hired more technicians from cities on Crete and mainland Greece, as well as men and women who know some German.

When word came that they were hiring office workers, uncle Yiánnis applied for a job. Because he understands some German and has banking experience, he was hired. As I understood it later, Dunbabin placed additional agents there. The Germans pay those hired workers with Greek paper currency, which is losing its value from week to week, if not from day to day—inflation moves fast.

For the menial work, the Germans use forced labor. Such servitude is called αγγαρεία (aggaría) in Crete. And because they are in a hurry to build the airport and don't have all the necessary equipment, they look for many more laborers than they would normally need. In a radius of 50-plus kilometers from the airport, there are several hundred villages, almost all of them in the mountains.

The Germans develop quotas of men that each village has to send to Tymbáki to work for the construction of the airport. Even if it appears that the quotas are based on the population of each village, the smaller villages have difficulty in meeting their quotas. The order each mayor receives includes the warning that failure to fully cooperate would result in the village being destroyed.

Vyzári's quota is fifteen men. A Vyzári team of that number of men has to go to Tymbáki to work at the airport for two weeks. At the end of the two weeks, another Vyzári team of the same size must arrive in Tymbáki, to relieve the previous team. And that's what occurs every two weeks.

Vyzári's population is 221 people at that point. After excluding the old, the women, the children, the ill, the handicapped, the two doctors, and our mayor, we don't have enough adult men to meet the German order. Makri Manólis, our mayor, is forced to recruit teenagers. He is called Makrí (long) because he is tall. So, I had just turned 14 when I found myself in the second group headed to the Tymbáki airport.

That day, the other men and I walked close to five hours to get to the airport site. We were taken to a barbed-wire-fenced area that had been assigned to the men from the eparchy of Amári. All the barbed-wire-fenced areas that I could see were across the river that runs on the south side of the construction area. At the barbed-wire side of the river, a lot of bushes and trees had grown on the riverbank. A donkey road separated the barbed-wire area from those bushes and trees.

A low-ranking (noncommissioned) officer and a Greek helper counted us. The officer spoke to us, with the helper interpreting. We, of course, didn't understand a word from the short and quick speech, so the interpreter said that he would visit with us later. After the officer left, the translator talked to us.

"It's good," he said, "that you are all here, so your fellow villagers can leave as soon as they come from supper. Five o'clock in the morning, and not a second later, you must be up and ready to go. If you are not, you will be punished. And when one of you is punished, your whole group is punished. This means that you stay for two more weeks of work, even if your relief group arrives."

He told us that an officer and a soldier will be at the gate at exactly five to pick us up. They will count the number of men from each village. They will then take us and the rest of the men from Amári to the construction site. While going there, we must stay in line without attempting to move faster or slower or to get out of line, unless we need to relieve ourselves at the trees and bushes at the riverbank, but then we must hurry back to the line. We will be taken to a large area, where other groups of workers will also be. At that time, work supervisors will select the men they need.

Then his voice became more threatening and his facial expression clouded.

"At the construction site you must do exactly what you are asked to do and nothing else. You must do it as quickly as you can. If you don't understand an instruction, there will be a local employee who speaks German. But be careful—don't ask too many questions.

"While you are working, officers on horses will be checking on you. These officers have the responsibility of making sure you work steadily, you are doing the work you are asked to do, and that you don't move around needlessly. These officers have long whips, and they readily use them if they think that you are not working as you should. Of those officers, the one riding a big white horse is the most dangerous. His name is Müller. Some men have already been maimed from his beatings. If you value your life, don't provoke him."

He continued with instructions: Meals are served at noon and evening, and they are served only to the men who work full time. Because of that, our first meal was to be at noon the next day. All meals are watery barley soup, and we are responsible for the cleaning of the metal bowl and spoon that each one of us had brought along.

He included the warning that even though there are a lot of soldiers around, escaping from the site isn't difficult. Should one of us escape, however, the rest of us will be punished, as well as our village.

"This is a warning," he told us before leaving. "If you want to live and go back to your village without an injury or without bringing punishment to your fellow villagers and your village, you must follow my advice no matter how difficult the next two weeks will be for you."

A German soldier with an automatic gun closed the gate and took a sort of relaxed stand outside. A good number of other Amariótes lay or sat on the ground in groups. After we visited for a few minutes, we slept on the ground.

At five the next morning, a noncommissioned officer and a local interpreter came. They called us out, the officer counted us as we exited one at a time, and we joined other groups. They took us toward the working area. After we passed a bridge, they moved us into a large area where other groups were assembling. Another officer, with an interpreter, awaited us. Farther away from our place, I saw another large area of assembling groups; another one of several others, I was told later. Officers with interpreters came, looked us over, and then selected one or more groups and took them. They avoided taking a few, including me. Among the few young remaining rejects, I was the youngest, I think, as well as the shortest.

While we wondered what would happen to us, a handful of officers walked up to us. The first one looked at each one of us carefully. Then the interpreter told me to follow him. And I do. Looking at him, I gathered that he was a high-ranking officer. I followed the man to his office. He made a phone call, and in a few minutes an interpreter arrived. He told me that the officer is a major and that I'll work for him for the two weeks I'll be there. I'm to clean the two-room office and the attached bathroom (concrete floor with a hole), take the major's clothes, towels and bedding to the laundry, make his bed, polish his boots, and whatever else he wants. He then told me where the locations of the various facilities were.

In the mornings, I'm to go directly to his office when my group is marched to the usual assembly area. Seeing the cloud on my face, he told me that the officer in charge of the morning assembly area has been so notified already. I must go to the meals at noon and evening, and after the evening meal walk to my barbed-wire area. Leaving, the interpreter told me, "This major is a nice officer, and you're lucky that he selected you for this."

After the interpreter left, the major signaled me to follow him. He took me to his car and drove with me to Míres, a town about fifteen minutes from Tymbáki. I was sitting in the seat next to the driver, with two briefcases at my feet. He took the fat briefcase with him and entered a building. He stayed in the building for a long time.

At some point, I noticed another officer coming to the door and looking at my direction. I was thinking about the briefcase at my feet, and I decided that they wanted to find out if I left with it. He wanted to know, I told myself, if the briefcase is safe. Sitting in the car wasn't a pleasant experience. Not only was I sitting for a long time, but I also wondered why the major was checking on me. That worried me.

Then, I attracted attention. Sitting in the passenger's seat of the German military vehicle, with no one to keep me there, raised suspicions. The expressions on the faces of the locals passing by varied from surprise, to curiosity, to disgust, and even hate.

When the officer came back, his briefcase was thin. Later that afternoon, we went again to Míres. This time, he took the skinny briefcase and left the fat one by my feet. The way he placed the fat briefcase by my feet, I guessed that he didn't want people to see it. Later that day, the two trips and the briefcases left me wondering if he is testing me. I wondered if he somehow would know if I had opened his briefcases.

The second day I saw him only briefly in the early morning. When he returned in the early afternoon, I noticed that, like yesterday, he looked carefully at his desk and then made a phone call. In a few minutes, the interpreter came. He told me that the major was going to Iráklio for an overnight trip. He wanted me to stay in his office, without leaving it, for the rest of the day and during the night. He was going to take care of my meals and he would make the necessary arrangements with the barbed-wire-fenced area's officer.

I didn't think it was strange, even though in just those two days with him, I realized that he didn't want other officers coming to his office, except two other officers and Mueller—the noncommissioned officer who rides the white horse. During those two days, all three of them came with briefcases, individually, to major's office twice. By the seriousness in their facial expressions during those meetings with the major, it seemed to me that whatever they were talking about must be important.

He left me plenty of bread and cheese. He already had found out that I like them. After doing all my chores, I had a lazy time. Immediately after his arrival, early afternoon the next day, he opened and checked all the drawers, cupboards and the lone closet in his office. It is a good thing, I think, that I only used his davenport to sleep on and bothered nothing else. After that, he seemed to be friendlier. His eyes, initially hard, now seemed softer, even if the rest of his face refused to do so. He also seemed to be more relaxed about leaving me alone in the office. I began to like him, and I felt comfortable being there.

Meanwhile, my job became a topic of conversation among the men from Amári. My own group was initially pleased, but I noticed that a couple of them seemed irritated when the conversation was about my rather easy job. Those men seemed to resent that the soldiers who dealt with us appeared to be sort of deferential toward me. I learned not to talk about my nice officer, especially about taking me along on trips to Míres.

The same day the major returned from Iráklio, the interpreter came to the office. He told me that starting that day, the major would take care of my meals, and that I'd also do some courier duties for the major, and he took me to three different buildings where I'd be delivering or collecting materials. The buildings had a large letter or a number on the door identifying them. He also told me that he is surprised about the meals and the courier duties. "Since the major came to Tymbáki, more than three months ago, he has never done this for his helpers," he skeptically concluded.

Before, Mueller did the courier service for the major, after his duty with the white horse, the interpreter mentioned, but now I'll be doing it while Mueller rides his horse. He asked me which village I am from. "I know where the Amariótes work. I'll show you," he told me while taking my hand to change my direction. As we walked, we saw at a distance an officer on a white horse galloping toward a walking man, with his long whip circling above his head. When he reached the man, the horse seemed to push him down and the officer repeatedly hit him.

I imagined the interpreter had seen such scenes before, as he took my hand and changed directions again. He seemed to be upset and didn't say even goodbye when he left me at the major's office.

The next day, the major gave me a sealed envelope having the letter R. I took it to the long and extra-wide building with the door having the same letter. After entering the hallway, I opened the first door to my right without glancing at the envelope.

In the large and long room, I faced a large group of noncommissioned officers and civilians working at chest-high tables. They were standing around the long tables, and I noticed a few of the officers and two civilians close by looking at me. I stood at the door somewhat confused, as I expected a small office. But at the far end of the room I saw my uncle Yiánnis.

I was ready to walk up there and visit with him. Watching the face of my uncle, however, I stayed put. He didn't smile and had a clouded, unfriendly, worrisome face. He wasn't the friendly uncle I know. I understood. I was now scared. As everyone in the room watched me now,

I put the envelope in front of my face and read the office number—5. I showed it to one of the civilians closest to me. He took the envelope from my hand, looked at it as we went to the door, and showed me the correct door farther down in the hallway.

During the rest of my days there, I continued feeling comfortable about my job. I didn't even mind the jabs I got about my association with the enemy. When I took sealed envelopes or packages to other offices, I made sure I went to the correct office and then strolled around leisurely before going back to the office, if I already had finished my chores. I did this strolling especially when the major went to Míres or Iráklio.

One day, I went close to the place where I thought the men from Amári were working. I didn't find them, so I was unhurriedly returning to the office. For some reason, I looked back and I froze. Müller, on his white horse, was galloping in my direction, with his big whip circling above his head. I turned to face him, expecting to die. The horse stopped, and the whip became limp. He came closer, looked at me, and looked again. The horse made a 180-degree turn. And so did I. I quickly returned to the office with my heart still pounding. I am thankful he had recognized me. I never walked slowly again at that place.

That incident made me much more thankful that I was working for the major. I had heard about the horsemen being mean, but I hadn't seen them working on the laborers until that man who, I understand, died, and the scare I had that day. Even though Mueller was reputed to be the worst of the horsemen, after seeing his behavior, I realized how horrible he was—and, I must admit, I was scared the next evening, when I saw him coming for another visit with the major. I'm sure he recognized my fear when he glanced at me for a few seconds.

The last three days of my second week with the major, he was working harder than usual on writing tasks. He hardly came out of the office, except to eat at noon.

The day before I was to leave, both the two lieutenants and Mueller were in his office. It was the first time that all three were there together. The next day, the major left for Iráklio. Leaving the office, he shook my hand smiling—and that was another first.

Going back to the barbed-wire sleeping quarters that evening, we found out that our replacements had arrived. The officer in charge signaled that we could leave, and we did. We started just before dusk arrived, and we walked until we reached Vyzári. My mother stayed up that night, sleeping on a chair, waiting for me, while my father and siblings were sleeping. My mother guessed that I'd walk back home that night.

That weekend my father and I went to Sáta.

Uncle Yiánnis goes to Tymbáki from Sáta every day. He walks to Klíma very early each morning where a friend of his keeps his bicycle, and then he rides the bike to Tymbáki. Klíma is a village at the foot of the side of Sáta Hill facing the Messara Plain. From there to Tymbáki, the road is level and passable for the bike and mechanized vehicles. And it is in Klíma where the military transports drop the Gestapo and soldiers when they come to Sáta or other villages in the interior.

That evening, he told me how much I pleased him for picking up on his mood when I walked into the office where he works. As he already had told Dunbabin and Kóstas, he had been surprised to see me there. "A catastrophe was averted," he said, and Uncle Kóstas began to question me about that experience. That's when I learned from Uncle Yiánnis that the men in that room were noncommissioned officers, while the civilians were paid workers as he is. That gave me the opportunity to ask him what he does. But he looked at Uncle Kóstas and Dunbabin, and simply said, "I'll tell you some day." In other words, "I'm not allowed to share that."

But he allowed that one of the noncommissioned officers he works with is Austrian and a member of the intelligence staff of the airport. He had been a university history professor in Vienna before the war and had befriended my uncle. He told my uncle that several changes are going on at the base. The major I worked for is an important man from Haniá. He was sent to Tymbáki for what had seemed to be a study of the work in the base. His departure from the base had been sudden. He left Tymbáki the day after I left. Following that, some big shots from Haniá had arrived at the base and stayed overnight.

A couple days later, almost the whole management team of the airport left the base, and a new team came from Haniá to replace them. According to the noncommissioned Austrian officer, there had been no explanation for the changes. Uncle Yiánnis, however, felt that his friend knew what happened and why.

Returning to Vyzári, I found my name on the list Makri Manolis had nailed to his store's door. I'm in the group returning to Tymbáki in the next trip there. I knew that this would happen, and I had made plans to seek the major and see if I could work for him again. His transfer killed that plan. Now I had to think how I was going to cope without the major. While working for the major, I carefully had studied the somewhat chaotic organization of the Germans' efforts to manage their workforce—in spite of their mean horsemen. According to an estimate from the major's interpreter, who is from Thessaloniki, most of the time they had over a thousand if not close to two thousand men working. He mentioned that there were a lot more workers than German military personnel in Tymbáki. And that showed in the amorphous, and at times brutal, handling of the workers.

While walking with my group to Tymbáki for the second time, I finalized details of a plan. It was somewhat risky, but I decided to try it, if the procedures on handling the workers hadn't changed. From my first time there, I knew that the workers from each village were counted only in the morning as they left the fenced area and in the evening after they all had returned to the fenced area. And the workers hadn't been counted by name—just so many from each village.

I had also noticed that the officer who led the group didn't mind that the villagers left the line and went into the trees to relieve themselves and then rejoined the line. But, when one rejoined the line, it wasn't at the point he left it. And since the officer led the group, he really couldn't see when the villagers rejoined the line. In addition, since our group and other groups were often split into different projects, in the evening the workers, after they ate, came on their own to the barbed-wire area.

So, I figured out that what really counted for the Germans, in the daily control of the number of workers from each village, was that the number of workers from a given village who come to the barbed-wire area in the evening is the same number as the number of workers who had left the barbed-wire area that morning.

When we arrived at the encampment this time, I noticed that the Germans who supervised us before were the same, and they were still deferential to me. After we settled down, I moved around the area and visited with members of the teams from other villages who had been there the past week. They all described the procedures to be exactly as they had been before. Now, the only thing I needed was the audacity to carry out my plan.

In the morning while being taken to the construction site, I went into the bushes by the river. I stayed there until the place was totally quiet—everyone had left. Then, I walked to nearby Kamilári, the village where our relatives who had helped us with the wheat are living. My old great-aunt was home—all others were working in the fields—so I surprised her. When I told her what I had done, she had a big laugh and held me tight.

I had a good breakfast and a good lunch. In the late afternoon, she had supper for me, and then I walked back to the barbed-wire hotel. I spend some time surveying the area before I got close. There was no one around. I walked into the bushes of the river bank and stayed there. When the workers began going by, I waited for what I thought was the right moment and then ran to join a small group of them. About half an hour later, the soldiers came. I did this for the full two weeks. I'm mildly surprised that my fellow villagers didn't become aware of my ploy. They thought I was still with the major, and I didn't say otherwise.

One night, sirens woke us up. In a few minutes, planes were over us. Antiaircraft batteries went on furiously while bombs were exploding. It lasted only a few moments, but it left us worrying about our safety.

On our way back to Vyzári, I told my fellow villagers what I had done. They were surprised; they had a hard time believing me. But, really, it was no mystery, since the situation was so convoluted. I told them how I did it. A few laughed. Most were pleased, but not all. Two of my compatriots weren't very kind, and a couple more seemed to agree with them. They felt that not only I had unnecessarily endangered my own life, but theirs, too.

In Vyzári, my ploy became the topic of conversation. Most of my fellow villagers were with me, but a good number asked our mayor not to put me in the same team with them. In a way, I agreed with their argument that my behavior endangered them, our village, and my relatives in Kamilári. But my great-aunt Kadianí, another sister of my paternal grandmother, even smiled, a first for her, when I told her the story.

The second week later, my name wasn't on the list for the team going to Tymbáki. The mayor reportedly said to the people who didn't want me to be in their team that he also didn't trust me. Because of that and for the safety of our village, he took my name off the records of the village. "He acted in such a reckless way endangering our whole village," he told them, "and I can't trust him."

The villagers who made most of the noise for my behavior weren't happy, but they didn't dare to complain. Many of the villagers were concerned, but my friend Evángelos mentioned that most were proud that I fooled the Germans. For my part, I was relieved. But I was also concerned, because I thought that the mayor, whose wife is my father's second cousin, was angry at me in earnest.

Eventually, I learned that Uncle Kóstas had intervened after two things occurred. Uncle Yiánnis' cover was blown. He avoided apprehension by the Gestapo because he was forewarned by his friend, the Austrian officer. Then, my father told me, someone from Vyzári met Uncle Kóstas in Kouroútes, a village southeast of Vyzári. He related to Uncle Kóstas the developing problem with the people who had criticized me.

Uncle Kóstas became concerned about my safety when I again had to go to Tymbáki, as I shared Uncle Yiánnis' last name, which probably wasn't a problem considering the way the workers were handled, but he used it as an argument anyway. One night, he slipped into our mayor's house at the southeast edge of Vyzári. Before leaving, the two of them developed a plan for erasing my name from the pool of villagers going to Tymbáki and how the mayor would avoid criticism because of that.

Up to that point I was rather innocently involved in the resistance and the intelligence network. Taking care of the Australian and New Zealand military men roaming in our area was a normal, natural act for any Cretan, young or old. And I, of course, was often in Sáta, where I mingled with the few Brits and other agents. But I was a visitor, not a participant—and, without being told, I knew that I must keep my mouth shut.

CHAPTER 16

Drawn into the Net

The accidental spy

It turned out that my Tymbáki experience became of interest to both my uncle Kóstas and Dunbabin. First, they were pleased with the way I coped with my unexpected encounter with Uncle Yiánnis. A couple of weeks later, they spent some time quizzing me about my time with the major and how I had been able to avoid working at the airport construction for two weeks. After that, both Uncle Kóstas and Colonel Dunbabin seemed to look at me differently. And in the months that followed, my life gradually changed.

The leaders of EOK in the cities, especially Iráklio, and Dunbabin established clandestine and well-functioning virtual avenues for moving people and documents to Dunbabin in Sáta. By using trusted professional truck and bus drivers, they brought both people and documents to trusted men in a few villages. My father helped in vetting the drivers. He practically knew all professional drivers on the island because of his well over ten-year experience in the island's transportation business.

From those villages, runners (couriers) took them for the last leg on foot to Sáta, as the little settlement is remote and isolated, and, when Sáta was compromised, to Aghios Ioánnis, another remote and isolated small village. Dunbabin and Kóstas decided that one of those virtual avenues ends at our front door in Vyzári and that I was to be the runner for moving people and documents from Vyzári to them.

Those people were men and women, at times full families, either running away from the Gestapo or individuals who for one reason or another needed to join the slim Greek forces in Egypt. Dunbabin and my uncle did the final vetting of those folks in order to establish their identity and for evaluating their need to move to Egypt—in clandestine night runs by British either submarines or speedy motor launches.

Following that, people started showing up at our front door. I was puzzled, but I never asked how those people found the operatives that sent them our way and how these men—I never dealt with a woman—once dropped by buses or trucks were able to find our front door without asking any questions in the village.

When those men, mostly one at a time, showed up at our front door, both my mother and I recognized them by their tentativeness in approaching us. Many seemed—and we understood why—to wonder who we were, or if we really were trustworthy. As I learned after the war, almost all of them didn't even know our name, although they were told to look for Maria—my mother's name.

Because Maria is the Greek name of the Virgin Mary, it is the most common female name on the island's villages. So they were instructed by EOK leaders and the field operatives of Advance Force 133 to use my mother's name, as a lot of women called Maria are around in every mountain settlement. At times, when I was the one at the door, they almost seemed ready to run, before I hurriedly called my mother.

At times, a runaway came at night or during the day, but almost always in the evenings, when the buses and trucks came or passed by from the city. It was up to my mother to feed them and provide them a place to sleep. The next morning, I helped them move on. For most journeys, I used our donkey, unless they preferred to walk—and many did.

They all knew that they were coming to our house. No one knew, however, where I was taking them. And it was the rare man who asked, as we walked, but I kept quiet and they got the message. Initially, I took them to Sáta and, after Sáta was compromised, to Aghios Ioánnis.

People interest me, so I liked taking them to Sáta because I spent about four hours visiting with them, while it was only about an hour and a half taking them to Aghios Ioánnis. Sometimes, we would make the trip at night, particularly if a person seemed to be overly anxious, nervous, uneasy, and worried, or he requested it. My mother and I had no idea why they were on the run and, of course, we didn't know their names, unless they volunteered their first name, and most of them did. All these men, except two, stayed anonymous to me, even after the war.

After the war, I learned that among the dozens of men I escorted was General Kelaidís. Even though I hadn't known who he was, I remembered him. He had impressed me from the moment he appeared at our front door. He was relaxed and trustful. He looked straight at me and smiled. He didn't directly ask for Maria. He was passing through, he said, and asked me if he could stay for the night, if Maria is here. Of course he could, I answered, and asked my mother to come to the door. She came and simply said, "You are welcome, I'm Maria." He smiled again and came in.

Unlike most of the others, some of whom were indifferent, uneasy, not nice, and some almost arrogant, he was extremely polite and apologetic to my mother for the inconvenience he was causing her on the night he spent at our house. The next day, during our four-hour-plus trip to Sáta, he on the donkey and I walking, Kelaidís kept talking to me as if I was an adult.

Of all the men I escorted to Sáta or Aghios Ioánnis, he was the least scared, the most humble, and the most pleasant—and he never asked where I was taking him. Even at that young age—I was not fifteen yet—I sensed an unusual self-assurance and seriousness about him. I liked him. Kelaidís was an air force officer, and he was going to Egypt to join the minute Greek forces there, I found out later.[12]

My biggest surprise came from Petrakis, the director of Koraís, the school I attended in Iráklio before the war. This time the vetting occurred in Aghios Ioánnis. When I met him now, he had his son along, who must be in his late teens. Petrákis appeared to be bothered by

---

12 After the war, he became the chief of the Greek Air Force.

something. He seemed to be overly agitated, and that reflected on his young son's behavior. I felt that he didn't trust us, as he looked around in a way that I thought indicated he suspected us. He even became upset about the length of the vetting procedures and the time he and his son had to wait until they were taken to their night rendezvous with a British motor launch.

Later, Uncle Kóstas told me that Petrákis was running from the Gestapo and he was anxious to take his son off the island and away from the reach of the Gestapo. Petrákis' wife is French, and serves as the instructor of French in Koraís. The son is their only child.

During the occupation, the jobs I'm asked to perform are done in other situations by a lot of other teenage Cretans, working for the intelligence organization of the resistance armies. What I do, probably dozens of other teenagers do for the British intelligence service agents on the island, and more yet for the partisan armies.

It has been easier for young children to avoid suspicion—not only on the countryside but also in the cities. At least until the Gestapo got wise or traitors pointed us out to the Germans—as happened to me in Sáta. Some even lost their lives. I'm among the lucky ones.

Sáta Is Compromised

Tragedy averted

Our family's farmhouse in Sáta is ancient. For several months, however, it served as the main base of the busy shop of Dunbabin. That stability allowed Dunbabin, with the cooperation of EOK's Cretan patriots, to form a loosely connected net of both British and Cretan agents.

This was especially so in the city of Iráklio and the German installations in that prefecture. The EOK leaders there recruited agents, especially good-looking young women, who applied for jobs in various German offices and installations. After the war, Dunbabin refused to name those agents, unless they were in danger of being punished for their association with the German officers.

It was during those months when, one evening, coming to Sáta with my father, we found a team of British commandos eating with Dunbabin and my uncles in our house there. British commando teams were using the hamlet as a secure stopping station when they needed to do so. This was especially so when returning from a mission and the vessel to take them back to Egypt couldn't approach their embarkation point on the south shore of the island due to foul weather conditions.

That was the first time that I saw a British commando team. They were an impressive group. Big, robust, exuding action and danger—I was thrilled. But what surprises me most was the fact that they look no different than the small group of German officers I had seen in Vyzári just a few days before.

Sáta has hardly thirty souls living there permanently. The families living there year-around were willing to have the spy ring in their midst, even though they were aware that if the Gestapo became informed and they found the Brits during a raid, their homes would be destroyed and whoever was captured there would be executed.

Sáta is a difficult place to find. Only an unmaintained miserable donkey path leads to it from north and south. As already noted, the place is protected by high hills from all directions except the west-southwest. Even from that side, it is difficult to see Sáta from a distance, as the few modest houses are pretty much hidden among the olive groves.

The Germans have maps, but unless they have good reason to walk up to it, the place is out of their way. The hamlet is at the southernmost boundary of the Amári region. It is only a few hundred feet from the boundary that separates, in that area, the Réthymno and Iráklio prefectures.

One day, before midmorning, a patriot from Míres came running to the hamlet. The patriots in Míres, he reported, have learned, by a miraculous accident, early that morning that during the night the Gestapo was informed about the British presence in Sáta. Dunbabin and his group moved out in just a couple hours. Before leaving, they sent runners, including my father, to inform the mayors and local EOK leaders, working with them, in Amári and the éparchies around Amári, including the Messará Plain, of Sáta's compromise.

That night, the Gestapo brought a large contingent of soldiers and encircled the little settlement. It was their first raid on Sáta, but everyone in the hamlet was expecting it. The Germans looked inside, outside and on top of every building, including stables. The few empty houses were explained as farmers coming sporadically to work on their fields, and then they spread into the fields around the tiny place. There was not a single trace around ever of a British presence.

The Germans spent part of the night and all day methodically checking the area. They found just puzzled farmers going about their chores, once they were allowed to do so.

The departing British and local agents had not left any incriminating evidence of their presence. Their action not only saved the hamlet, it also left an impression on the Gestapo that their informer gave them a fabricated story. The Míres station of the Gestapo may have decided that the person who gave them the information lied or was mistaken— something that probably also saved the hamlet later, when they seemed to suspect certain people there.

That the hamlet was compromised was a surprise. No strangers went through it, except for the roaming black-market merchants, but it had been more than a month since the last one was there, and the British were careful not to venture out of the house when strangers were around.

The villagers from other villages who own properties there and come occasionally to Sáta were fully trusted. Also among the trusted outsiders were two farmers from Klíma. Uncle Kóstas had been the godfather of one of those farmer's sons. Uncle Kóstas approached them.

"Yes," one of them said, "I did mention the British to my koumbáro (best man) in Bómbia, but I fully trust him." Uncle Kóstas knew that man and had been in his house in Bómbia. Kóstas visited him, but he claimed that he hadn't talked to anyone about it. My uncle went to Míres. He visited with their main contact there. They decided to ask the Sátanás partisan army to investigate the incident. Eventually, Kóstas found out that a communist had betrayed Sáta, and that the partisans had taken care of him.

It took more than two weeks before we were advised that our house in Sáta had been abandoned. My mother found herself in a difficult position. By local standards, our family's properties in Sáta were extensive, but we also had significant properties in Vyzári and in Ághios Ioánnis. She needed to find a way to supervise properties in three villages.

Mother asked me to sit with her and review the problem. We spent some time examining various possibilities. At the end, we came to what we thought was an acceptable solution, even though my mother had some reluctance in approving it. As the eldest male remaining in our family and as someone with some familiarity with the house, the hamlet, and the area, I was the logical choice to take over that responsibility.

The two of us talk often and at length about the family's affairs, but it was still a surprise that my mother had faith in my ability to cope with that responsibility and signed off on that decision. When I think about it now, looking at the fifteen-year-old boys around me, I wondered what made us feel that I could be fine alone in Sáta.

The next day, I left on foot for Sáta.

CHAPTER 18

The Case of the Microbirds

Becoming a farmer

I had been in Sáta many times, but as a visitor, not as a resident. And I quickly learned that there was an enormous difference between visiting and residing in that little place.

When I arrived, three surprises were waiting for me. The first was that a family had moved into our house. My second surprise was that there were no animals in our stables, save a pair of oxen and a donkey. The chickens, goats, and sheep were all gone. "What the hell has happened?" I asked myself. If the first two things were surprising, the third one was devastating. Except for salted olives, there was no food left. No potatoes, no legumes, except koukiá (fava beans). There wasn't even any bread or grain to mill for flour. It was a shock; yet, I still didn't fully realize the enormity of the trouble I was in.

Mihális Tyrákis, Tyromihális for the locals, is a distant cousin of my paternal grandparents. His is one of the six permanent families living in Sáta year-around. Another three families have properties in the area, but they are minor. They have built small houses, but they come to Sáta only when they need to do some work on their properties.

Bárba (old uncle) Tyromihális, whom I knew well from previous trips to the hamlet, came to the house in late afternoon to take our oxen and donkey to hamlet's communal spring to water them. He didn't seem surprised to find me in the house. He welcomed me and asked me for dinner that evening. I gladly accept the invitation.

There, my theia (aunt) and two of their grown children, Maria, who is married to a local man, now with Dunbabin and Kóstas, and Nikolís welcomed me. After dinner Nikolís and I got together to talk while the women did the dishes. Barba Tyromihális joined us. "Do you know what happened here the last couple weeks?" my theio asked.

"Yes, Ippokrátis told us about the German raid." Ippokrátis is a member of EOK from Fourfourás, the former home village of Barba Tyromihális, who now proceeded to tell me what happened during the raid. His version wasn't different from Ippokrátis' version. I just listened as if it were the first time I'd heard it.

But this gave me the opening to bring up what I found or, rather, I didn't find at our house, this afternoon.

"Uncle Mihális, I spent the afternoon wondering about the present state of our house. A family is in our house. All the food supplies are gone, and there is no bread or wheat. Except for the donkey and the oxen, the other animals have disappeared."

"I thought you seemed perturbed and irritated while visiting with you this afternoon."

"Yes, I had been, and I'm still so. What did happen in our house?"

"First, Kóstas asked me to take care of the donkey and the oxen until you got here."

"Did my uncle know I was coming here?"

"Yes. Kóstas told me that he is going to send word to Maria."

"But my mother never got such a message. We found out about the need to come here from Ippokrátis."

"Maybe Ippokrátis was the one who was supposed to bring the message to your mother and for some reason he was unable to do it sooner. That explains why it took you a long time getting here and the fact that you didn't bring any supplies. Listen, my nephew, if you need help, let me know. I want to help you settle in."

"Thank you, Uncle Mihális. What happened in our house?"

"When the Germans decided to build an airport on the south shore of the island they selected the Messará Plain, and Tymbáki was in the way. The Germans moved into the town and displaced all of the town's residents. The town folks had to leave with just the clothes they are wearing."

That I knew already. But I kept quiet, and my old uncle continued.

"Most of the Tymbáki families found refuge with relatives in other villages. The rest were taken in by friends or by total strangers in other villages. As you know, your uncles are friends with Vangélis, the mayor of Tymbáki, who has a relatively large family."

Apparently, Vangélis was too proud to ask my uncles for help, and he moved his family to temporary housing in Zarós. When my uncles located him, they invited him to come to Sáta after they found a house for his family. While looking for a place for Vangélis, my uncles heard that the town's tailor, who was new to Tymbáki, had no friends or relatives around, because he had come to Crete from the mainland.

When Uncle Kóstas received word from Vyzári that my great-aunt, Aggelidomanólena, would allow Vangélis to move his family into the house she has in Sáta, he asked Vangélis to move there. Then as my uncles were leaving in a hurry with the British, they asked Tyromihális to ask the tailor to come to Sáta and stay in our house and in the room in which he is now. Both families moved to Sáta a few days before I showed up.

"What about the animals and food?" I asked.

"I believe most of the animals and foodstuff were consumed by the wandering British soldiers and the operatives of the spy ring. And according to your uncles' directions, I gave the chickens, goats and sheep to Vangélis' family. It also appears that the tailor may have taken whatever food supplies had been left in the house."

The way he said "may," and not looking at me, I guess that he knew where the foodstuffs had gone.

"My nephew," my old uncle continued, "your uncles had quite a few people here for a long time. Even though we all helped, I imagine that their supplies have been exhausted. Again, since you have been so late coming, if anything was left, the tailor could have taken it for his family."

"Well, I guess I'll have to find ways to survive," I grudgingly and silently admitted to myself.

"Mihalákis, your uncles and your father had to leave your house suddenly and in a hurry. I imagine they had hoped that you would bring supplies with you."

"Oh, now it's my fault," I think, before saying, "Yes. I realize that now."

"Mihális, I now think that your father and your uncles assumed a lot about you coming here, without letting your mother know what is going on."

Looking at me for a while, he asked, "Now that you're here, have you thought yet about how you're going to face this?"

"To tell you the truth, Uncle, I don't have any idea right now as to how I'll cope. For now, anyway, I will take care of the oxen and the donkey, and thank you for taking care of them until my late arrival."

Nikolis, who is about ten years my senior, and I walked around the hamlet for a short time and then we sat out outside my house and visited for a long time.[13]

The next day, I went to my Barba Tyromihális' home for breakfast, lunch and supper. After the evening meal, Barba Tyromihális, Nikolís, and I visited again.

During the day, I had spent a lot of time trying to answer my barba's question on coping with my present situation. While playing with various possibilities, another question had surfaced. That is, "What do I do after I solve the present problem of supplies?"

The way the war was going, it seemed that there would be years before it ended. We had also solved the problem for bread for now, but that problem could return. "So, what shall I be doing in Sáta during those

---

13 That was the beginning of a warm friendship that lasts till we both are old.

years?" It took some time, but I finally thought I had an answer to my own question.

Now, during our visit when I found an opening, I looked at my old uncle and addressed him. "Bárba, you mentioned yesterday that you are preparing to start cultivation and planting as soon as the rainy season starts. I would like to start planting too. Since my uncles left the oxen, I might as well use them. I'll need some wheat seed. Could I borrow some from you?"

My barba stayed silent for some time, looking at me a couple times before he finally spoke.

"Have you ever cultivated, Mihalákis? Have you ever planted anything?"

"No."

"I thought so. It isn't easy, my nephew. It's hard work, long hours and little sleep."

"As you know, Uncle Mihális, because my father worked in the cities, we never had the need and means to cultivate our properties in Vyzári, so we have other people do it for us. After the difficulties we had last year, running out of wheat, I feel the same situation could develop for next year too, and since my uncles have the oxen and the necessary gear, I would like to try producing our own wheat.

"Yes, I haven't had any experience in farming. And I'm sure that it is as difficult and exhausting as you say, but my mother has sent me to take care of our family's properties, and that's what I'll do. I don't know anything, but I can learn. I want to learn."

My Barba looked at me sort of askance. He either thought I was ridiculous or he doubted me. "And he is right," I thought, now that I came to visualize the enormity of what I had said. "How the hell am I going to do all this?"

Tyromihális must have realized my thoughts and it took a long time for him to react. He finally said, "Mihalákis, I'll come to your house tomorrow, and we will start your lessons in cultivating and planting. You must be awake and ready by daybreak."

He said that with a hint of a smile. I realize he thought I would not be able to get up before daybreak. But I was up when my theio came before the sun made its appearance. We inspected the gear for saddling the oxen, and then we moved the equipment and oxen to the field next to our stables. We saddled the oxen. Those beasts seemed to know what we were doing, and they cooperated. We attached the gear to the plow, so the oxen would pull the plow in the fields. My uncles' plow is steel-made, easy to operate for grownups, but it was heavy and its handles were too high for me—I realized that it will be difficult, but I postponed worrying about it.

Then, together, we saddled the donkey and we loaded on it all the equipment. We did both the oxen and the donkey together a couple times. Then he asked me to do it alone. It was an effort for me, but when I was through, I didn't see a sarcastic smile on him. He seemed satisfied that I could do it. Now the old man seemed more serious. I felt he was almost pleased. We went to feed and water the oxen, and he explained how to do it, always looking at me—I suspect he was checking if I was paying attention.

The next day, as early as before and while he was observing me, I repeated yesterday's work and then I recited what he had told me in his lecture the day before. He asked me to put áhera (straw) in the manger of the oxen, and after they ate, I took them to the spring, while he followed every step I took.

The third day he brought some wheat seed. Going to our field next to the stables, he showed me how I should spray it on the ground, and how much seed in a small part of the field before cultivating it, and then do the same on next part of the field, until I finished the whole field. The fourth day, I did all of those things while my silent Bárba watched me. At the end, he looked at me and said, "I will loan you the wheat seed."

After all that, we moved to the kitchen. I had nothing to treat him, so we just talked. He told me that a good farmer wakes an hour before daybreak to feed and water his oxen. At daybreak or soon after, the good farmer loads his donkey with cultivating gear and seed and leaves with his animals for the field to be cultivated, but watering them first. When the sun is setting, he loads his donkey and heads home, but stopping at the communal spring to water the oxen. At home, he spends the evening feeding the oxen and then he goes to bed.

During all this time, the old man watched my facial expressions and other body language, but I watched him too. At the end, I felt that he was feeling that I might be able to make it, but it was obvious he still had some doubts. Before leaving, he invited me to come to his house for lunch and dinner. I thanked my old uncle—who isn't really very old, even though he looks it—for the lesson, for his concern about my situation, for offering to loan me the seed, and the invitation to lunch and dinner. He listened with a faint smile.

At lunch, even my theia invited me for supper. As I was leaving that evening, my aunt invited me for all of the meals the next day. And this went on for more than a week. It was nice, but I eventually became embarrassed about accepting their invitation for that long. I came to think that I shouldn't depend on the goodness of my bárba and theia, even if they assured me that they liked having me eat with them. Besides, I realized, I must collect myself and get serious about my life in Sáta. First of all, I decided, I must become self-sufficient and cook for myself.

The thought occurred to me that I can go to Vyzári with the donkey and bring back supplies. But I promised my mother that I would be able to cope with any adversities here. How could I go back home right after facing the first difficulty I encountered? It would be a disappointment for my mother. Deciding to cook for myself means that I have to cook the only foodstuff I have, koukiá—the fava beans. I like none of the legumes, and I dislike koukiá more than the rest of the legumes. And that's the reason I hadn't looked at the koukiá all this time. And now it was koukiá or nothing else.

When the koukiá plants flower, flying insects deposit minute eggs on each of the flowers. Those minute eggs become part of each bean. In time, the minute eggs hatch into little worms. Those worms eat a hole in each bean. After the holes reach the surface of the bean, the worms are metamorphosed into small flying insects. Those insects will, in turn, lay eggs in the flowers of the next season's plants of fava beans. Koukiá are giants among the legumes, much larger than any of the rest of the legumes. The farmers keep a part of their fava beans, as much as they need for seed to plant the next planting season. The rest of the koukiá are treated so that the eggs will be destroyed. The simplest such treatment is to put them in hot oven.

One evening I told my aunt Tyrákena (wife of Tyrákis) that I had found some koukiá and salted olives, which was true, so I was going to use them for my food. She attempted to object to my decision, but after a glance at her husband, she stopped. What I planned to do was to cook the koukiá in the morning and eat them for breakfast, lunch, and supper.

We always ate koukiá, and the rest of the pulses, with bread, but in this case I had no bread. So, I was going to boil them, salt them and sprinkle olive oil over them. Early the next morning I put a pot of water on the fire. After the water started boiling, I picked up some of the fava beans. Taking them to the pot, I noticed holes in them; I froze. I looked at them again. Holy Ghost! Every single one of these fava beans had a hole with a living insect in it. My uncles had kept them for seed, and that's why they weren't given out or taken away by the tailor.

What to do now? I already had detached myself from the Tyrákis' table. As much as I wanted to, I couldn't bring myself to go back, especially since I noticed last night's expression on bárba Tyromihális' face—his thoughts, I decided then, were the same as mine. That is, "It's time that I must learn to take care of myself." Anxiety and hopelessness suddenly took over my whole body. Not only couldn't I eat, but also my hopes of becoming self-sufficient evaporated instantly. I sat on the clay floor while the water was boiling loudly. I was defeated.

By noon I was hungry. So, I tried to get rid of the "micro-birds" from the beans, but they didn't cooperate and stubbornly stayed inside their holes. I put some beans in a pot of water and waited for them to exit their holes. Only a couple decided to do so, no matter how long I waited for them to use their tiny minds. I reasoned that if two of them left their holes in cold water, the rest of them would leave when the water became warm and then warmer. I put the pot with cold water on the fire with all the koukiá I wanted to cook. Now I waited for the micro-birds to become alarmed as the water warmed up.

I stood over the pot waiting to see their mass exodus as the water got warmer and warmer. But they do not seem alarmed at all. Only one came to the top. I wondered if the water was hot enough, and I put my finger in to test it. Ouch! The water was hot! And then it started boiling.

Apparently, these little things died fighting for their right to stay in their holes. Those little devils would rather die than leave their nests. Just a couple more float on top of the water. I had come to the point where I became angry at those stubborn little insects. Why did they stay in their holes? Why did they refuse to cooperate with me? After all the trouble I went through to coax them out of their holes so they could live. It was maddening to realize that what I have done hadn't worked out.

Not knowing what else to do, I kept cooking the koukiá until they were soft, before taking them off the fire. I had skipped breakfast. Now I had a choice: eat the koukia or skip lunch too. But, I was hungry. I needed to eat. Yet, how could I eat the koukia knowing that dead little things are inside them? I could even see some of their heads close to the outer edge of their holes. I shivered, and my skin was suddenly covered with little sharp bumps when I noticed that they were watching me with their dead open eyes—as they had been when alive.

I chose to skip lunch. I made myself busy taking care of the oxen—they seemed to recognize me now; we were becoming friends. Evening came. The problem returned. And now I was not just hungry, I was desperate. I finally admitted to myself that I had no choice. I could skip eating again, but the koukiá would be there tomorrow morning as well.

So, I decided.

I put a small bowl of koukiá on the table; I added lots of salt and olive oil, and tried to avoid looking directly at the beans. I sat there contemplating my next move. I'm thinking how they will feel in my mouth, when I crush those little devils with my teeth. The more I thought about it, the more I lost my resolve to eat the beans.

Then, I sobered up. No matter how they felt in my mouth, I had to eat them. I picked up my spoon. I put the spoon in the bowl, still avoiding looking directly into the stuff. I closed my eyes. I brought the spoon into my mouth and emptied it. I hesitated for a few seconds and then I bit the stuff.

I hesitated again for a couple seconds. Then, I started chewing. Surprise! No difference from the other times I had eaten koukiá. I ate koukiá the next morning, noon, and evening and the next day, and the days after, but always closing my eyes and always hating the stuff.

It was getting close to the rainy season. Once it starts, I was told, it doesn't stop, especially the first couple of months. I visited Nikolís Tyrákis. Could he take care of the oxen for three or four days? Nikolís told me that he would.

My mother had a good laugh at my predicament with the koukiá and had no argument for or against my decision to become sort of a full-fledged farmer. "If that's what you want to do and if you feel that you can do it, go ahead," she told me, as she looked at me, smiling—that smile betrayed, I think, not just her approval but also a hint of pride.

I stayed home that evening, but the next couple evenings I spent a few hours in the kafenio with friends, playing préfa (a popular card game for the mountain folks) or backgammon, and catching up on the local gossip. The morning I left, I put on my clean clothes, loaded the donkey with the provisions my mother prepared for the next two to three months, and went on to Sáta.

I was now eager to begin cultivating our fields and producing our own wheat grain. "The rains should start soon," my mother remarked as I left home, and Bárba Tyromihális agreed with her when I went to thank Nikolís for taking care of the oxen.

But before the arrival of the rains, I had a surprise visit.

My Uncle Yiánnis
Confession time

One evening, upon coming to the house, after watering the oxen at the communal spring, I used the back door to enter the house from the stables. Reaching the kitchen, I saw my uncle Yiánnis standing by the parathýra of the front room. He gazed at the leviathan expanse in front of him. A multi-green sea of olive groves stretched seemingly all the way to the Libyan Sea. Not far from the shore the Paximádia, two small islands patiently sat on the dark blue sea next to each other. It was the best view that the hamlet offered.

Uncle Yiánnis must have been deeply absorbed in what he saw and in his thoughts, as he didn't hear me, when I came into the kitchen from the stables, until I addressed him. His visit was a surprise, as he was the first member of the spy ring to visit Sáta, after the German raid. Even though my uncle's arrival seemed to break the unspoken rule of the spy ring on visits to the hamlet, I was elated to see him.

Of the three brothers, I know Uncle Yiánnis more and deeper than even my own father. The two years I had lived with him, while going to school in Iráklio before the war, he had guided me in gaining confidence in my social positions. I had been free to discuss and argue with him about wrinkles in the social happenings, as well as positions in philo-sophical principles or theories as applied to politics and religion.

Now, I suspected that he had a serious reason for coming. Yiánnis didn't keep me in suspense for long. He told me that his health had taken a turn for the worse, to the point that not only is he concerned, but so are Kóstas and Dunbabin. Arrangements have been made for him to go to Egypt. There, Dunbabin, through the British military intelligence corps, had arranged for him to enter a British military hospital in Cairo.

Now I knew why my uncle was so absorbed looking at the Libyan Sea—the Mediterranean waters touching the shores of Libya and Egypt and extend north to also caress the south shore of Crete. The ostensible reason for coming to Sáta was to see how I was doing and to bid me goodbye before leaving. Knowing my uncle and observing his serious, if not defeatist, mood, I suspect he is most likely wondering if he will ever be able to cross back these waters from Egypt and return to Crete again.

So, what he wanted, I guess, was to take another look at the place where he had lived and loved for many years—a look that might be his last one. He justified my suspicion before we went to bed by asking me if I could go with him to look at some of our properties the next day. And so we did.

After supper the next day, we talked about the work in Sáta and my life there. He started reminiscing about the years he and I shared a room in Iráklio. He, working in a bank, and I going to a private school—the same school that both he and Uncle Kostas had also gone to many years before.

In time, my wise Uncle Yiánnis came to the time I was sleeping with Mrs. Elli, our landlady. When he started the reminiscing, I thought we would end up on that episode, and I felt it was time to tell my dear uncle the truth. I often felt that I shouldn't have lied to him about that affair. Besides, my uncle was ill, leaving for Egypt, so I had to square off with him by telling what I didn't tell him before.

But for some reason, before telling him about Mrs. Elli's bed, I shared with him my travails at Vangelió's parents' house almost two years before I slept with Mrs. Elli. This is the very first time I talked to anyone about

Vangelió, and I had some emotional difficulty in telling my uncle about her. Vangelió was my very first love. We both were about eleven years old and so innocent that we didn't realize why we kissed and hugged each other. The only thing we knew was the feeling we had when we hugged each other tightly and kissed—it was such a nice feeling!

It was the first year I was away from Vyzári, having enrolled in the Iráklio private school of Koraís. I was living in Vangelió's parents' house, as has been arranged by my mother. Both of Vangelió's parents are Jehovah's Witnesses, and Vangelió's mother is a distant cousin of my mother.

When Vangelió's mother found out what her daughter and I were doing, she became hysterical. She told Vangelió that the Devil had sent me in order to punish them. So the hugging and kissing stopped, but that's not all. From then on, I was forbidden to eat with them, and I became their slave. I ate alone, I washed dishes, I cleaned floors, the bathroom, and the courtyard, and whatever else Vangelio's mother ordered me to do. I was freed from all that only at the end of the school year, when my father came to take me home to Vyzári.

It was also the first time I had shared my experience with Mrs. Elli with anyone. Talking about that experience, though, was like reciting a review of a book I had read, without the emotion I felt when talking about Vangelió.

Over two years later, while living with Uncle Yiánnis and still innocent sexually, I was invited during a cold winter to sleep with Mrs. Elli, a widow in her early fifties, and her son. Their room was heated by a hearth, while our room wasn't heated. She had cleared that with my uncle, who felt that it was a kind offer by a kind lady.

It turned out that the kind lady had an agenda. Before the winter was over, she had slowly, carefully, and methodically, even kindly I think, awakened my sex drive, and introduced me to the pleasures of sex, while using me as her sex toy. During that process, my uncle noticed changes in me and attempted to find out if anything was going on. When he questioned me, I was able to lie convincingly.

My uncle listened attentively, never interrupting me and never letting his gaze fall away from me. When I finished, Yiánnis continued his silence for some time. I knew my uncle, and I was waiting for some light rebuke about lying to him.

"When it comes to Vangelió," Yiánnis began, "I believe you paid a stiff price for what you did. You actually didn't do anything wrong, nothing at all. It was so innocent that I'm disturbed that these people treated you in such a terrible way. It is something like it that makes me distrust religion, any religion.

"Religion blinds you most of the time from looking objectively into life's path. The Jehovah's Witnesses, as you know from your mother, are so brainwashed that they have become logically frozen by the sea of the sophomoric messages they receive from their clever organization. And it is not just them, all religions strive for that.

"I know you are a good man, my nephew, and I realize now how you feel about Mrs. Elli and about your relationship with her. Still, Mihalákis, she did take advantage of you. What puzzles me is why she did it. She is not a pretty woman, but she is not ugly either. She is skinny, which might repel some men who like their women somewhat plump. She could have found an adult lover. It is hard to fathom why she picked you for a lover, a little kid, in my eyes anyway. And, at your age then, I cannot envision you fornicating with Mrs. Elli or with any other woman."

"Well, uncle Yiánnis, after the war when we go back to Iráklio, we shall ask her."

"If we ever go back," was my uncle's pensive response.

PART THREE

RESISTANCE

CHAPTER
20

Daily Life in Sáta
A farmer's life

The work of the farm didn't stop after my escape and return. Part of the reason I decided to farm is that I didn't want to disappoint my mother, but the strongest factor is the fact that our family went hungry just a year ago. I don't want that to happen again. Like my father, I have no desire for farming. And having no previous experience in farming, I'm not aware how difficult and exhausting the life of a farmer is.

But once I commit to farming, even if it's only until the end of the war, I want to do it like the successful farmers in Sáta, as the ones Barba Tyromihális has described. I sense it will be difficult, but like having to eat the koukiá with the little animals inside them, I have to overcome the obstacles I will encounter. In my innocence and inexperience, I move by instinct rather than by a well-thought-out plan and a clearly defined goal. I simply react to the circumstances I encounter. I realize why I'm in Sáta, but how I proceed to meet that "why" is in thick fog—a fact I hadn't recognized at that time.

By the onset of the rainy season, the oxen and I are well-acquainted with each other, and Bárba Tyromihális spends part of an additional day with me teaching me how to handle the oxen and the plow, how to sow and plow the fields. Taking care of the oxen is a routine operation, but it has to be done with diligence. And since they don't eat all day during cultivation, it's important that they are fed well, especially in both morning and evening.

Each feeding session is a few successive mini-feedings, about fifteen or so minutes apart. In each of those feedings, a small quantity of straw is put into the manger of each individual ox. If the manger is filled with straw, the oxen will push most of it out of the manger onto the floor, wasting it.

The first two or three mini-feedings are easy. The oxen are hungry and eat the straw. After that, however, they slow down or would refuse to eat much more, pushing the straw out of the manger. Since the oxen will be working in the fields all day without stopping to eat, I have to entice them to eat more straw. I do this by adding rόvi to the straw. Rόvi is a type of harsh-tasting legume which is produced for that purpose. The rόvi is soaked in water for some time before given to the oxen, and the oxen love it, especially when it has sprouted a bit.

When the oxen stop eating, I take them to the communal spring, which is a short distance outside the hamlet. Returning to the stables, they might still eat some άhera (straw). If they stop eating, I mix a handful of wet rόvi with the άhera. Since the oxen love rόvi, they try to eat it. But the wet rόvi is now attached to άhera, so they continue eating the straw looking for more rόvi.

The whole process requires that I get up each morning more than an hour before daybreak, seven days a week, because we are in the fields not much later than sunrise each day, and every day, including Christmas Day and New Year's Day. The routine of work at home and in the fields is hard, much harder than I had expected. And it never stops.

I get up way before daybreak, I feed the oxen and water them at the middle of that process, I load the donkey with the cultivating equipment and seed, I stop at the communal spring to water the oxen again, and I seed and cultivate all day, with a few minutes of a break at noon for some bread and salted olives, while the oxen stand by. As the sun is setting, I load the donkey, I stop at the communal spring to water the oxen, I get home and I unload the donkey, I feed the oxen following the identical routine as in the morning. While feeding the oxen, I do the house work, cook my dinner or warm up leftovers, I eat, and after the last feeding of the oxen, I go to sleep.

In the fields, I follow Barba Tyromihális' directions. At the beginning it is tough, very much so. After a couple of weeks or so, it becomes a bit better. But it still is more difficult for me than for the adults. The steel plow is too heavy, making it hard to maneuver. The handle of the plow is too high for my short stature, which makes my job even harder. And there is hardly a field that isn't full of rocks.

I made a comical figure behind the oxen, as I found out later, so the adults had fun watching me cultivate. And, of course, I was awkward and much slower than they. I find that I plow half as much ground, if not less at times, than the average adult farmer. One thing I know, however: Barba Tyromihális is surprised. I don't think he has doubts anymore about my commitment and ability to work in the fields. But, of course, he knows, and I suspect, that I still have a lot to learn.

All of the families in Sáta work on the same schedule during planting season. The difference in my case is that there are several helpers in each family, while I am not only a family of one but also a grossly inexperienced young farmer.

When planting is done, I have time to have Manolítsa teach me how to play the mandolin. She is my senior by a few years and a cousin several times removed. Her father is one of the farmers from Fourfourás who have a few properties in Sáta, and they come for a few weeks each season to take care of them. I'm not a good pupil, though, so at times she stops teaching me and begins playing the mandolin for me. Sometimes, my friend Nikolis would join us playing the lýra—a distant cousin of the violin.

It is also during those days that I have time to spend with the meandering black-market merchants coming to the hamlet. They come on a donkey or mule to exchange their goods for grain or legumes, and rarely for olive oil. Since I have few needs and no spare amounts of wheat and legumes, I'm only interested in the peddlers from the fishing villages fairly close to us and who also take olive oil.

Among the peddlers, there is one who says he is a Cypriot. He speaks "funny" Greek, and we all think that's the way Cypriots talk. He tells us he had been among the British colonial forces that defended Crete (Cyprus is a British colony). It is strange for us that he is asking about the possibility of meeting resistance partisans or British agents, and that he is still on Crete, when the last Anzac men had left months before.

He always looks sad, and we sympathize with him, especially when he is saying how much he misses his children and that's why he now plays with children. Still, when he is overheard asking the children if they have seen foreign men around, we start cutting short our visits with him. Eventually, his visits to Sáta become rare.

The few girls in Sáta are much older or much younger than I. Only a couple of girls are close to my age. But that really doesn't make any difference. The community is so small, and the mountain villagers' social etiquette is such that even flirting with the girls will alienate the adults in our little community, and I need their friendship for company, moral support, and the security they can provide.

And, after my escape, I do feel insecure. The insistence of the Gestapo in specifically visiting our house and the thoroughness of searching it every time they raid or pass through Sáta signals that they haven't forgotten my escape. Even though I hadn't been in the house all those times, it is by pure luck. I'm seriously worrying, especially during the nights.

Staying in Sáta, especially during the nights, has become dangerous. I have a serious problem. My presence in Sáta is needed, but I must be careful. During the daytime hours, I feel somewhat safe—all my fellow villagers, from little kids to old adults, look out for me. The nights, however, are the most dangerous time. Giórgis Voskákis, one of the men in Sáta, who is a member of the spy ring sought me out, during a short daytime visit to the hamlet. "Your uncle Kóstas," he says, "asked me to see how you are getting along."

After telling him about my concerns, he asks me if I would like to have someone to help me. "I would," I answer, and he recommends a couple from another village. "They are very poor," he tells me. "Both the man and his wife are good workers, and I assure you that both are also fully trustworthy."

The next day, I ask my friend Nikolís to take care of the oxen and I leave. I visit with the couple Giórgis recommended. I like them. I ask them to come to Sáta, and they accept. Next, I go to Vyzári to visit with my mother. Even though she doesn't know the couple, she agrees with me. About a week later, they and their children move to Sáta and take residency in our farmhouse. The couple have two teenage daughters and a son about twelve. With the family of the tailor already residing in the house, it is rather tight quarters, but somehow we are able to cope—even though some friction in the use of the kitchen does surface occasionally.

The arrival of the helpers allows me to sleep outside of both the house and the hamlet, and gives me the freedom to visit Vyzári more often and have longer stays there. The additional time with my mother and siblings is welcome. That freedom also allows me to become more involved in the Advance Force 133, including manning a clandestine radio for listening to Greek language broadcasts of Radio Cairo or London and dispersing the war news.

The first couple of weeks after the arrival of the family, I spend my time working with them. The husband and wife are indeed hard workers and quick studies. Meanwhile, during those days I notice that the teenage daughters of the couple have two distinct personalities. The older one, Anna, is about my age, possibly a year older, and she is a pretty young lady. She has a fair complexion and dresses better than her sister, but she is bashful, stand-offish, and reticent.

The other one, Léna, about a year younger than I, is plain, but has an outgoing, vibrant personality. She is devilish, dynamic, a pistol—smart, funny, and fearless. In contrast to her sister, she has a ready smile and a boyish way of acting. We instantly develop a cordial relationship and, almost automatically, we become friends. I like talking to her, and she likes to surprise me with practical jokes.

A few months pass. I begin to notice two developments. The family seems to leave Anna and me alone in the house for unnecessarily long periods of time. Then, the younger daughter's attitude and behavior around me is changing. Léna is solemn and reserved, looking kind of strangely at me when I'm talking to her sister. She avoids me. No jokes and kidding anymore.

It is about then that Anna seems to somewhat come to life and to seek my company, often enough to arouse my curiosity—while Léna is putting more and more distance between us. Even though it is easy for me to quickly fall for a pretty girl, I haven't shown any interest in Anna. I like her looks, but that's all.

One time when I'm going close to their village, their mother asks me to take Anna back to their home-village, as it is close to my route. She needs to go home in order to take care of their cats. From then on, every time I take that trip, I'm asked to take Anna to their village. In a tiny settlement, as Sáta is, everyone is aware what is going on in each household. And, of course, my trips with the pretty girl are noticed. One of the times I go to Vyzári, my mother asks me what is going on with the pretty girl. I'm not surprised that someone has sent word to her on what is going on in such a little community. I tell my mother not to worry.

One day at breakfast, the mother of the girls tells Léna to go home tomorrow to take care of their cats. For weeks, I am wondering how I can get Léna alone for enough time, so I'll be able to visit with her about the trap her mother is setting up for me. So, I casually say, "Léna, I'm going that way tomorrow, so we can go together up to your village." She loses no time saying, "I will like that." I notice that both her mother and Anna don't like it.

Léna and I have a lively trip, in contrast to the boring ones I suffered with her sister. Still, we don't touch on what is going on with her mother, her sister and me. When we are close to her village, she says, "Mihális, I have a good friend who would like to meet you. Can you stay at my house a few minutes, while I bring her there?" I have no problem with that, so I stay outside her house while she goes to fetch her friend.

When she returns with her friend I almost faint. What a beautiful girl, what elegance, and the promises for lots of things in the way she moves. Oh, my gosh! What a girl! From the first look at her I am paralyzed. The rather tight dress, the movements she has, and her delicious

smile as she zeroes her eyes on mine totally obliterate any rational thinking for me. I'm in love, instantly.

Both girls notice. "This is Agápe," Léna says. "My God," I think, "even
her name is Love." Agápe says that she is going to have a few of her cousins for dinner that evening and she invites me to that little party. I imagine she has seen, how couldn't she, the star-struck impression she made
on me, looking at her coming down the hill. I just can't refuse. So I stay.

That evening, Agápe's polite mother welcomes me. She remarks how
the Paradisanós brothers are friends of her husband, the judge, and how
happy they are that I escaped from the Gestapo. We have dinner and
then a few of Agápe's cousins show up. Agápe and I sing and dance together; we laugh, kid and joke all evening long. The girl has been raised
in the city, and her mother is almost as much fun as the daughter. War
brought them to her father's home-village.

When Léna and I leave their house that night, I want to ask her if I
could come back, but I'm not brave enough, even though as I'm looking
at her eyes, I'm almost sure that she would have asked me the same. Late
that night when I leave Léna's house, Léna asks me if I like her friend.
"Yes, I like her, very much," I reply. Léna looks at me smiling and says,
"I noticed."

She keeps quiet for a few moments and then she asks, "Would you
like to meet her again?"

"Yes, I would."

What I don't say to Lena is that I will love to meet her again, but to be
just the two of us. The girl has the presence, air, and attitude of a glamor-
ous girl from Athens, I think—even though I don't know any girls from
Athens. Leaving that village, I'm thinking of how I can get together with
her in a private meeting with just the two of us. But even if she cares to
meet with me, I know it isn't possible for such a private get-together in
the village. No such thing could happen in this or in any other village
around, no matter how liberated the girl might be, because of the conservative mores of the mountain folk.

A few weeks pass before Léna and I find ourselves alone—I suspect, Lena has arranged that, somehow.

"You told me that you like Agápe," she begins.

"Yes, I do," I reply after some hesitation; I'm wondering why she is asking.

"She is a very good friend of mine," she says with a hint of pride.

"Yes, I have gathered that."

"She likes you too."

"I know," I answer without a trace of humbleness or humility.

"She wants to meet with you."

"How do you know?"

"She told me. Do you still want to meet with her?"

"Yes."

"I can arrange a meeting with her."

With astonishment I say "Αστιένεσαι;"—Are you kidding me?

"No, I am not kidding. I can do it."

"How?"

"When you go that way again, she can meet you in our house."

"How can that be done?"

"On Friday, next week, I have to go to our house and check on our cats. She and I have already talked about it. If you can come, she will meet you in our house on Saturday noon."

I can't believe it. And the anticipation of such a meeting is so strong that I don't even think of, or question, her motives for her doing this. Later, I realize that it is jealousy. She is jealous of her pretty sister, and possibly resentful of her mother's machinations, and that's why she has taken the initiative to introduce me to Agápe.

"Léna, I will leave for my trip a couple days before you leave, but I'll be at your house on Saturday noon." She looks at me with a crooked smile and says, "That's better, yet." The plan has been put together by the two girls, and it works. When I walk into their house expecting to find two girls, the only one there is the beautiful Agápe.

⸻

Soon, summer is upon us. And I'm glad I have helpers. I had been alone during almost all of the planting season, but now I have help for the harvesting of the wheat I planted. Just like all other farming tasks, harvesting of the wheat is hard work. The three women of my helping family are in the fields all day, under the hot summer sun, cutting the dried stalks of the wheat.

They line up at a section at a time. They grab a small bunch of stalks, and using their scythes cut them close to the ground. They place the small bunches on the ground. The boy picks up those bunches and assembles them into larger bundles. The father picks up those bundles and forms bales. He loads the bales on the donkey and takes them to our alóni, which is by our house in the hamlet.

The alóni is the stage at which the wheat stalks are thrashed and the grain is separated from the stalks. It is a circular stage built on a location exposed to the prevailing winds. A rock wall is built around it. That wall is step-high, low enough to walk into the alóni's floor, except from the back—the side that no prevailing winds blow into the alóni. On that side the wall is fairly high. Our alóni is on our property next to our house; the field I had to go through the night I had escaped from the Gestapo.

Like any other alóni, the floor of ours is earthen—just the soil. As the cutting of the wheat stalks is nearing its end, we start to prepare the alóni for the threshing of the wheat stalks. We wet the bottom and then we walk over it pressing down as much as we can. We repeat that process a couple of times.

Meanwhile, we all begin to collect the fresh droppings of our oxen and the fresh droppings of other oxen we find on the road. We keep them moistened in large troughs. When we have enough, we mix them well and, using them as a paste, we treat the bottom and sides of the alóni with a thick base of it. We let that coating dry well. It becomes very hard. That's the stage at which the threshing of the wheat stalks takes place.

The threshing is done during the hottest time of the summer days, around noon. Lots of stalks are spread on the stage, the floor of the alóni, making an extra thick heavy coat. A special wide and long wooden board is put over the stalks. On the bottom surface of that board, small, skinny, and sharp pieces of special extra-hard rocks have been embedded into the wood.

Our two oxen are brought in. We saddle them to a yoke, and through a chain we attach to the yoke the board with the embedded sharp rock pieces. I get on the board. Standing, I hold in my left hand the reins of the oxen and in the right hand a long enough stick with a short sharp needle embedded in front of it. Using the stick, I lightly encourage to oxen to begin walking. They do, and they ferry me on the board around and around the threshing stage.

The reins are more for my stability as I stand on the board than anything else, as the oxen know the routine and stay in the aloni ferrying me around and around, without any further encouragement from me. After a half an hour or longer, someone from my helping family comes and replaces me. And this changing persons on the board goes on until that day's threshing session ends. As this is going on, members of my helping family and I move the uncut stalks to the path of the oxen with the board and bring more bales in. This goes on at each noon session for days until enough of the stalks are threshed—almost pulverized.

Once the stalks are threshed, the oxen and the board are removed. Then we move all that matter on the middle of the stage in a long pile, covering the diameter of the stage and facing the incoming prevailing winds. Now, we just wait for the prevailing winds to start blowing, which normally happens in late afternoon, most of the time.

The wait is hours sometimes and occasionally days. But even when the wind comes, it must be with the right intensity for the purpose we want it to help us. What we do is we use special wooden implements to take parts of the mixture of grain and the pulverized straw and repeatedly toss it in the air—and that is a learned skill. The wind takes the straw away and the grain falls down in place.

The wind must be strong enough to take the straw away, but not so strong that it will also take the grain too. When the wind is just right and after many repeated tosses, the grain falls in place, without any straw. The wind has taken the straw, which is now piled against that higher part of the alóni's wall. And this is important for us, as it is that straw that we will feed the oxen during the next cultivating season.

The grain is sacked. It is taken to the house and is put in πυθάρια (pithária)—large ceramic containers, which are wide and almost as tall as I. The áhera (straw) is also sacked and taken to the aheróna (straw room), in the stable complex. The roof of the aheróna has a hole, through which the áhera is poured into the room. Then, a special cover is put over that hole. That cover saves the áhera from the coming winter rains.

Almost always the grain and the straw have been processed and stored by June.

Aghios Ioánnis
A brave little village

That year, a few weeks after harvesting the wheat stalks, pro-cessing them, and then finishing that work by storing the grain and straw, I decide to take a break from work.

I like all fruits, but I love figs. Among my mother's prop-erties in Aghios Ioánnis, there is a field in Kiminári, a place fairly close to the village. I'm enamored with that little field in the summer. There is an extra-large, huge fig tree in the field and a wonderful spring of cool water adjacent to the field.

At noon of a hot summer's day, there is no other unadulterated plea-sure like spending a couple or three lazy hours under the shade of the trees, eating figs, drinking the cool water, pondering life's twists and turns and taking a nap or two.

So, that's where I go for my break.

Since my preteens, Aghios Ioánnis is among Vyzári and Sáta as my most favorite villages. Two of my dearest people, my mother and my pa-ternal grandfather, whose first name I carry, had been born there.

Ághios Ioánnis is a poor village, but its people are kind and hospita-ble. During the German occupation, the villagers also show an unusual collective bravery—just like the families in Sáta. The villagers allow the operatives of the spy ring to come and go as they need, always knowing that if a traitor let the Gestapo know, their homes will be razed and any of their men found there will be executed.

Aghios Ioánnis is perched on the side of a giant steep hill. One could say that the village is clinging precariously to the steep side of the hill, as perilously as a man clinging for dear life on the side of a sharp mountain precipice. But that, of course, can be said for hundreds of the Cretan mountain villages.

Now, why would a village take a root in a place like the one here? Well, it had been simple in Crete, where water is scarce in the summer. From ancient times, a settlement, small or large, develops around a spring with enough water that can sustain it during the hot summers.

There is no noticeable level area on the side of the Aghios Ioánnis hill and hardly any level place in the village. The villagers have to cut into the hill to build their homes, streets and tiny squares. The lone kafenio, owned by Leonídas, a first cousin of my father, is actually built into the hill, with only its front wall seeing the sun.

Moving from a street to the next street above is hard work, as it's almost straight up. Often the flat clay roofs of the single-story houses on a street are on the same level as the next-street above them. One could easily walk from that street to the roof of a house below. And walking on the roofs, which are of heavy and compact clay, doesn't differ much from the street.

Visiting with my mother about her young life in Aghios Ioánnis, she mentions once that she had seen my paternal great-grandfather, Giorgákis Paradisanós, bandaged up a few times. Apparently, Giorgákis liked his wine much too much. Once in a while on a dark winter night after getting drunk in the kafenio, he becomes disoriented on his way home.

As a result, he accidentally walks on the roof of a house all the way to the other end of the roof and then … you guessed it. He falls in the street on that side of the house or to the front yard of that house. My mother's comment is, "It is a good thing that the houses aren't too high and he is loose because of his drunkenness." The legend about Giorgákis has it that once he tasted wine, he never drank water again. That, of course, couldn't be quite true, but he did like his wine. The tale ends when he dies at the ripe age of 106.

It is a small village—hardly two hundred people live there. The men cultivate the fields with oxen and primitive plows. Most of the crops are legumes, barley, oats, and some wheat. Most of the villagers use the legumes for their meals every day. The flour for their bread is from a mixture of wheat, barley, and oats. Depending of the proportions of the flour from those grains, the bread is usually dark and hard. The fields are filled with small rocks, at some places a boulder or two and oftentimes even more than that. All fields are on steep ground, all the way down the creek at the bottom of the deep ravine.

The solitary cash crop of the village is olive oil. But even the best fields for olive trees are owned by a handful of families, while the rest of the villagers work on their little land and supplement their meager income working for those with more properties and large olive tree groves. They all scratch a lean living.

The communal spring produces just enough water for the village's households and their animals—chickens, domesticated rabbits, sheep, goats, oxen, and donkeys. The little water that escapes from the main spring is shared by a handful of villagers who are fortunate to have small plots of ground downstream and right next to the spring.

The millennia of continuous cultivation, the topography, and the torrential rains in winter have robbed the village's fields of their fertile soil. Cultivation is done with little or no terracing of the land. Thus, when the rain comes, it takes the soil downhill, a long way down to the creek flowing at the bottom of the seemingly bottomless ravine. The creek takes it to the river, and the river takes the soil all the way to the sea—the Libyan Sea.

That creek, with an orientation of east to west, is at the bottom of a deep ravine formed by the almost vertical sides of two high hills—the one I call Aghios Ioánnis Hill on the south side of the ravine and the longer one coming from Vyzári, on the north side.

Aghios Ioánnis is one of the most isolated villages in the region. Because of the hills and the deep ravines, it isn't an easy place to reach. And reaching Aghios Ioánnis is done only on foot, over donkey and goat paths.

The closest way to do so by the Germans is from Vyzári, on the north. And that is a bit over an hour by strong legs. Traveling during daytime via that donkey path, travelers, especially Germans, could be seen from Ághios Ioánnis going down on the north side of the ravine, in order to pass the mostly shallow creek, often impassable during the rainy season, and then scale up the south side of the ravine to reach Aghios Ioánnis.

Approaching Aghios Ioánnis from the south is a much longer undertaking, on foot again, over unfriendly topography, but not as bad as coming from the north. Additionally, the Germans had to pass a few villages and hamlets, and thus they would run into the danger of having the villagers send runners ahead to warn Ághios Ioánnis. Coming from the east and west isn't better because of Mount Psilorítis from the east and Mount Kéndros from the west.

These factors permit the British intelligence unit to feel safe enough to use Ághios Ioánnis as a rest station. Whenever the spy ring's base is on the areas of Mount Psiloritis or Mount Kéndros close to Aghios Ioánnis, the spy ring operatives descend to the village. After weeks in the fields, besides eating home-cooked meals there and having plenty of wine and raki, they take a bath and have their clothes and bodies deloused. I didn't count how many times I walked to the yard of the village's mayor, my great-uncle Koronákis, who is married to Maria, a sister of my paternal grandfather, that I witness the following scene.

In the middle of the yard, which is open and next to the churchyard, there is an oversized zinc or tin tub. A nude operative, Brit or Cretan, sits in the tub. My great-aunt is bringing, by the bucket, warm water from the kitchen to the tub. My great-uncle, is helping the man sitting in the tub soap himself. At the end, the man stands up, and Koronákis rinses him off.

This scene is duplicated, a few times, in other households of the village. All is in public, without embarrassment by the ones involved in the cleansing process or the villagers at large. There is no running water in the village, or in any other village for that matter, and no toilets, and the resulting mess couldn't be inside the small houses.

Although the location of Aghios Ioánnis is an important factor for the spy ring, the most serious consideration for Dunbabin is the human factor. The three Paradisanós brothers have strong connections to Ághios Ioánnis. Their father is from there. Manólis' wife, my mother, is from there. Another Manólis, Manólis Papadoyiánnis, a prominent resistance leader, is from there.

Between the Paradisanós clan and the Kaparós families, my mother's clan, that is, most of the villagers are their relatives. Add to that the Papadoyiánnis clan, and practically all villagers are supporters. And if they aren't, they are strong patriots, and no matter what their political or social orientation, they keep quiet.

One of the places by Aghios Ioánnis that Dunbabin and his men often use, especially the ones with wireless radio, is the Perdíkis' Metóhi. Perdíkis is a shirt-tail relative. In his early twenties, Perdíkis built a small farm cottage in his olive grove located on the north side of the ravine, exactly opposite the village.

Perdíkis is old now, and the olive trees around his little "house" have grown so large that one can't see his cottage from the village. After his wife died, Perdíkis moves to his farm "house" and made it his primary living quarters. Because of that, the men in Aghios Ioánnis baptize the place as the Perdíkis Metóhi (Perdíkis' Hamlet)—population one.

If one doesn't know its existence, the place couldn't be easily found, as there aren't any roads or paths leading to it.

Eventually, Aghios Ioánnis is punished by the Germans. Aristédis' father and mother, my great-uncle and great-aunt, Stephanís and Póppi, as well as Evangelía Dandoulákis are lost at sea when the ship they are in is sunk by a British submarine. The SS had been taking them to the mainland and then to a concentration labor camp in Germany.

It is a double tragedy, as Aristédis has sent the message to Cairo of the ship's trip.

Also, Antonis Zoidákis, another shirt-tail relative, is killed in an altercation he and Leigh Fermor had with a German patrol. My great-aunt Póppi, the mother of Aristedis, and Mrs. Dandoulákis are sisters of Papadoyiánnis.

This time, after I have plenty of figs and more than enough rest, I fill with figs two large baskets my father had made from dried cane, load the baskets on the donkey, and take them to Vyzári. Besides eating them fresh, Mother also dries them in the sun for the winter months.

When I bring figs home, not only do my mother and siblings enjoy them, but also my friends. Among them is Evángelos, a special friend. He is the son of Haríklia, one of the sisters of my paternal grandmother.

Evángelos, a first cousin of my father, is my only adult and closest friend in the village.

Anna

An unusual love affair

Evángelos is around ten years my senior. He is of slight build, a rather melancholic and moody man who avoids fights and large groups. He is peaceful and private. He listens to gossip and raunchy stories told by other men, but he rarely has much to say, and his laughs are miserly. Every time I go to our village from Sáta, I make sure that I spend some time with him, no matter how short my visit is.

On this visit, Evángelos mentions that his father, my great-uncle Pantelovangélis, is pressuring him to get married. "Your mother and I are getting old," his father had said, "and it is time to bring another woman into the family to help with the household chores and the fieldwork."

Almost all wives in Cretan mountain villages rear the children, do all the housework, weave the fabrics from which they sew the clothes for the members of their household, take care of some livestock, and assist in the harvesting of the crops, olives, and grapes, as well in the production of wine and rakí.

Evángelos is not pleased with his father's plans. "I feel," he tells me, "that I am not ready for married life's responsibilities and obligations." After a brief break, he continues, "I know, however, that my father is right about the need to have more help in our household, and I will do as he suggests." No surprise there; he is an obedient son.

"Besides the fact that I don't feel like getting married," Evángelos goes on, "I'm worried about what sort of a wife my father will choose for me, as he already has engaged a proxenitís (matchmaker)." Vangélis joins us as we are visiting about this. A few years back, Vangélis had bypassed the traditional marrying bazaar by eloping with one of Evángelos' sisters. Addressing both of us, Evángelos now in a contemplative mood, states, "I trust my father's judgment, but I always dreamt of choosing my own wife."

Vangélis, who is watching him with a quizzical expression on his face, speaks before Evángelos has a chance to continue. "Your father is a fair and reasonable man, so there may be a way out of this. As I understand it, some fathers have given the opportunity to their sons to reject a proposed wife for them." Evángelos perks up. He likes the idea. Vangélis suggests that Evángelos should sit down and have a heart-to-heart visit with his father. He would request to be allowed to visit any prospective bride before his father would commit him to the marriage. Furthermore, he should request the privilege of rejecting any prospective bride that he doesn't like.

The following day Evángelos reports that his father has agreed to his request. He is a happier man. Before the month is over, I return to the village, and Evángelos has news. His father has located, through the proxenitís, a young lady who fits his father's expectations for a prospective daughter-in-law. Evángelos is told that she is from a proper family, a hard worker, very important for a farming family, and she has an adequate dowry. In addition, her moral reputation is stellar. This is critical, as a girl who is reputed to have lost her virginity or just being a flirt, isn't desirable for a daughter-in-law.

The young lady is from another village, some distance from our own. The contrast between the two villages can be called significant, if not dramatic. Her village is on the mountain slopes, and it hardly has any conveniences. It is mostly a village of shepherds. Its people are known for their rough and aggressive nature, their exploits as sheep and goat rustlers, and their liberal use of guns and knives.

Our village lies lower, on the southeast corner of the Amári Valley, where Mount Psilorítis meets the Valley. Even though small, Vyzári is the commercial and medical center of the area. Its inhabitants are known for their enlightenment and peacefulness. Of course, not all inhabitants of our village are enlightened and genteel, and not all inhabitants of the young girl's village are sheep and goat thieves or killers. Evángelos notes that his father assured him that his proposed in-laws are good people.

The young lady's name is Anna. Apparently, her father is most understanding of the desire of Evángelos to look over his daughter before his father commits him to the finalization of the plans of the two families. Evángelos has made plans to visit his prospective bride and had asked Vangélis to go with him. They have discussed the trip and had agreed that Evángelos will signal Vangélis when he is ready to leave, in case he doesn't like the young lady. When I leave for Sáta, no date for Evángelos' meeting with Anna has been set.

News to Sáta travels slowly, always. As we have seen, the hamlet is off the main traveling roads, so one has to have a specific reason to go to, or pass through, it. About a month later my distant uncle Trullinós from Fourfourás, the father of Manolítsa, comes to Sáta to check his few properties there.

He mentions that Evángelos has become engaged. I thought that things have moved a bit too fast, and I wonder why. Engagements are considered serious affairs and take some time to finalize the official announcement and prepare the celebration. More often than not, engagements provide the opportunity for the two young people to begin knowing each other and for their respective families to begin acting as relatives. Because of that, celebrations for engagements usually take substantial time to be planned and organized in a proper manner. "Well," I think, "Anna must be quite a girl, for Evángelos to move that fast."

When I journey back to our village, I effusively congratulate Evángelos. But he is solemn. He is downright unhappy. He is a wreck.

"She is not pretty," he almost whispers. "She is ugly," he continues a bit louder, "she is skinny, very skinny." A young woman having some meat on her is desirable—the idea being that she can withstand hard work better.

"Her legs are like toothpicks," Evángelos goes on, "and she is so bashful that she avoids facing me. I think there is something wrong with her. She isn't what I had been thinking of as a wife of mine. No, no, she is not," he says repeatedly in desperation and total defeat. I express astonishment about his becoming engaged to such a girl when he had planned everything so well. After a long pause, he recounts to me his engagement story.

The matchmaker sets up the date for the visit. Early in the morning that day, the two men get up on their respective donkeys and leave for Anna's village. It is like a holiday for them. They are joyful and confident. After all, they don't have to work in the fields that day, and they expect a fun trip. They will look up the girl. If Evángelos likes her, they will have a nice time there celebrating with his future relatives.

If he doesn't, the trip will still be a nice one, as it is the first time for both them going to that village. It is customary on such visits for the prospective groom to carry a piece of jewelry to give to the prospective bride, a gesture taken as "an engagement to get engaged." At the suggestion of his father, Evángelos takes a piece from his mother's lean costume jewelry collection.

When they arrive, Anna's family welcomes them warmly. Anna's parents and all her brothers and sisters are there. There is hardly a place to sit down in the room, as a good number of Anna's uncles, aunts, and cousins are there, too. That is a surprise, as they expect a quiet, small, intimate visit. It is also strange that Anna is nowhere to be seen.

But this is the first time both of them have been in such a situation, so they brush off their first impression, as the atmosphere quickly becomes festive. Raki runs freely and various nuts, cheeses, and homemade goodies are in abundance. "These are good people," Evángelos thinks. Then lunch comes, and it isn't a mere lunch.

There is baby lamb roast, a delectable stew of wild rabbits with onions, and partridges cooked with rice. It is a banquet. The family-produced wine has replaced raki, and it is also flowing, as its source is inexhaustible. As is customary, only the men sit down to eat. Since there are so many of them, crude carpenter's horses support the makeshift table of long, rough wooden planks.

The women serve the meal, and a few of them stand by to replenish whatever is needed. At the end of the meal, one of Anna's cousins starts playing his lýra, and the rest of the men start to sing mandinádes (rhyming couplets). Their two guests are caught in the festive environment and, having had enough drinks, sing along with them.

At that point her mother brings Anna in and sits her across from Evángelos.

"My heart sank to my heels," he whispers to me. He is thunderstruck. She is nothing like he has hoped for. He immediately takes a strong dislike of her. Then, his dislike increases after he spends the better part of an hour with her across the table, while she is avoiding looking directly at him. He makes up his mind. He signals to his brother-in-law.

Vangélis stands up. Silence! All festivities cease. "We would like to thank the family for the splendid welcome we received," Vangélis begins. "The women cooked an excellent meal and served it most politely and efficiently. The whole affair has been like a king's banquet, and we are very much obligated to you all for such wonderful treatment."

Changing the tone of his voice he announces, "The hour is getting to be late, however, so it is time for us to leave for home." Then, looking at Anna's father, he reports, "After we visit with Evángelos' father, the proxenitis will arrange a proper time for the two of you to get together."

At that announcement, Anna's sisters, aunts and female cousins who had come in the room appear becoming gloomy, as if their balloon had suddenly burst. But her mother and the men seem to take it in stride. Anna's father stands up to respond to Vangélis' thanks. In a polite and amicable tone, he starts. "We also are impressed by the two of you. You seem to be most polite, you reflect the kindness of good people, and you behave as genuine Cretans. Both of you are a credit to your families."

Then he continues, "Before you leave, however, I would like to visit with you for a few minutes." He then looks at the women in the room and asks them to leave the room. The women, including Anna, waste not a moment before they all are out of the room, as one of Anna's brothers closes the doors. The two guests and Anna's male relatives are left in the room.

The father directs his gaze at Evángelos. He looks at him contemplatively for a few moments. Then in a calm and soothing voice, "Do you like my Anna?" he asks. "Evángelos' surprise and confusion shows," Vangélis states to me when he joins us. "What could I say?" Evángelos murmurs. "The young girl is his daughter, and I'm a guest in his house," he adds. So, he nervously, but politely, replies that he does.

"Then, why are you leaving," asks the father with a shade of a faintly accusing tone in his voice, "without letting her know that? Why aren't you offering her some indication of your feelings?"

"Both of us become dumbfounded," Vangélis states, and according to him, Evángelos' face goes "white like fresh snow on Psilorítis." "I look around the room," Evángelos recalls, "and I see nothing but cold stares." Slowly but for sure, fear starts to crawl into his heart—flashes of gruesome stories about the deeds of mountain men start to go through his mind.

At that point, Vangélis attempts to interfere. He isn't only older than Evángelos, but also taller and more robust. "We need to go home and discuss this with my father-in-law," he states matter-of-factly, after he rises from his chair.

"But," asks Anna's father, looking at Vangélis, "what is there to discuss?" And then, with his glance moving from one man to the other, he keeps on. "You came to our household as our guests, and we have treated you well. Haven't we? You have seen our relatives, and I am sure the proxenitís must have related to your folks that we are a good and close-knit family, and that my Anna is a hard worker, a caring person and a virtuous girl. Your father-in-law's gesture of allowing the two of you to come here indicates that he already has approved the betrothal of Evángelos to my Anna."

There is no stopping of him, as he now proceeds with a vociferating tone. "Also, several people have seen you come to our house. Our neighbors have heard of the celebration. Our fellow villagers must have guessed by now that you have come for Anna. If you depart now without leaving some indication that Evángelos is committed to her, there will be vicious gossip in the village. Anna will be hurt, terribly. My family will become the laughingstock of the village. This will be spread to other villages. The respect our family enjoys in the area will be seriously damaged, and my daughter will be ridiculed."

Then suddenly changing to a soothing tone, "But besides all these facts, Evángelos has already said that he likes my Anna. We really don't see why this affair cannot proceed as is customary."

"Apparently," Vangélis joins in, "the rest of the men in the room must have seen the confusion and fear in us, as it is here that the eldest of Anna's brothers stands up."

"Look," he announces, "my father is too polite to tell you what I believe you're thinking." He stops for a second or two and then moves on. "You are not fooling us. You came to our house, you had a good time at our expense, and now you want to go to your village and tell the proxenitís that you don't want to marry my sister."

With more emphasis in his voice now and still looking at Evángelos, he continues. "Do you do this every time you visit a girl who you claim to be a prospective wife? It's nice to have good times at the expense of their families and make fun of them afterwards. Isn't it? I don't know about the rest of my family, but you made me very angry. You see, this will shame not only my father's family but also all of our clan. So, I am telling you this. If you leave now, without getting engaged to my sister, both of you will never reach your homes."

After a short pause to let the threat sink in, he puts his right hand on the handle of the threatening large knife he is wearing in its sheath under his waistband and starts again, with an unfriendly smile and almost whispering. "And, if you think that after you declare your affection for her now, then go to your village and dissolve the affair, I will hunt down both of you, and your days will be numbered."

It isn't unusual for a mountain Cretan to carry a gun or a menacing knife in its sheath tucked under his belt or waistband; it is an indication of manliness and bravery, as well as a warning to his enemies.

At that point, one of Anna's uncles, the most fearsome one in looks and the one who has a gun tucked in his waist, joins the "conversation." He doesn't even bother to stand up when he addresses them.

"Look. What my nephew just told you will exactly happen," he starts with a strong voice and then proceeds in an even louder tone, "but not by him alone. I, my sons, and the rest of the men of our clan who are here and the ones who couldn't come today will help Anna's brothers in their quest to properly punish you." He stops for a second to caress the handle of his pistol, and then, with a stern look, he concludes, "I assure you, these aren't idle threats." The all-male chorus in the room, except for Evángelos and Vangélis, move heads in agreement.

Evángelos and Vangélis exchange looks. Vangélis inquires, "Would it be possible that Evángelos and I discuss this proposition in private?" They are shown to an adjacent small room. "Standing there, we spend some time assessing the situation," Vangélis relates. "We know that we are trapped. Is there any way that we could escape this trap? At the end, we see no way out of it. It is clear to us that these folks mean business. Their threats are real."

The two men have entered another world, a world unfamiliar to them. They have heard stories of forced marriages and killings happening in mountain villages. But nothing like that has ever happened in their village. Not a single man in our village wears, at any time, a knife or gun; no one has even idly threatened someone else with bodily damage, much less death, and as far as they know, no man has ever been forced to marry a woman without the appropriate traditional marriage procedures.

"We consider the possibility of accepting the terms of Anna's family," Vangélis starts describing their thoughts at that point, "and then Evángelos will refuse to honor them, once we are safely at home." He then adds, "I'm fairly sure that, in such a case, the threats against me wouldn't be carried through. The threat against Evángelos' life, however, is serious, and it must be taken as such."

"They will kill you," he states to Evángelos, who has come to realize that on his own, "and since this seems to be a powerful clan, in terms of the number of male members and their apparent closeness to each other, you can't expect much protection from anyone."

They feel that the proxenitís didn't do his research well, or he is in cahoots with Anna's family. They are facing a ruthless bunch of men who would do anything in order to get Anna married to Evángelos. The other thing that they discuss is the possibility of this affair becoming the beginning of a vendetta. There is more than Evángelos' life to consider here. When Evángelos is murdered, it will be the duty and honor for a relative of his family, or a very close friend of his father from another rough village, to kill one of Anna's close relatives; in turn, they might decide to kill one of Evángelos' relatives, which would lead to the murder of another one of Anna's relatives, resulting in Anna's relatives going after another one of …

Once such a thing starts among the mountain people in some regions of the island, it is difficult to stop it. The two men are scared. The Cretan police and courts are always ineffective in clan and family quarrels, but now the German occupation forces have rendered them totally impotent, so they couldn't expect protection from them.

Panic isn't just setting among the two men; it has taken over. As much as they hate it, they move back to the large room. Evángelos addresses Anna's father. "I will marry Anna," he simply states.

Even that, however, doesn't relax Anna's father, who has his steady sight on both visibly shaken men. "I thought that for a fleeting moment I saw amusement in his expression," Vangélis recollects.

"Do you," Anna's father asks of Evángelos, "have with you something that you like to give to my daughter?"

"Yes," Evángelos replies.

"Well, that's fine gambré mou (son-in-law of mine). You will present it to Anna, when the women come in." And then he follows by placing another order. "The two of you are staying here tonight. During the rest of the day and tomorrow, my sons will take you around to introduce you to our friends and to the rest of our relatives in the village." He looks at the two men and sees no reaction. "I will presently leave for your village," he continues looking at Evángelos, "to let your father know about your agreement to marry my Anna and to discuss with him the necessary details for your forthcoming wedding."

And that's exactly what occurs.

For the balance of that afternoon, Anna's brothers take Evángelos and Vangélis to the homes of relatives. They go from house to house. In each house, they are offered treats and drinks. They are also taken to the kafenio where they are congratulated and treated to drinks by the men there. By this time, the two men have decided to act properly and so they do, even though they don't like their forced parading around.

The two men stay with Anna's family that evening. Anna had been reserved, looking embarrassed. She hardly looks at the two men. She disappears pretty early and doesn't reappear the next morning.

Late that morning, their donkeys are brought to them, and they leave. During their time on the road, they evaluate again the possibility of Evángelos reneging on his promise to marry Anna. But their conclusion is the same as before. The two men also wonder about the motives of Anna's family in trying to marry her to a man who doesn't want her. For a fleeting moment they consider the possibility that either the proxenitís or Evángelos' father or both might be involved, but they readily discard it.

Another possible reason, they feel, might be that Anna's family wants Anna to marry in Vyzári, a nicer place when compared to theirs. Of course, the fact that she isn't a beauty enters their minds. They feel, however, that since they had gone to all this trouble to get Evángelos to marry her, they would have done it with any one of her previous suitors.

They agree, however, to keep the reason of Evángelos' engagement between them, to save embarrassment for both of them—Evángelos for caving in to the threats of Anna's family, and Vangélis because of failing to save his brother-in-law. But, eventually, somehow some of their relatives and other people in Vyzári become aware of some of the details. I don't go to their wedding because I have to move some documents from Zarós to Aghios Ioánnis for Colonel Dunbabin.

During the time of Evángelos' engagement and marriage, my father is in Egypt on a trip for training and rest. On his return, he visits me at Sáta, and I relate to him the Evángelos saga. He is puzzled. He knows Anna's father and some of her relatives. The story the two men have told me just doesn't fit in. So, he becomes curious. Later, when the opportunity is presented to him, he approaches a friend of his who is a member of the resistance and one of Anna's relatives. It turns out that my father is right, and he relates to me, what really has happened.

Anna's family isn't the vicious and murderous clan they portrayed themselves to be to Evángelos and Vangélis. It is a fine family of peaceful and good people. The affair, however, is much more complicated than the two men ever suspected. Anna's father and brothers do have a serious problem. No young man from their village has ever shown a serious interest in Anna. Apparently, after Anna has become of marriageable age, some prospective suitors from other villages had come to look Anna over. They go home, sending back regrets.

The family has come to the conclusion that Anna will become a gerondokóri—an old maid, a most undesirable status for a Cretan mountain woman. This is bad enough, as it is considered a most dishonorable situation for the men of a proud mountain family. They will be looked upon as if they don't have what it takes to find a husband for Anna.

In addition to that, however, there is another problem for them, which is potentially much more serious. It is the tradition in the Cretan mountain villages that sisters marry according to their age—the oldest one first, next the second oldest, and so forth. Most often, no girl may consider marriage as long as an older sister is still single. Because of that, it will be a rare, a most rare occasion indeed, that a proxenitís will consider approaching Anna's father for one of his younger daughters, as long as Anna is still single.

The men in Anna's family are in trouble, and they know it. So, they proceed to orchestrate a confidential scenario by which they hope to trap a husband for Anna, and they enlist the help of some key men of their clan. While up on the mountain slopes tending to their sheep flocks, the men rehearse the prime elements of the scenario. But they have to choose the candidate wisely in order for the trap to succeed. They decide to take their time in both honing and refining their scenario and in selecting the proper candidate.

As it turns out, unexpected help comes their way.

When villagers from our mountain region go to the city Réthymno, they normally eat lunch at Apostóli's, a restaurant catering to workers and mountain villagers. Two or so weeks before his father started to press Evángelos for marriage, the old man had taken olive oil to the city's oil merchants. As usual, he goes for lunch at Apostóli's before shopping and then taking the old bus back home. As he is going to sit at his table, he is pleasantly surprised in recognizing Anna's father at another table.

Each Cretan village has a patron saint. On that saint's day each year, after church services, the village holds a public celebration that lasts late into the evening—and sometimes until the next morning. Villagers from other villages, close by and from afar, come to partake in the celebration and fellowship—young men and young couples, as well as older couples bringing their daughters to show them off.

In that process, friendships are developed or renewed among men from different villages. Evángelos' father and Anna's father had formed such a friendship when they were young, and they have maintained it in such celebrations from time to time. But it had been years and years since they had last crossed paths.

Evángelos' father approaches Anna's father's table. The two of them eat lunch together. During their small talk, they bring up their current family situations. Anna's father quizzes his friend about his son. He likes what he hears. At the same time, Evángelos' father likes Anna's father's description of her. By the time their second bottle of wine is almost empty, the two men have decided to become relatives by marrying Anna to Evángelos.

Two months pass, after their marriage, before I get to meet Anna. It is a surprise. It's nothing like I expected. Sure, she is thin. Her legs are not the massive legs of a hardworking mountain woman, but they aren't like toothpicks either. Her face is not ugly. It is plain, all right, but once you visit with her for a while, it embodies a strange attraction. It isn't long before I realize that her bright eyes, her readily shown impish and shy smile, and the warmth and friendliness of her demeanor combine into transforming her appearance from plainness to a sympathetic, somewhat attractive young woman. I like her.

Unaware of Evángelos' father's involvement in the affair, Anna's initial welcome to the village is rather cool. So, every time I go to the village, I stop at Evángelos' house. I found Anna to be witty, intelligent, open-minded, and most of all kind. And it is readily apparent that she loves people.

More than a year passes. Evángelos and I are visiting. On our last few visits, I have noticed a gradual transformation in his behavior. He is surer of himself, has a better grasp of the politics of the village, takes diligent care of the family's properties, and mostly stays home during his free time, paying only short periodic visits to the kafenío, and has stopped reading cheap romantic novels. I note those things to him.

He meets my eyes, "I am in love with Anna," he calmly states. I look at him with my mouth half-open. He is glowing. "And, you know," he continues, "she is in love with me." I can easily see that he is very proud of that. "I couldn't have found," he goes on, "a better wife than Anna."

I'm stunned. After all, this is a woman that he practically hated when he was forced to marry her. "How did this happen?" I inquire, rather incredulously.

"I really don't know," he replies. After a pause, he carries on. "The only thing I know is that when I woke up one morning, I found her standing by our bed smiling at me. I didn't know how long she had been standing there smiling, but at that moment, I realize that I love her." He immediately goes on, without allowing me to ask clarifying questions. "I know that you think that she is cute. I don't understand now why it took me so much time to see that. She is so adorable when she smiles, isn't she?" he concludes.

In our following conversation, it becomes apparent that Anna had won Evángelos' heart sort of incrementally. "The first few months of our marriage," he relates, "my behavior toward her had been sort of indifferent. But no matter how coldly I treat her, she always looks at me adoringly. So much so, that initially I'm flattered, but as time goes by I feel embarrassed, and I start having guilty feelings about my behavior."

Her shyness combined with her love-making innocence make her sexually attractive to her husband. As the months go by, she becomes "a tiger in bed" is his evaluation of their current bedtime activities. She proves to be an amazing quick study, which brings him to realize that she uses her shyness to camouflage her acute mind. "She is smarter than I am," is his admission, which is amazing when said by any Greek man, but especially by a Cretan.

She also has a strong will, which she allows to emerge only rarely, and then at strategic moments. She respects his folks, and she holds no visible hard feelings for the initial treatment she has received from him, some members of his family and the community. His conclusion is that "She is a very dear and special person."

Her intelligence and good nature start a transformation in the way the villagers treat her. She becomes one of the most liked women in the village. Her kindness, her resistance to cheap talk, her refusal to gossip, the way she carries herself, her devotion to her husband, the love she shows for her husband's parents, the respect with which she treats her elders, and her willingness to lend a hand where it is needed without being asked win over even the most skeptical and cynical of the villagers. And our village is a village of cynics.

Traitors

There were some snakes

One evening in Vyzári, Uncle Kóstas passes through and stops to eat supper. He tells me that a group of patriots is meeting in Aghios Ioánnis tomorrow and they want to talk to me. When I ask him why, he says that they will tell me.

When, the next day, I arrive at Barba Koronákis house, I find a half a dozen men whom I don't know. They are discussing security problems. They are visiting with local men about the possibility of traitors in the area—but especially the whereabouts of some men whose names they already have. When they switch to me, they have questions about the wandering black-market merchants that have the habit of coming to Sáta. Actually, during the last few months there are only two such merchants, besides the fishermen from Aghia Galéne and Kókkinos Pýrgos.

One of the merchants I hadn't met because I had been in the fields, the other one is the Cypriot who has the habit of popping up there once in a long while, even when he has nothing to sell. Apparently, someone else had talked to them about both of those two as well as the fishermen, as my meeting with that group is short. It seems the only thing new to the group comes when I tell them that during the last few weeks or so the Cypriot has come only once, on foot apparently coming from the Messará Plain and passing through the hamlet on his way north.

One of the problems facing both the Cretan resistance leaders and the British intelligence operatives is the devious actions of traitors who provide information to Germans. The Gestapo uses both men and women. It's difficult to put the informants in specific categories, but what the partisans, the intelligence operatives, and EOK patriots uncover is a rainbow of informants.

Some are handsomely paid. Before the war, Crete has had a lot of poor families, both in the cities and the villages, and the occupation made things worse. A lot of families are destitute, but there are also people who will do anything if they are paid well. Others are caught breaking the German security dictums and the Gestapo has spared them and their families, as long as they become informers. There are some people who use the Germans to settle past grievances or real and perceived injustices.

And then, there are some who move by political motivation, especially the leftists acting against the British, as it happens for Sáta. Members of EAM, especially the communists, move because of ideological motivation, or resentment toward the "plutocrat British," a common pre-war motif.

At any rate, I'm sure that there aren't many, but during a meeting some of the agents tell me how wrong I am. Because of the traitors, I'm told, hundreds of whole families have been apprehended by the feared SS and have been sent as slave workers to concentration work camps in Germany or liquidated, and hundreds of men have been executed—many in groups and all without a trial—and villages have been razed to the ground.

Still, it is a surprise that the effectiveness of the British intelligence group on the island isn't even dented, and of the several partisan armies, none has been eliminated—not even the smallest ones. In Amári the most serious two occurrences of betrayal had been the Sáta occurrence coming from the Messará Plain. and the one in the village of Gerakári coming from the area's leftists.

And then there are some puzzles or conundrums. Even though there are so many destroyed villages, there are settlements, like Sáta and Aghios Ioánnis, that are still standing, even though the Germans have had some reason to suspect them for association with either intelligence or partisan activities. And, even though, practically, all the Amariótes must know that the British spy management is among them, it appears that not any one from Amari ever apprised the Gestapo even for their presence, much less for their specific location.

Those who manage the British intelligence feel that most of the information the Gestapo receives is outdated, incomplete, or erroneous. There are several theories about that. The theory or guesswork that most intelligence operatives and partisan leaders seem to agree upon is that the Cretans are what else but …Cretans! Even though there are some "spoiled eggs," it is an honor for a Cretan to hurt an oppressor, no matter of what political color that Cretan is.

Still, the information the Germans receive has often led them to punish innocent people and, at times, wrong villages. Good examples are Giórgis Tyrákis of Sáta who is tortured and executed because an informant mistakes him for his first cousin Giórgis Tyrákis of Fourfouras, who actually is deeply involved with both the British spy ring and the partisans, and the destruction of several villages close to Ano Méros and Gerakári because of the abduction of General Kreipe, while only Ano Méros and Gerakári had been somewhat involved.

This becomes more pronounced when the leftists of EAM in Crete become more active at the closing years of the war. This is something that has come from the EAM practices in the Mainland. During my peripheral involvement in the resistance, it is possible I have been more than once in the company or presence of traitors. This we know, as in Vyzári, EAM members turned us into the Gestapo, which in turn has the SS come to our house in order to have the whole family either liquidated or taken to work in a concentration work camp in Germany.

Each partisan army has its own way of attempting to avoid breaches of security and to punish the offending person if they are able to identify the traitor. Advance Force 133 has an intense, multilayer vetting process, as my mother and I are advised when the men and documents from the cities begin showing up at our front door during the first year and a half of the occupation. If Force 133 suspects a breach of security, they refer that case to one of the partisan armies, and it is up to that army to investigate and punish the perpetrator. During my association with Force 133, I have heard a few descriptions from partisans, who have witnessed, had been told, or have participated in investigations of security breaches and in some cases the subsequent punishment. Some investigations are quick and others protracted. Some of the punishments are also quick and humane, while others are protracted and gruesome.[14]

---

14 The problem is that after all these years I'm not sure today which detail goes with what case and, I'm not even sure how exactly those cases had come to my attention. So, in the next few chapters I have reconstructed the case of one such incident in which I personally know the traitor, and I had been peripherally involved. In that reconstruction, I have attempted to incorporate as many of the elements of the stories that apparently impressed me enough to be able to remember them. And again, because a few of the participants are still alive, or their children and grandchildren are unaware of the actions of their progenitors, names and locations have been changed in order to avoid embarrassment or raise the possibility of vendettas.

This vendetta problem visited me a few years back when I started writing the first rough draft of the manuscript for this book. I had sent it to a friend who had been one of the heroes of the resistance. I had asked him to check the manuscript for incorrect or objectionable items. He had no corrections except on a story covering one of the incidents in which he had been involved. Since I hadn't witnessed it, I had written the story according to what I had been told by colleagues of his. So I asked him to revise the chapter. I translated his version into English and I incorporated it into the manuscript, and that pleased him. A few weeks later, however, he wrote that his sons have asked him not to allow me to publish it—because of the fear of vendetta, he admitted.

The Water of the Vultures

A possible informer

The prisoner is forced up the mountain. His hands are tied—but not close together, leaving him some ability for helping himself in scaling the mountainside. It is obvious that the hours it had taken, well before daybreak, in climbing that far up the mountainside for the balance of their trip, hadn't been easy for him. He actually had an arduous time, as his two captors admit. Their voices, however, reflect no pity. To the contrary, they crudely cuss and taunt him with their knives. One can easily see that his wrists are bleeding from the rough rope they used to tie his hands.

Ten men are waiting for the prisoner and his captors that morning. The place is high up on the forbidding rough mountainside terrain. It is at the tree line fringes and higher than Nída—a large plateau on Mount Psilorítis. All the waiting men are sitting around a small spring with icy cold water. They are eating brunch, at midmorning.

Nine of the men are wearing side arms and each has a submachine gun next to him. All, except for the British man and two others, have a large knife in a sheath tucked under their belts. The tenth person, a seemingly old man, has long and unruly beard and hair, and his clothes haven't seen soap and water for months. He is sitting some distance from the others, and next to him lies a katsikáki—a young goat, tied to a rope. Strangely enough, he doesn't seem to belong.

The spring is known as The Skarónero—The Water of the Vultures.

When the two new men with their prey arrive, no one moves. They just observe them impassively, as if they are objects of little interest. The new arrivals don't bother to give any greeting or any form of recognition to the men already present. They all know that in the time that will follow the situation won't be pleasant. One of the men with the captive gives a strong push to their prisoner, and the prisoner lands on the rocky ground. The prisoner grimaces from pain but keeps quiet. The two men then proceed to the spring water, to quench their thirst and wash the sweat from their faces.

The first one of the ten men to move is Alékos. His real name is Pat—a captain in the British military intelligence corps. He moves toward the prisoner. Both of the prisoner's captors, however, move quickly to block his way. At that point, Kóstas, the apparent presiding member of the group, and one of the Cretans without a knife under his belt, asks the two men to allow the British officer to do as he pleases.

Pat, who speaks Greek fluently, asks for a knife and upon removing the rope from the prisoner's hands helps him rise and escorts him to the spring. The prisoner drinks water as if he had not done so for days, stopping often because of the coldness of the spring water. After the prisoner washes his face and the blood from his wrists, Pat escorts him back to where he had been lying. Pat points to a flat rock and, in English, tells the prisoner to sit down—and he does.

The prisoner looks around. One could see from his expression that he quickly realizes that even if he is able to somehow escape he won't get far. The ground to the south and immediately below the spring falls sharply, almost vertically, probably almost one hundred meters down; even if one has all the time in the world, one couldn't scale down that side without the proper gear. The ground east and west of the spring rises a bit, forming sort of a short and shallow canyon, and then fall sharply. The ground north, above the spring rises up fast and it is strewn with small rocks. He knows from his journey to the spring that those rocks are unstable and slippery. The large rocky expanse above the spring is like a lunar landscape. There isn't a single tree around. As a rule, vegetation isn't welcome much in this area of the mountain.

It's a rough but fascinating place.

The Mitáto

A shepherd's home

I t is two days before the Water of the Vultures meeting when nine men, from different parts of the island, assemble at Gerothanásis' mitáto. Bárba Gerothanásis is a shepherd, and his mitáto is his workplace up on Mountain Psilorítis.

Gerothanásis must be barely fifteen years older than the oldest of the nine men. Cretans, who have an inborn respect for old age, call any man significantly older than themselves, bárba—the Cretan colloquial term for θείο (theío)—uncle. In this case, though, the moniker "bárba" comes naturally, as "Gerothanásis" has been derived from the merging of géros (old) and Thanásis (his Christian name).

In addition, the hard life of a mountain shepherd shows on the harsh deep lines on Gerothanásis' face, while his hair is long and unkempt, and he sports a long, unruly beard and a thick and giant mustache on his craggy face, adding several years to his appearance.

His mitáto is his permanent base in that part of the mountain and is so honored by the rest of the several hundred of shepherds on Psilorítis. As is normal for a Cretan shepherd's mitáto, this one includes a spiliá (cave) and a mándra (an outdoor fenced area for containing the animals). Gerothanásis uses the cave for protection from the elements, housekeeping chores, and the staging area for processing the milk from his flock into cheese.

Less than twenty-five yards north of Gerothanásis' large cave, there is another cave. Its small opening allows entry into a long, narrow cave that leads to another cave, which is not only larger than his housekeeping cave but also much deeper into the mountain, cold and complicated as other caves continue into the mountain. He uses that cave for curing the cheese.

Gerothanásis' main mándra is a large fenced area a few yards from his main cave. The sheep are kept there in the evenings. Its fence is made from logs and branches of mountain-grown trees and mountain bushes. A small mándra is next to the large one. It holds a good number of lambs and a few kids, young goats—they are being weaned. Gerothanásis has also a couple of goats tied to ropes just outside his mándra.

The mándra is large enough to accommodate more than 300 sheep. He says that his present flock is a few more than 270 sheep, as in the last few months rustlers stole more than 20 of them.

Gerothanásis isn't happy about that and he notes that he has become more alert and careful in safeguarding his flock. He also indicates, looking in the direction of where a rifle and a semiautomatic gun are standing against the side of the cave, that if he catches a thief stealing any of his flock, he will kill him. By the calmness of his voice and the manner in which he says it, one knows he means it.

Kóstas and Pat are first to arrive. Gerothanásis always welcomes guests to his mitáto. A shepherd's life on the mountain is a lonely one; quite often several weeks go by without human contact. This time he is especially happy to see those two. Kóstas and Gerothanásis exchange the customary hugs and perfunctory kisses that Cretan men use to greet male friends and relatives they had not seen for some time. Pat does the same, having adopted some Cretan customs.

Kóstas, who has provided the framework of several of the stories in this book, is my uncle Kóstas—one of my father's brothers. He has been in the mitáto quite a few times before, either passing through or whenever the British intelligence service uses it as its floating headquarters. Pat is serving his second tour as part of the core of the British intelligence on the island and has also been at the mitáto previously.

"Bárba," Kóstas addressing Gerothanásis, "we are expecting seven more men, soon. We will have dinner and sleep here, if that's alright with you."

"But, of course, it's alright with me, my son," says Gerothanásis, whose massive furrows give Kóstas a contemptuous frown, with an extremely reproachful look. "You should know by now that my place is your place," Gerothanásis continues, "and you offend me, Kóstas, when you ask for permission to stay here."

Kóstas, looking at a special large set of high-power binoculars, a present to Gerothanásis from Dunbabin, ignores the rebuke and continues addressing Gerothanásis. "Barba, have you checked the blankets lately?" "Yes, Kóstas," Gerothanásis answers, a bit peeved.

Gerothanásis uses the binoculars to scout out the area to look out for Germans and suspected sheep rustlers. In a location away from his mitáto and when the sun is shining, he can even distinguish the color of the blankets aired by the women of a relative of his in the second-floor windows of their house, in Fourfouras—his village. If one is red, Germans are in the vicinity, if two, there are German transports with antennas used to detect the source of wireless communications.

Gerothanásis knows better than to ask why Kóstas and Pat are there and whom they are expecting. He and the rest of the shepherds on Psilorítis are conditioned to expect the sudden, sporadic and unexplained comings and goings of both the partisans and of the operatives from the headquarters of the intelligence service. In that process, the shepherds have learned not to question the comings and goings, even if they are itching to find out what is going on.

Since Gerothanásis is going to have guests for dinner, he decides to roast an arnáki—one of the lambs being weaned. He picks one, takes it to a nearby spring and butchers it. After he skins it, including the head, he severs the head's mandible, in order to clean the animal's mouth, and meticulously cleans the intestines, including the stomach. He brings all to the mitáto and salts them.

Near his cave, Gerothanásis has constructed two fire pits—a large one and one much smaller. He had done that by excavating the soil and using rocks for building short walls for resting the skewers and to contain the embers. He has also built with rocks thick and fairly high walls around them to minimize the danger of embers escaping from the pits. When the wind is strong and he needs to light a fire, he lights a single one inside the cave.

After starting the fire in both fire pits, in order to generate lots of embers, Gerothanásis, with the help of his two guests, cuts a lean but firm tree branch and a number of small ones. The three of them use the larger branch to skewer the lamb. While Pat is rotating the roasting lamb in the large fire pit and tending to the fires, Gerothanásis and Kóstas start cutting into small—walnut-size or smaller—pieces the lamb's tongue, heart, liver, lungs, stomach, kidneys, and the fat taken from the insides of the slaughtered lamb.

After that, the two of them use the smaller branches as skewers for those pieces. That's done by alternating the cut pieces in the small skewers, then they use the cleaned intestines to wrap them around what they have skewered. After that, they wait until the rest of the group arrives before they start roasting the meat on the smaller skewers.

Now, Gerothanásis settles into his normal routine. He goes to the area where his flock is feeding. With the help of his several trained dogs, the leading males of his sheep, which are wearing small cowbells on their necks, and using his loud whistling, by inflecting it in various sounding ways, he directs his flock toward their mándra.

He leaves the sheep just outside the mándra, with his dogs standing around the periphery of the sheep. He then allows the sheep, one by one, to enter the mándra. He seems to know which ones are currently producing milk, as he stops those sheep and milks them. Kóstas has, several times before, seen him do this, but he is amazed again how quickly he does it, while estimating that it took Gerothanásis well over an hour to let all the sheep in the mándra.

The next person to arrive is Giórgis. Gerothanásis grows even happier when he sees him. Giórgis is the senior officer of the Petrakoyiórgis partisan army. A personable and handsome man, he is legendary among the partisans, admired for his bravery and native intelligence. The Petrakoyiórgis army occasionally uses that general vicinity of the mountain as their liméri—clandestine base.

During those times, Giórgis and Gerothanásis have become close friends. "Eh, Bárba," Giórgis says, in giving the customary hugging and kissing greeting to Gerothanásis, "I haven't seen you for over six months and you seem to be getting younger, even though your clothes could use some soap and water." "Ande sto Diávolo pseftoandárti, (Go to Hell, phony partisan)," is Gerothanásis' greeting rebuke.

The rest of the members of the group arrive, one by one. Antónis' village had been destroyed, and the men found there were hunted in the streets and slaughtered. Níkos, Epaminóndas and Leonídas are former mayors of their corresponding villages in parts of the island other than Amári. Their villages are totally or partially destroyed by the Germans. Hrístos and Miltiádis are the last to arrive.

Two of Hrístos' young brothers had been executed by the Gestapo. Miltiádis had lost a son and a son-in-law in the same way. Since a few of them hadn't been on Psilorítis before, Pat remarks to Kóstas later that he is wondering who had given them such good instructions in scaling the mountain, and especially in finding the mitáto.

Before dinner, Cretan men in the cities like to have one or more glasses of oúzo with some mezédes (appetizers)—salted and roasted garbanzo beans or peanuts, bite-size pieces of tomato, cucumber, fruit, salted sardines or olives, deep-fried gizzards, or whatever else the place has for such occasions.

While the "guests" are arriving Kóstas has put, each time, one or two of the smaller skewers in the small fire pit. Kóstas' roasting provides the kokorétsi—a mountain man's tasty delicacy. The mountain villagers and shepherds follow the pre-dinner custom of the city folk, especially when they have guests. But they substitute rakí for oúzo, and in this case the roasted kokorétsi, cut into bite-size pieces, makes delicious mezédes—better than the city ones. Bárba Gerothanásis' mezédes that evening are some of the most tantalizing ones available anywhere on the island. As

Gerothanásis' guests arrive, they readily join the ones already there in partaking in the mezédes and rakí.

Some of the men sit on the ground, while others prefer to use large flat stones as stools or benches. The group switches to Gerothanásis' fairly good wine while they help themselves to the tender roasted lamb and paximádia (oven-dried bread that has just been wetted to soften it). Gerothanásis offers the head of the roasted lamb to Kóstas, to the mocking dismay of Giórgis.

Gerothanásis doesn't know the six newcomers, and no introductions have been made. Before the evening is over, though, the conversations during the rakí, wine, and courses of the simple but tasty meal allows Gerothanásis to find out the names of all involved and guesses from where they have come. After the meal, each man takes his metal dish and fork, as well as the tin can he has used for drinking to the nearby spring where they wash them. Six of the men sleep on the ground, inside the cave. Kóstas, Pat and Giórgis also sleep on the ground, but at three different strategic points a few hundred yards away from the mitáto.

Normally, Gerothanásis sleeps with his weapons and two of his dogs at one of the strategically located points, away from the mitáto, changing the location often. He does this in order to safeguard his flock from rustlers and to detect, as early as possible, any unpleasant night visit by the Germans, even though a night scaling of the mountain by the Germans is unlikely, because of the difficult mountain topography.

Since Kóstas, Pat and Giórgis have taken over the strategic positions, Gerothanásis stays in the cave. He feeds his dogs first with the bones of the lamb, then bread and finally any left meat. In the meantime, he processes the milk he has obtained earlier from his animals into cheese, and then he sleeps there with the others. All sleep with their clothes on.

At the break of dawn, Gerothanásis is up from his short sleep. He lets his sheep out of the mándra and moves them to one of the feeding locations he uses, leaving his dogs with the sheep. Coming back, he feeds the baby animals he is weaning and his goats with some wild greens and the leaves of bushes and three branches, then begins preparing breakfast for his guests. Tiganítes (fried dough), myzíthra (a soft, tasty cheese) he had already processed, as well as honey and bread are on the menu.

Kóstas takes Gerothanásis aside. "Bárba, we will leave later today for Skaróner, we have a mission to complete, and we will be there for at least two days. Our guests have brought bread and salted olives, but all of us could use some cheese and Giórgis, Pat and I some bread also." Gerothanásis, eying my uncle with some appreciation of the little information he has been given, is more than willing to help. "Of course, Kóstas, I will get some for you. And my son is scheduled to come tomorrow and stay for a few days. Should I bring you some food to Skarónero?"

"As you know, it's some distance from here, Bárba, and we are going to be busy. No need for you to do that. But thank you, Bárba." Gerothanásis asks each of his visitors for his vourgídi (homemade backpack). Into each one of them he puts plenty of cheese, and for Pat, Giórgis, and Kóstas, he also puts some salted olives and dried bread. Not long after that the group leaves.

Rules

Getting ready

When the nine men arrive at Skarónero, they take turns drinking the spring's icy cold water and washing their faces. After that, they relax while visiting with each other about the situations in the places that each of them has come from. Because of the presence of Gerothanásis the previous evening, the men avoided updating each other at the mitáto. The unspoken rule is that security matters aren't discussed in front of a nonmember of the active underground, no matter how trustworthy the listening person appears to be. Unfortunately, that security rule has apparently been broken at times, either by innocence or carelessness. And it appears that the breaking of a security rule such as that has necessitated the Skarónero meeting.

The next morning, they sit down for a formal meeting, after they have bread, olives, and some of Gerothanásis' cheese. Pat and Giórgis sit next to Kóstas at a position next to the spring. The rest of the men have taken places to the left and right of the three men, in a sort of lazy semicircle. After everyone has finished eating, Kóstas, standing, looks from left to right of the rough semicircle—and starts the meeting, which takes most the day, with a few breaks, the longest in early afternoon for some relaxation.[15]

Kóstas begins the meeting with a summary with the reason the group is at Scarónero.

For months things had been going wrong for the resistance in several areas. The Germans seemed to know not only some of the resistance actions, either before or immediately after they had occurred, but also names of the patriots involved. Several of the people who had been informers have already been unmasked and punished.

But there is a case that has been baffling because the resistance leaders have been unable to find out who is responsible for some of our colleagues having been killed by the Gestapo or the SS. Finally, exhaustive research by a group of patriots has apparently uncovered the person responsible for those actions.

As Kóstas states that he had been told, "The problem is that there is no definitive documentation of the guilt of this person. All of you have had some relationship with the man suspected to be the informer." He stops here, and looking at the men, waits for any reaction. Seeing none, he continues.

"So, you have been selected to come here and come face to face with the suspected man. The group of patriots that sent you here hopes that the collective weight of your testimony will help to break down this man, or otherwise decide if he is responsible for the death of our colleagues and even more innocent civilians.

"But that's not all," Kóstas tells the group. "If we find him guilty, if he is the informer, we must pass judgment on him, and then we must carry out the warranted punishment." Kóstas stops and gives a searching glance, panning the length of the rough semicircle. There is no reaction that he could detect. He feels that they are with him, but he has to be sure. So, he continues.

---

15 What follows in this essay is a very short and rough summary of what my uncle recalls and, in turn, what I recall from the main points he makes, heavily interspersed with scenes and actions from other similar events I have been told about, which are witnessed by other operatives.

"We are here on a discovery mission. But that's not all. Our colleagues who sent us here expect us to be judges and, if warranted, executioners. I imagine each one of us has known that before coming here or, at least, had assumed as much. At this point, however, I must have the assurance that not only do we all understand this, but also that all of us are totally, and I repeat totally, committed to completing this mission. If you didn't understand this before, or if you've changed your mind, this is the time to leave us. You will have five minutes to make that decision and there will be no discussion on it." More than five minutes later, no one had moved, and Kóstas continues.

"The seriousness of our mission demands that we must do the first part of it in a logical and rational manner. To do this, we must have a set of parameters, some basic and simple conditions or rules that we have agreed upon before we start our proceedings. Furthermore, we must be fully committed to observing those rules. And, again, I emphasize this, that we will totally abide by those parameters. Again, there will be no discussion on this, and I must have a unanimous decision on it. And again, if you don't agree you must leave now. If you agree, raise your right hand." All hands are up, so Kóstas continues.

"Alright! My first proposal is that each proposed parameter is to be adopted or rejected by at least five votes, a majority vote among the nine of us. If you disagree raise your right hand." No one disagrees, and Kóstas instructs his colleagues to raise their right hand each time, if they agree with each proposal. Then he continues.

"Normally, it is not unusual that enacted regulations must at times be changed, as conditions change or as other serious reasons emerge. Changing rules, however, especially during the proceedings that they govern, is a drastic action. Because of that, I propose that in order to change or amend any of our regulations, or to eliminate any or add new ones, it will take six votes instead of the five. Do you agree?" All hands are raised.

"I propose that Pat will be the person who will monitor us on the appropriateness of both our questions and our actions regarding the prisoner."

Pat doesn't object, and the majority of hands are up.

"I also propose that Giórgis will advise the prisoner of the charges against him." No reaction from Giórgis. All hands go up, and Kóstas moves on.

"I was told that two men are bringing the prisoner to us. I am sure that some of you know them, but still I will mention that their first names are Hárris and Demítris. I propose that they will be the ones who will encourage the prisoner to answer our questions."

Pat speaks before there is time for the hands to be raised. "That would be fine, as long as I will agree to their actions in advance, Kóstas." Kóstas agrees with that stipulation and asks for the vote. All hands are raised, and on goes Kóstas.

"We must now consider what to do with the prisoner if we find him to be guilty or innocent of the charges."

Pat raises his hand.

"What is the problem, Pat?" Kóstas asks.

"Well, I feel that the two conditions should be separated and each one put to vote on its own merits." The rest of the men move their heads in agreement.

"Do we all agree on this?" No objections, and Kóstas continues.

"I propose that we allow the prisoner to leave the mountain, if we find that he is not guilty or if serious questions are raised about his culpability."

Without waiting Giórgis speaks. "The problem I see is that even if we find him innocent, it doesn't mean that he really is innocent. So, I feel that we should return him to the people who sent him to us and have them decide what to do with him."

Pat agrees with him and moves to amend Kóstas' proposal to reflect Giórgis' thoughts, then Antónis stands up. "Look, it took months for several patriots to investigate and research the events that led to the capture of this man. I imagine most of us know these patriots, and we know that they are level-headed men who don't act lightly at any time. They couldn't have zeroed in on this person without some serious evidence.

They chose him because he is guilty. We shouldn't even think that we would allow him to leave here, not under any condition."

Leonídas raises his hand.

"Antónis, I understand your position and I appreciate it. But Giórgis' proposal simply gives us the authority to return the prisoner to the people who sent him to us if we find reason to have some doubt about his guilt."

Antónis, however, is adamant.

"This man is the reason so many of our relatives and friends have been executed or slaughtered like animals in the streets of their villages. In no way should we allow this criminal to leave here alive. We are never again going to see our parents, brothers, sons, nephews, cousins and friends that the Germans have killed. Death is the end—the absolute end. Period. This man took them away from us and put them to death before their time had come."

He stops for a few seconds and then he speaks even louder. "I'm wondering now why we are here. Why are we spending all this time to pass judgement on a man who is guilty of the death of so many of our relatives and friends? We should cut his throat and do it slowly, the moment we see him."

Leonídas takes the floor again.

"Antónis, as you know, I lost several members of my family, including my father—God bless his soul and forgive his sins. I am with you. I want the people who are responsible for those atrocities to pay with their own lives." He stops for a second or two to collect his thoughts.

"You and I, Antónis, have mourned too many times for too many of our friends and relatives. I would have objected to Kóstas' proposal. I am, however, in favor of Giòrgis' proposal. I don't want to kill a man who might not be guilty." Leonidas stops again, and, looking at Antónis, he raises his voice.

"Yes, Antónis, we all have witnessed the finality of death. But, do we really want to be like the Germans and kill innocent people? Would you really feel better about the loss of your people if we kill a man without being sure that he is the guilty one? I don't think so, Antónis."

For a minute or two, Kóstas waits for a reaction from Antónis or others. When no one speaks, he asks for a vote in accepting his proposal as amended by Pat. It carries six to three. Kóstas continues.

"Giórgis has studied the actions of this man. He also had close contact with the group that examined the apparent and suspected leaks among the resistance forces. I think he should be the one who will decide on the punishment of this man, if we find him guilty."

Giórgis shows surprise for a second or two, but then speaks with clear voice.

"I propose that if we find the prisoner guilty, he will be executed."

Pat speaks.

"Normally, I would object to this proposal. A condemned man should have the choice to appeal his sentence. In this case, however, we have been placed in a bind. If we find him guilty, we have no way to detain him, so that he could challenge our decision, unless we pass him over to the Cretan police. But that really isn't a viable option either.

"We know that the Cretan police force has been dealt powerless by the German occupiers. Additionally, we have discovered that some police ranks have been infiltrated by Gestapo collaborators. We really don't have a choice."

Kóstas calls for the vote, and all hands go up, and he continues. "I propose that Hárris and Demítris carry out our judgment."

Hrístos objects. "Look, Kóstas, I lost two brothers. This man, we have been told, is responsible for that. I want to be the one who would carry out our judgment. You rob me, Kóstas, of the pleasure of avenging the death of my two brothers."

Miltiádis joins in. "I, too, lost a son and the husband of my oldest daughter because of this man. I also want to be part of the punishment that would be inflicted upon this traitor."

Kóstas asks for further discussion but no one indicates interest in additional comments. He repeats his proposal, and the vote is five to four in favor of it. He then turns to Giórgis.

"Giórgis, you felt that if our prisoner is the traitor, he should be put to death. How should that be done?"

Giórgis' answer comes out immediately. "By gun."

Four men stand up.

"I suspect we again need to have some discussion," Kóstas says after surveying who the standing men are. "Who would like to start?"

Hrístos speaks.

"Kóstas, you just took away from me the right to avenge the blood of my brothers. Now Giórgis, and I suspect you and Pat agree with him, proposes that we make it easy for him to die. I am asking you, and all of us, not to make it easy for an animal like our prisoner to end his life. I propose that we cut his throat and do it as slowly as possible."

Miltiádis, Antónis and Leonídas move their heads in apparent agreement with Hrístos, and they all four start talking at the same time.

It is then that Giórgis stands up and with a strong voice asks to be heard.

"I would prefer that the prisoner be shot. But I am not the executioner. We already have chosen the executioners. We gave them that chore without even consulting with them first. So, I withdraw my initial proposal. Instead, this time, I propose that we allow the executioners to choose the manner in which they will execute our prisoner."

Kóstas asks if there are any objections in allowing Giórgis to withdraw his first proposal. There are none. He then observes that there were two proposals remaining on the floor. He suggests that they vote first on Hrístos' proposal for cutting the throat of the prisoner. There are no objections, and by garnering only four votes, Hrístos' proposal fails.

Kóstas looks at Hrístos, realizing how hurt he is, as he has lowered his head, in the submissive gesture of a defeated man. Kóstas keeps looking at the direction of Hrístos and waits for a few minutes before calling the vote on Giórgis' second proposal, which will allow the executioners to decide the manner of the execution. Giórgis' proposal passes by a vote of five to four.

It had been a long day. Kóstas closes the meeting.

"We have come to the end of these deliberations. This could have been a very difficult undertaking. However, even though some of us aren't totally pleased, the important thing is that we have developed a framework that we can use when the prisoner is brought to us.

"You made my job easy, and I thank you. Now let's eat, visit, and go to sleep early. Tomorrow is going to be another difficult day."

Gods, Heroes and Turks

Short respite

At daybreak the next morning, all the men in the Scaróne-ro group are up. They tend to their morning needs, then Kóstas addresses the group.

"As I noted last night, the party we expect should be here possibly by midmorning. So we have at least two, maybe three, hours before then. I have also noticed that four of us have never been on Psilorítis before, and an additional one has never been on this part of the mountain range.

"Because of that, I visited with Giórgis last evening. Giórgis and his fellow andártes have, occasionally, made their liméri on this part of the mountain. I have asked Giórgis to give us a short tour of this area. As a matter of fact, even the rest of us could use a refresher look at this fascinating area."

He asks the group if they care to take the time now to have breakfast now or wait to have a brunch later. They decide to wait.

Giórgis stands up, which is a signal to the rest that the tour is starting. Walking on any side of the mountain isn't easy, and so it is at the Skarónero area. As far as the eye could see are small rocks and pebbles, as well as larger boulders and flat slate. The ground is uneven with fairly short sharp drops and rises.

But all men are familiar with rough topography, so there is no problem for them here. Giórgis, walking unhurriedly and explaining what they see, leads them to one of the small rises on the ground, some distance from Scarónero. When they reach the rise, they are on the edge of a sudden and sharp, deep drop.

As Giórgis notes, the expanse far below them is the Nída Plateau, which lies a few hundred feet directly down from where they stand. "The Lassithi Plateau, which is on the eastern mountains of the island and is somewhat comparable in size of Nída's, has become famous for its windmills bringing up the water lying underneath it," Giorgis remarks, and then continues.

"In contrast, however, Nida is arid, as are most of the rest of the plateaus on Cretan mountains. Because of this, sheep and goat herders use Nida to graze their flocks." Seeing Nida is a thrill for all, but especially for the men who hadn't been there before. They had heard stories about Nída—from the ancient times to the Roman and Byzantine epochs and, of course, from the Greek mythology. More recently, they have heard about the use of the area, by the partisans working against the German occupiers. They also are aware about the dreaded goat and sheep rustlers that come from the villages just below Nída.

Giórgis points out toward the direction of the Idéon Andron cave. It is located farther away to the north, close to the fringes of the plateau. The Idéon Andron has always been a mysterious cave for Giórgis, so he never misses a chance to talk about it. According to Greek mythology, that's where Rhéa's mother Gaéa, brought baby Zeus, in order to save him from Krónos, his father, swallowing the baby.

While the other men move back a little, the ones who had not been there before stay at the edge of the drop-off listening to Giórgis and asking him questions about the area around Nida and Skarónero. Then they join the rest of the group. Giórgis asks the group to follow him. They follow a fairly gentle rise of the ground, and after a while they come to the ruins of man-made shelters. Giórgis stops there and points at the first one.

"These shelters have been abandoned since the late 1800s. They were built by Ottoman Turk shepherds, when the Ottoman Turks were the masters of the island. They had been built close to the tree line for security reasons. Even if Cretan revolutionaries or goat and sheep rustlers had been successful in scaling the mountain unnoticed, they would easily be spotted in this nearly barren environment."

According to Giórgis, the shelters had been constructed entirely of stone and without mortar to bind the rocks together. Because of that, and to increase the protection from the fierce winds, the walls are thick. No roofs remain, but those too had been made from rocks. Logs from mountain trees were brought up and placed across the width of the shelters—that is the reason the shelters are rather narrow. Smaller branches placed above the logs made the base for the rock-roofs.

There are a lot of flat slate rocks around. The Turks selected thin ones and placed them on the roof to protect the shelters from the rain and early snow. The reason one of the two long walls is shorter than the other is that the roof slates had to be put in such way that the incline is steep enough to have the rain run down from slate to slate. Some shepherds constructed two-room shelters, especially if they had any women with them—the women had to retreat into the inner room whenever men other than their own are present.

After studying the landscape for sometime, Kóstas eventually has to ask the men to head back to Skarónero.

The Trial

Judgement day

When the group returns to Skarónero, they find Gerothanásis sitting on a rock by the spring with a katsikáki (a baby goat) tied to a rope by his side. Gerothanásis meets Kóstas' quizzical glance. "What is this?" Kóstas asks.

"Well," Gerothanásis hastily babbles out, "you said that you would be here for a couple days. So, I thought I would bring you a decent lunch. You are probably getting tired of the olives and cheese I gave you."

Now, all the members of the group direct their attention to Kóstas and Gerothanásis.

"No, Bárba, we aren't getting tired of the olives and your cheese."

"I bet the rest of your men don't share your opinion, παιδάκι μου (pedáki mou)—my little child," Gerothanásis says while looking at the rest of the group.

And, indeed, the rest not only follow the conversation, but also begin to be amused by the verbal exchange between the two men, plus they seem to be looking with strong favor over what Gerothanásis has brought.

Kóstas notices.

"And what is this katsikáki doing here?"

"I thought that tonight you could use a roasted katsikáki for your supper."

Kóstas doesn't seem to appreciate Gerothanásis' gesture, but Pat almost breaks into laughter, and Giórgis is trying hard not to show his wide grin. Kóstas keeps his cool.

"Bárba, we do thank you, but this isn't necessary as we aren't staying here tonight."

"I have guessed that much," pitches in Gerothanásis, "and that's actually the reason I brought the katsikáki. You can take it with you and have your hosts tonight will roast it for you."

This information is much too much for Kóstas, who couldn't help but shout at Gerothanásis. "You must be out of your mind, Bárba. How the hell we will be able to take it with us?" And when Gerothanásis replies innocently, "Well, that's why I have brought the rope," Pat and Giórgis, who had been joined by the rest of the group, have now doubled up laughing.

"Did you walk all night to get here?" Kóstas asks.

"No. After my son came yesterday, I walked to Grigóri's mitáto, where I spent the night."

Kostas advises the men that they will be busy for the rest of the day, so they probably should have a good brunch before their prisoner comes and start their deliberations. The men, who are eager to find out what Gerothanásis brought, happily agree.

Gerothanásis had brought in his vourgída (huge locally made backpack and a second smaller bag), enough for an army. Roasted lamb, myzíthra, salted psaroliés (a certain type of tasty olives, that are picked one by one from special olive trees), and bread. After they wet the dry bread, they all sit down around the spring and start eating. Gerothanásis takes his food and sits where he has tied the rope of the katsikáki. At one point Pat, Giórgis, and Kóstas, while talking about the men for whom they are waiting broke security rules and agreed to allow Gerothanásis to stay for the proceedings. "Even responsible leaders break rules at times," Pat mentions later in another meeting.

They still eat their brunch when the prisoner and his two captors arrive. After Pat seats the prisoner, Kóstas stands up. He tells the two arriving men that there is plenty of food and they, as well as their prisoner, are welcome to have lunch. Pat volunteers to take some food to the prisoner.

While eating, the two men who brought the prisoner sit by the spring, close to Kóstas. Kóstas takes the opportunity to speak to them, in a low voice, about the "chores" that the group assigned to them. Both of the men show no emotion, nor do they have any questions or objections about the assignments.

After they all finish eating, Kostas rises. He asks Hárris to bring the prisoner close to him and have him stand just next to the spring. Kóstas then addresses the prisoner. "My name is Kóstas. You are here because a group of patriot leaders sent you to us. The men around me and I constitute a group selected by the leadership of the resistance organizations. We are going to ask you a number of questions. We expect you to answer those questions. Furthermore, we expect you to tell us the truth in answering our questions. None of us is part of the group that sent you here. Most of the men here, however, have either met you before or have information that implicates you in some of the crimes for which you are accused. One of my colleagues will advise you on that.

"You will be allowed to take as much time as you need to speak in your own defense. You will not be allowed to speak, however, unless you are spoken to first or when you are answering our questions. Finally, Hárris and Demítris, the two men who brought you here, have our permission to treat you as they please when you refuse to cooperate with us."

Kostas sits down, and Giórgis, staying seated, looks at the prisoner and talks.

"My name is Giórgis. For much more than a year, a number of German similar actions indicate that the Gestapo must have peripatetic informants in the central and west region of the island. Because of that, a group of patriots have spent many weeks examining facts that would help them identify the informants. Their conclusion is that there are not several informers, and that you are the only traveling Gestapo source." Giórgis stops for a few seconds, observing the prisoner; sensing no reaction from him, he continues.

"The reason you have been brought here is that we were asked to visit with you and attempt to find out if you actually have been collaborating with the Germans. Normally a proven traitor would be eliminated immediately. But there are a number of reasons that you are still living.

"To begin with, even though the patriots who sent you here believe you are guilty, the fact is that all the evidence they have is circumstantial. You also have spent some time with people who have testified that they like you; they think you are a nice man, so they have serious doubts about your culpability. Then, we know you are a Cypriot, but even so, we have a hard time believing that a Greek, even if he is from Cyprus, has done these abominable deeds to the Cretans. After all, we are not only Greeks, we also are fellow islanders. And finally, if you actually are guilty of the charges, we want to find out the reason you betrayed us."

The prisoner keeps silent as Giórgis scrutinizes him. Kóstas then addresses the prisoner.

"You heard Giórgis, so I am asking you, did you provide the Germans any information at any time while you have been on this island?"

"What can I say? It appears to me that you have already decided that I am guilty. Where is the evidence that I actually cooperated with the Germans? I don't like them either. But answering your question, no, I have not been an informant."

Kóstas looks at the group and asks if anyone would like to question the prisoner. Epaminóndas stands up. He asks, "Do you remember me?"

"Yes."

"Do you remember when you visited my village? It has been almost more than a year ago, and five British soldiers had stopped there."

"Yes."

"Do you remember asking me what would happen to them?"

"I remember something like that, but not exactly."

"Do you remember my answer?"

"No."

"How long after that was when my village destroyed by the Germans?"

"From what I have heard it must have been several weeks."

"It wasn't quite a week. And the Gestapo asked for the five British soldiers, as well as for me by name at that time. It just had happened that I had not been there. How could they know about me and the British soldiers?"

"I don't know."

At that point Hrístos asks the prisoner, "Do you know me?" After the prisoner said that he didn't, Hrístos goes ahead with his questioning.

"When you had been in my village, the two young men who brought you to our house to eat and stay overnight are my younger brothers. Two days later, I find out from them that you had asked questions about my connection with a spy ring on the island. As they told me, they had admitted to you that I have been an operative of the spy ring and that they themselves are at times used, by the spy ring, as runners (couriers).

"They were too young and foolish to know that they mustn't have visited with you about this. They paid for that with their lives. Not quite a month later, they are picked up by the Gestapo, our house is destroyed, and my wife and parents are taken to a concentration camp in Germany. Were you the one who informed the Gestapo about them?"

"No, I wasn't. I am sorry about your brothers, your wife and parents, and the dynamiting of your house, but I had nothing to do with all of that."

"How did you know that the house was dynamited?"

"Eh? Well, isn't that the way the Germans destroy houses?"

Antónis stands up.

"No, it is not the only way. But I want to visit with you about something else. Even though I have seen you in Aghios Ilías only once during the past year, I'm told that you have been there often. "As a matter of fact, you actually had developed a relationship with the widow Hrysí. Is this correct?"

"Yes, it is."

"Do you know where Hrysí is now?"

"No."

"How can that be, since the two of you have been very close? Did you know that she and the other women had been allowed to leave my village, before it was destroyed and before its male population had been butchered?"

"I heard that the village had been destroyed and that the women and children have been taken away, but that's all," the prisoner says, and Antónis continues.

"Later, we found out that the Gestapo had separated Hrysí from the other women and children. Those women, who have no children, have been sent to a concentration work camp in Germany, while the others are allowed to leave with their children. Now we have word that Hrysí has been seen living in Iráklio. Since she had been your lover, I ask you again, how come you didn't look out for her?"

"Well, I just didn't."

"You mean that you did not even care what happened to Hrysí?"

"Yes, I did and I do care. But I thought she had been shipped to a concentration camp, with the other women. Also, if I had made any inquiries about her, the Gestapo will, most likely, discover me through their local informers—and there seem to be a lot of them. And since I am an escapee and I also sell guns, they will summarily execute me."

Leonídas raises his hand and proceeds to question the prisoner.

"Your name is Vassílis, isn't it?"

"Yes. It is."

"More than a year ago, you had stopped with your donkey outside my kafenío in Aghía Sofía. Do you remember that I had bought a sub-machine gun and two pistols from you?"

"I remember."

"Then let me tell you a story. Before your arrival, we had several visits from the Germans, since the only motor road in the region goes through Aghía Sofía. Those visitors had been regular army and friendly. After your visit, we noticed that we no longer have visits from companies of the regular army that had visited us before. Instead, we have visits by Germans who seem to be Gestapo officers. We had thought it to be strange, but we decided that some traitor had told them that you had been coming to sell guns.

"One day, when I'm in the city purchasing supplies for the kafenío, I find it necessary to stay there overnight. That night the Gestapo raids Aghía Sofía. The strange thing about that raid is that they had gone only to the homes of the men who had bought guns from you. The men in the households in which guns had been found are executed on the spot. They ask my wife about the guns you had sold me. Luckily, I had been wise enough not to tell her that I had made that purchase.

"For some reason, they believe that she didn't know that I had purchased any guns, and they found no guns even though they do a very careful search of my house. After that, they order all villagers to leave without taking anything with them. Then they loot all the houses and take all the animals, except the donkeys and mules, which they kill. After that, they destroy the houses in which they had found weapons, as well as mine.

"Tell me, Vasílis, how did the Germans know the exact name and type of guns you had sold me? And, how did they know the names of the rest of the men who had purchased guns from you?"

"I don't know."

"Some of those men had been careless in hiding those guns in their houses, and they pay for that with their lives."

"I hadn't been part of that. Again, it appears to me that you blame me for all the misfortunes you have suffered for almost two years, now. I am not a traitor. Even though I am not a Cretan, I still am a Greek and I would never hurt my fellow Greeks. It also appears that you implicate me in these events because, by coincidence, it happens that I have been there at some time before; how about local Cretans who could have been the traitors?"

Níkos takes the floor. "I am from Krýo Neró. How many times have you been there?

"None."

"Do you know where it is?"

"I think so. I rarely have gone in that part of the region because there aren't any villages there—just a couple hamlets, as I understand it. Besides, I have been told it's difficult to get here and that people there are very rough and they don't like outsiders."

"As you must know, my little metóhi lies hours away by foot from the closest highway. It is high up on the mountainside and, as you just said, it's difficult to approach because of the treacherous goat paths we have for roads. Because of that, even the black market weapons merchants had never come to sell us their goods.

"Once in a while, maybe a couple times a year, someone from another village pays a visit to a relative there, but as long as I can remember, we have never seen a total stranger show up. Yet, someone appeared there several months ago who has no relatives in any one of our half dozen goat-shepherd families in the hamlet. That stranger was there for only a few hours and then disappeared. I had been taking care of our flock on the mountainside at that time. My young son befriended the stranger and brought him home for lunch. That man, as my wife describes him to me, looks exactly like you."

"Your wife must have seen a different man. As I already stated, I have never been in Kreyiónero."

"You fit my wife's description so closely. If it hadn't been you, then he must be a twin brother of yours. Do you have a twin brother?"

"No."

"Incidentally, how do you know the colloquial name of my village?"

"I don't know. I must have heard it at some place."

"But you already said that you hardly have been in that region."

"Yes, but that does not preclude the possibility that I must have heard reference to it at some village close to that area."

"Oh, well, let's move on. During the time you, or your identical twin, spends in my house, you and my wife visit about the resistance and the fact that two of our young men had joined the Badouvás partisan army. Another one joins the same army, after your sudden appearance and disappearance.

My wife tells me that you are a kind man, away from your home, lonely, and willing to help the resistance. Did you know, but you must know, of course, that the Germans had never been there before?"

"No, I didn't know."

"But after your visit, the Germans undertake the laborious effort to scale the mountain, and during the night at that. They encircled the hamlet and methodically and meticulously search for both weapons and men by name—and the names they have are those two men in the Badouvas army, but not the name of the young man who has joined the same army after you had visited our hamlet.

"Most of the men had suspected your sudden appearance and quick disappearance. So, as precaution, we had been sleeping in the mountain caves close to our flocks. So, we have been saved, but not our families. Before destroying our hamlet, the Germans execute the two old males they find related to the two young men who had joined the partisans. Did you know, but of course you must have known, that our families, including my wife and son, have been shipped to a concentration camp in Germany?"

"I did not know. I am sorry."

Miltiádis decides that it must be his turn to visit with the prisoner.

"I, too, haven't met you before. I have been told, however, that when my son, Leftéris, and my son-in-law, Theóphilos, came down from the Petrakoyiòrgis liméri to attend a party in Kamáres, you somehow are able to attach yourself to them. All three of you, as I understand it, have had a good time all night eating, drinking, and dancing. At that time, you must have found out that Leftéris is sweet on a young girl in that village. Also, somehow, you must have found out about the day that he will be coming down again to visit her.

"About a month later, Leftéris and Theóphilos come down to Kamáres. The Germans encircle the village early that night, and the Gestapo takes away my two sons, and no one else. The next thing we hear is that they had been executed."

"Yes, I had been with them, and we did have a good time. But why would I send two men to death who had befriended me and for a night had shown me a good time, when I hadn't had a good time since I left my home in Cyprus more than three years ago? I couldn't do that to them."

Giórgis addresses the prisoner. "Vassílis, you said that you sold guns to the villagers."

"Yes. Presently, however, the demand for them has disappeared."

"Now, let me ask you, where did you find the guns you sold?"

"They had been collected from the dead paratroopers. Others have come from the retreating British forces. My supplies have come from the villagers who collected them. I did give back to the villagers all the grain I had received from selling their guns, for helping me to avoid capture."

"Are you absolutely sure that guns you sold have come from those two forces?"

"Yes. Absolutely."

"Do you see that fellow who helped you earlier?"

"Yes."

"That fellow's name is Alékos, and he is a British officer. He is also an expert in identifying firearms. He has examined one of each type of the guns you sold to some villagers in Sfakiá, Aghios Vasílios, and Amári, and parts of areas neighboring the Messará Plain. In that process, he has found out that some of the pistols you sold had been older than the ones that the paratroopers or the British soldiers carried. Why do you think that is so?"

"Eh, I don't know. That couldn't be so. Maybe he is wrong. He must be wrong."

"But, Alékos has been trained specifically to recognize all German weapons and to be able to associate them with the units of the German army using them, presently and in the past."

"It seems to me that you are trying again to implicate me in affairs for which I am totally innocent. But if this agent is actually correct, then I will visit with the villagers who have supplied the guns and find out what has happened."

"Incidentally, what are the names of the men and their villages who supplied you those arms?"

"I promised them that I'll never give out their names, even if my life depended on that. I'll have to ask them for permission to do so."

Giórgis looks at him and continues. "Oh well, we will see about that. As you already heard, after the destruction of Aghios Ilías, we learn that Hrysí had been taken to Iráklio. Did you know that?"

"No, I didn't, but I'm glad she is safe."

"Don't you think that's sort of strange?"

"No. Hrysí is a beautiful woman, so a German officer could have saved her."

"Local operatives," Giórgis continues, "have been able to find the house that the Gestapo has taken her."

The prisoner now seems to pay more attention to the proceedings. Giórgis notices and goes on. "As I understand, you know Andréas Aggourákis from Ághios Ilías. Do you remember him?"

"Yes, I do."

"We had moved Andréas to Iráklio and we had posted him in a patriot's house from which he can observe the house where Hrysí is staying. He had been able to see you visiting that house once and staying there for two days.

"He asks one of our local operatives there to follow you around in the city. That man reports to Andréas that you seem to move about the city without any precautions. You just have said that you didn't know Hrysí's whereabouts. How do you explain all of these developments?"

The prisoner stays silent for a few minutes.

"Yes, I have been there. I hadn't wanted to say anything because I love Hrysí. One of her relatives had contacted me, so I took the chance to visit her. She told me that she escaped from the Germans, and through relatives moved to that house, where she has been hiding. But I suspected that she has been the informer responsible for the destruction of Aghios Ilías."

"Yes, we, too, suspected that. A few days ago, however, during one night, two of our operatives in Iráklio have been able to get into her house. By morning they have a different story. She has told them that you are the informer. She says that you had asked the Gestapo to take her to Iráklio.

"We then found out that the owners of that house are Jewish and had been taken to a concentration camp in Germany. The Gestapo had asked her to avoid leaving the house often and had someone regularly bring her supplies. She also has stated that you have been in that house about a dozen times since she moved there."

"She is lying. When I was in that house, she told me that because of the work she had done for them, the Gestapo had forgiven my escape and that she had arranged for me to surrender. It is because of that that I don't use precautions in moving about the city. So, she has lied to me and she has done the same to your men."

Kòstas, Pat, and Giórgis admit later that there is some question about the culpability of their prisoner. There are no hard facts connecting him directly to the crimes for which he is accused. A lot of damaging circumstantial evidence, but is that enough to pass judgment on the man? Too many coincidences, for sure, and his answers to the questions are suspect.

But, even so, is it possible that the prisoner is telling the truth? Is he a victim of all those coincidences? The seeds of doubt appear in their minds. Could it be that they have the wrong man? Their attention now switches to the "jury" members. All three of them, but especially Kóstas and Pat, begin to wonder if this is the proper group to judge this fellow.

When they ask the "jury" to pass judgment on the prisoner, they feel that the jury group members' apparent prejudicial feelings and the amount of circumstantial evidence they have will lead the "jury" to find the prisoner guilty. And a guilty decision is tantamount to a death penalty. They could actually kill an innocent man.

It is then that Hárris, one of the men who brought the prisoner, raises his hand and asks Kóstas to recognize him as he has important information. Kóstas tells him to go ahead.

"The other day, when we are taking the prisoner through Voríza, we stop for the evening in the home of one of our contacts, in order to get information for another problem. In addition to us, he also has two more guests. They both are from the Badouvás army. After supper, one of them takes me aside and asks for the name of our prisoner. He tells me that he is from Kryghiónero and that he thinks our prisoner resembles a stranger whom he had momentarily seen in his hamlet once."

Hárris is just finishing when I arrive at the Skarónero gathering carrying a thick envelope. There is hardly a piece of my clothing that is dry because of sweat. So, let me backtrack a little.

Because of the potential military importance of the Tymbáki Air Force Base, the British intelligence service, with the help of Uncle Kóstas who knows the region and its people well, has recruited local operatives in that area to keep an eye on the activities on and off the base.

The town of Míres is important because of its proximity to the air base. The spy ring has supplied Míres' operatives with the best and most up-to-date photographic and surveillance equipment. The envelope I give to Uncle Kóstas has photographs which are among a large number of photographs from the Tymbáki airport and the area around it, including Míres, taken by the patriots in that area. The significance of some of those pictures doesn't escape the operatives in Míres. They had felt that the photos, especially the last few, should be delivered immediately.

A young operative takes all the photos they have and brings two bundles of them to Sáta. He is told that I'm in Vyzári and continues walking until he finds me. I take the envelopes to the Perdíkis' Metóhi, where Dunbabin's shop had moved a couple of days before. When I arrive, Aristédis is alone. Dunbabin is in Ághios Ioánnis, he tells me. I run down the hill to the river and up the opposite hill to Aghios Ioánnis.

I find Dunbabin and my father eating a brunch at my great-uncle's house, Mayor Koronákis. After I tell him who has brought the envelopes, Dunbabin stops eating and takes out the contents of the envelopes—a long note and a good number of pictures. He reads the lengthy note and then spreads the pictures from the envelopes on the table. There are a lot of them. He is always dour-looking, but this time his face seems to relax—he even looks pleased. He goes over the note and the pictures again. He seems to be in deep thought for some time.

Then, he carefully selects a few photographs. He asks the mayor for a piece of paper. Referring to the note that came with the photographs, he writes a short note. He puts his note and the pictures he has selected into one of the envelopes.

Dunbabin looks at me for a few seconds, as though he is examining me. "Do you know where the Skarónero is?" he asks me.

"No."

"I know you have been in Lohriá, do you know where the kafenio is?"

"Yes."

"Have you eaten anything today?"

"No."

He asks my great-aunt Maria to prepare something for me. She does. It's what my father and Dunbabin are eating, a bowl of boiled of chick peas with a generous portion of olive oil poured over them and a large piece of dark bread. I'm hungry, so I eat well. Then he hands me the envelope. "Ο θείος σου (Your uncle) Kóstas is at Skarónero," he tells me. "I want you to deliver this envelope to him as quickly as you can."

Dunbabin looks at my father for a moment and then continues. "The kafetzís (kafenio's owner) in Lohriá is a friend of your father and mine. Introduce yourself and tell him that I told you to ask him for directions for Skarónero, and that it's most important that your uncle receive this as early as possible tomorrow."

Having known where the kafenio is, I find the kafetzís. I introduce myself and I tell him what Kýrios Yiánnis told me. He looks at me and he looks at the envelope I am carrying. "I have a better idea than that," he tells me, "Just wait a minute." A few minutes later, he comes back with his son, Pétros, about the same age as I.

Looking at both of us, he tells me. "Pétros will take you close there. I need him early tomorrow so he can't take you all the way there," he tells me, "but he will take you close enough to make it there early enough tomorrow." Turning to his son he instructs him to take me to a certain location, the name of which I don't remember, sleep there, wake up at daybreak, give me directions for the balance of the trip, and then return home as fast as he can. He stops there and faces me.

"Mihális, where Pétros will leave you is close to the Scarónero, and if you move fast, you can easily make it there before noon." Pétros leading, we do quite a bit of the climb before and some after dark. We sleep among the trees. At daybreak, he again gives me directions for the balance of the trip and leaves me. I stay until it is a clear light and then I move. Later, I felt amazed that I had been able to find the spring, but I do.

At Skarónero, I stop for a second to view the group and to take a couple deep breaths. I am surprised to see the Cypriot peddler who used to come to Sáta. He looks at me, and he too seems to be surprised. Uncle Kóstas doesn't miss our interaction even though neither of us makes an outward movement indicating that we know each other. I walk to the place where uncle Kóstas is seated. From the way he looks at me, I know that he is also surprised by my sudden appearance.

"Theie (Uncle), Kýrios Yiánnis asked me to bring to you this envelope. He says that it is very important."

"Thank you, Mihalákis. Did Kýrios Yiánnis ask you to go back and report to him?"

"No, he didn't. But he asked me to tell you that he will be in the Lohriá area this evening."

"Good. If you are hungry, there is some food left that Barba Gerothanásis brought, so go and have something to eat."

"I will." Then, lowering my voice, "May ask why this Cypriot peddler is here? I know him."

"I noticed. He is our prisoner. I'll talk to you next time we meet in Aghios Ioánnis. Now eat. And after that you may leave, or if you want to stay for while, you may do so. If you do, sit next to Gerothanásis." I look at Gerothanásis, whom I had met in Fourfourás, and he smiles at me, it is as if he knows what my uncle has said.

Not having anything to eat since I left the Koronákis house, I am hungry. So, after I have some water and wash my face, I go for Barba Gerothanásis' goodies. And they are good—cold, but good. While eating, I catch the prisoner looking at me once in a while. It's just fleeting moments but, as I find out later, it didn't escape the attention of the trio, Kóstas, Giórgis, and Pat. Meanwhile, I am wondering what the prisoner is thinking.

While I'm eating, Uncle Kóstas opens the envelope. Right after the first look at its contents, he asks the rest of the group to give him a few minutes. He reads the note and passes it over to Pat and Giórgis. Then, the three of them go through the pictures, first almost feverish manner and then slowly. It is obvious that all three are surprised and pleased. Then they have, in a barely audible tone, what appears to be a serious discussion. Finally, Kóstas asks the rest of the group to forgive the three of them for the interruption and takes over the proceedings again.

"Vassílis, as you heard, we have a partisan who has placed you in Kreyiónero. You told us that you never have gone there. Do you have anything to say about that?"

"As I said before, I have never been in Kreyiónero. The partisan is wrong. He must have mixed me up with another person. It is not my fault that so many people think that I look like strangers they have met a few days, months, or more than a year before."

"Now Vassílis, I must warn you. We have solid evidence for the following question. Think carefully before answering it.

"Have you ever been in Míres?"

The prisoner appears to weigh his response more seriously than in the previous questions, and he takes a longer time than previously before answering. He then says firmly, "No, I have not. I know where it is, but I have not been there. That's why I have taken some time trying to recollect if I ever had been there."

"Vassílis, it is not just the Germans who have operatives watching the Cretans. The Cretans also have operatives watching the Germans. And some of those operatives are in Míres. It so happens that those operatives have seen you visit the Míres Gestapo offices, more than once."

"No! No, I have not. As I have said, I know where it is because I have been in Bómbia selling goods, which is close to Míres. But I have never been in Míres because I was told that there is a Gestapo contingent staying in that town."

"Vassílis, let me explain a bit. A few people from our local operatives in Míres have observed for longer than a year and a half now a man who comes to Míres, always at odd hours at night, enter the Gestapo building there and then leave a little later or just before the crack of dawn.

"He seems to be a Cretan, and they are puzzled because of the night curfew the Germans have for the local population. A week ago, however, he broke that routine. He had come in late afternoon. We believe that person is you."

"It couldn't be me, as I have never been in Míres."

"What I haven't told you, Vassílis, is that our agents were able, during that last visit, to take several pictures of that person entering that building that day. A number of those pictures are in that envelope that my nephew, whom you seem to know, just delivered to us."

Kóstas asked Hárris to take two of the pictures to the prisoner. Looking at the pictures, the prisoner's demeanor visibly changes as he looks at the pictures. His body stiffens, and his face clouds.

Kóstas asks: "Isn't that the Gestapo building that you are seen entering and exiting? Also, according to the note that came with the pictures, we have just placed an operative in that building, and according to that person, you had a meeting with two Gestapo officers there, the senior officer there and another Gestapo officer, who had come from Iráklio."

The prisoner stays silent. But his head is up, raised even more than previously. His expression is that of an angry man—a defiant man. Kóstas understands. "This man won't break easily," he thinks. He has Harris retrieve the pictures and take them to the rest of the group. Then, he proceeds.

With a soothing voice and patronizing tone, he says, "Vassílis, help us to understand what forced you to turn against your own compatriots. You seem to be an intelligent and brave man. All of us know that in a war, especially as this one, a lot of things can happen that change a person. We will take under consideration any special circumstances which contributed to your behavior. Please let us know, before we deliberate about what to do with you. Believe me, it will help you."

The prisoner's stance doesn't change. Actually, his eyes now show contempt and a fearsome hatred. Giórgis then stands up and addresses the group.

"We have spent a lot of time in examining the deeds of Vassílis. If we had any thoughts of doubting all or part of the evidence provided to us by our fellow patriots before, and by what we found during this session, the pictures dispel all such doubts. I'm convinced that the group that sent this prisoner to us is correct to single him out as the traitor responsible for the havoc that we have gone through for well over a year now."

"This man, our prisoner, is guilty of the acts for which he is blamed," Kóstas states. "If you agree, with Giórgis, raise your right hand."

All hands, almost in unison, come up, and Kóstas continues, "What punishment is proper for this prisoner?"

Leonídas shouts, "Death."

Kóstas asks for a showing of hands, if they agree.

All hands are up.

I think that I should leave but I want to stay. I look at Uncle Kóstas. He looks at me for a second. I see no displeasure toward me in his look. I decide to stay a little longer.

CHAPTER 29

The Confession
The end

fter the vote, Kóstas turns to the prisoner.

"We still will like to hear your side of this affair. A man like you surely wouldn't have sent so many people to death and so many innocent women and children to prison and work camps without an important reason. People who had done you no harm—some of them had actually befriended you and provided you with food and shelter."

The prisoner looks at Kóstas and, forcefully, spits in Kóstas' direction.

Normally, the gesture wouldn't have been as shocking as now. However, Kóstas is liked and respected by all. In spite of the emotions and preconceived ideas that most of the members of the group had brought to these proceedings, they feel that he had gone out of his way to hold the hearing with dignity and fairness. Even Pat, who normally is restrained and careful in his pronouncements, can't help but react.

"A vain and unfortunate blunder," he murmurs.

And as it turns out, Pat is proven correct. Demítris is angered by the prisoner's disrespect of Kóstas. He inquires.

"Will you allow me, Mister Kóstas, to try my hand in dealing with this fellow?"

Before Kóstas could answer, Pat speaks.

"Demítris, are you going to physically torture the prisoner?"

"No."

"Alright, then."

Kóstas followed, "Go ahead, Demítris, but keep your promise to Pat."

"Yes, I will. I promise. But, I would like to have the katsikáki that my Bárba over there is holding."

When Demítris says that, I notice Hárris smiling. As Hárris later told Uncle Kóstas, he knew what Demítris had been up to, as he has used various forms of that trick before in other trials, and it always had worked.

Kóstas asks Gerothanásis if it is okay with him, and it is. Demítris then takes the katsikáki by the rope and brings it in front of the prisoner. He gives the rope to Hárris and then, looking at the prisoner, he addresses him.

"You heard a few minutes ago that you are to be put to death. What you didn't hear is the way by which you are to die. That's because it has been decided that Hárris and I will execute you and, as you already know, we have no pity for you. After we listened to what you have done and viewing the way you treated Kýrios Kóstas, it will be a pleasure for us to take your life."

He stops. Then, smiling at the prisoner, he continues, with a stronger voice and slower pace.

"The other thing that wasn't said is that they left it up to us how we are to put you to death. Did you hear me?" And louder yet, "Did you hear me? It is up to Hárris and me as to how we are to end your miserable life."

Demítris, taller and more masculine than the prisoner, stands in front of the prisoner and tries to intimidate him. But he doesn't succeed. It is noted, however, that the prisoner, without showing any emotion, pays close attention to Demítris' movements. Demítris continues.

"I don't know how long you have been on our island, or if you have heard how some of us settle our differences here. So, let me tell you. It is either with a gun or a knife. Most prefer the gun. I, however, prefer the knife. Actually, I love settling arguments with my knife.

"Do you know why?" He stops for a few seconds and then adds, "No, you don't know." He stops again, and continuing to smile at the prisoner, he continues, "Because it doesn't take a smart fellow to tell you that death with a bullet is quick. There is no lingering pain and no agony. You take a bullet and all is done. But … are you listening?" And louder, "Are you listening? Oh, you are. Good. Then pay special attention to this. Death by knife can be slow, very slow. It's up to the one using the knife to make it maddeningly slow process with terrifying pain and worse yet, protracted agony.

"This time, friend, Hárris and I would prefer to use a bullet each. But if you don't give the information that Kýrios Kóstas asks, I will use my knife. I see you are listening, so listen even more carefully yet. I will be very careful in increasing your pain, by precisely cutting your throat in a way that will prolong your agony. And I know how to prolong your agony as long as I care to do so.

"You will be pleading and pleading and pleading and pleading, agonizingly pleading to finish you off fast. But I won't. The more you plead, the longer I will leave you in that terrifying agony. Again, listen and think about it. I can prolong your pain and agony as long as I please, and I will do so. Maybe you don't believe me, or you think these folks would stop me, but you are kidding yourself. They already have left the choice up to us as to the manner by which you will be executed."

Demitris asks the prisoner to address Kóstas and to answer Kóstas' questions. The prisoner with his eyes on Demítris doesn't respond. For a few minutes Demítris and he eye each other. Then, Demítris takes over, again.

"So, now, I want you to watch, and to watch very closely, how death by knife comes. How death by knife will come to you." At this point, Hrístos leaves his seat and joins Hárris. Demítris moves back where Harris and Hrístos hold the katsikáki. They have a whispering short visit. The three of them kneel and force the animal to lie on that spot. They hold it there. The katsikáki doesn't seem to like it, as it is crying and doing its best to escape their hold, but it is forced to finally settle down.

Demitris stands up. "It is good you have watched" he tells the prisoner, "as that's the way you will behave when Hárris, my friend Hrístos, and others will have you on the ground, as I get ready to work on you. So, continue watching how you are going to die." Demitris kneels down again. Then in a slow process and with devilish grin looking at the prisoner; he takes his time caressing the neck and throat of the katsikáki.

"This is the way I'll caress your throat, when we have you on the ground, just before I cut it," he tells the prisoner. He stands up, takes his knife out of its sheath. It is a large knife, a menacing knife, and Demítris holds it theatrically above his head, waves it around, and then holds it against his own throat. The prisoner watches.

Next, Demítris kneels again and starts to lightly caress with his knife, in very slow motion, the throat of the animal and, looking at the prisoner while saying, "That's how the knife will caress your throat, too, before it starts doing its job."

Visible sweat appears on the prisoner's forehead. I can see that he doesn't want to watch but either from pride or because he can't help it, he won't remove his eyes from Demítris' hand.

Demítris, who, according to rumors has a lot of experience with a knife, as I'm told later, goes on.

With the slowest motion he could muster, and in a way that the prisoner couldn't see exactly what he is doing, he begins to cut, just a little niche on the side of the neck, being careful not to injure any vital parts of the throat of the katsikáki. Demítris makes sure the prisoner doesn't see that cut, or the following ones, which aren't lethal. But he makes sure the knife, Hárris and Hrístos get bloodied.

The animal is in complete panic, and its cries reverberate throughout the ravine. In that small canyon, the echo of its cries sharpens further the intensity of the dramatic impression of that tragic scene. The animal starts desperate gyrations. Hárris and Hrístos have a harder time in controlling it, while Demítris, still having his devilish smile fixed upon his face, continues to have locked eyes with the prisoner.

Without disengaging his eyesight from the prisoner, Demítris cuts a little more of the katsikáki's throat. Its cries now are pathetic. After seconds that seem like minutes, Demítris cut a bit more of the animal's throat. The little animal has gone now into almost uncontrollable gyrations and sickening crying.

Demítris, still having locked his eyes with those of the prisoner, now cuts a bit of the throat of the animal and asks Harris and Hrístos to let the katsikáki free. By now the clothes of all three men are covered with blood.

The dying katsikáki attempts to get up, again, and again, and again. It gets up on its knees and then falls, up on its knees and then falls, up on its knees and then…

The prisoner with a half-open mouth is looking at the doomed animal, listening to its muffled death throes. Now, his entire face is covered with sweat.

Demítris still has his devilish smile as he keeps his eyes on the prisoner's eyes. He leaves the katsikáki to suffer for what seems to be hours. Finally, when the animal stops showing signs of life, Demítris cuts off its head. Then he stands up, and standing with legs parted, like a Roman gladiator in Rome's Coliseum in a gesture of victory, he raises the head of the katsikáki above his own head. He still is smiling at the prisoner, but his smile now is a smile of triumphant pleasure.

At that point, the prisoner falls down on his knees, covers his face and starts sobbing. During his crying, the prisoner mumbles, but no one seems to understand what he is saying. It isn't just the prisoner who is affected by Demítris' absurd real-life theatre. The gallery of men, including Gerothanásis, has been mesmerized. In his time in Crete, Pat had seen the butchering of several animals by knife, and all of the rest of the men had butchered lots of lambs and baby goats, as well as grown animals.

But no one had done it with such a deliberate, slow process which leaves the animal to suffer for such a long time. Even I feel sorry for the

katsikáki, even though I have butchered a couple of them by knife before. It is Pat, the Englishman, who summarizes the scene.

"Bloody brutal, but effective."

At that point I look at Uncle Kostas. He makes a signal that means to
me that it is time for me to go. And I do.

It takes some time for the prisoner to regain his composure, as Uncle
Kostas tells me weeks later. And, right after that, Pat asks the prisoner in
English from what part of Cyprus he has come. "Nicosía," is his answer.
And what part of Nicosía is the next question, and the prisoner gives
him the name of his neighborhood. At this point Pat speaks to him in a
language that the others don't understand. The prisoner answers also in
that language. The prisoner is a Turk Cypriot. Pat asks him for his real
name. The prisoner replies, "Kemál."

Pat had served in Cyprus twice, as part of the British garrison there.
That's where he learned to speak both Greek and Turkish. As he explains
later, he had started to suspect, at some point in the proceedings, that
Vassílis might have been a Turk Cypriot. What made Pat sure was that
when Kemál broke down crying he was saying in Turkish, "I will tell, I
will tell, I will tell, I will…"

Pat had witnessed the simmering friction between the Cypriot Greek
majority and the Turkish minority. The British used that situation clev-
erly in order to control the island's population—it was after all their mo-
dus operandi in controlling their large number of colonies. Most of the
mountain Cretans, including me, almost all of us with limited education,
aren't even aware of the ethnic population dichotomy of Cyprus, much
less of the underlying friction, as Pat does. Pat also knows that almost all
of the Cypriots, Greek and Turks, have learned English. In addition, because of the large Greek majority, most Turks have also learned to speak
Greek, albeit with various skillfulness.

All the men maintain their seating, while Demítris and Hárris sat
one each side of Kemál, facing the group. With encouragement from Pat,
Kemál starts his story.

The Anzac expeditionary force that defended Crete had also included a few dozen Cypriots. Among the hundreds of prisoners captured by the Germans there were also some Turk Cypriots. A little over a dozen Turk Cypriots are separated from the other prisoners and taken to a holding facility close to the Iráklio airport.

"There, we are interviewed by German military intelligence officers," he says, "and we are told that we are under the care of the Gestapo, and after we are appropriately trained we will become members of the Gestapo. When one of our men stated that he prefers not to participate, the captain in charge takes his sidearm and shoots him dead."

There, they spend more than a month in training. A Greek professor, who had come from Athens, takes them through different training scenarios in approaching people, observing, how to ask questions which might bring intelligence information, how to get villagers to feed and give them needed shelter, as well as in the Cretan topography and the social life of the Cretans.

The last couple of weeks, they are free to roam in the city, as long as they avoid drawing any special attention to themselves. After that, they are allowed to travel to Réthymno and Haniá, and are instructed to visit the Gestapo offices in those cities. They are given plenty of money to spend as they please. Few of them have the impression that they have been followed.

Coming back, they split the group according to their assignment—some for the cities and others for the villages. At the end, each man is called out of the room and is given his assignment in private. A Gestapo lieutenant picks him up and brings him to Míres. His assignment, as a black-market wandering merchant, covers certain villages in the Messara Plain, and the éparchies of Amári, and Aghios Vasílis, and later extended to a few villages into the Haniá prefecture.

They instructed him to visit the Míres or Réthymno stations once a month, but immediately if he has found crucial information or if he is in need of help. All his visits in Míres must be at night, and he is given a code to pass the night curfew when challenged coming and leaving.

"The last time I visit the Míres station," he continues, "I didn't follow those directions. While in Ambadiá, I find out that an investigation is underway to identify the source of the leaks, and I become seriously worried. That's why I got there in a hurry and during daylight, which angers the Gestapo officers. As it turns out, they had been right."

The local officers feel that it could be a serious problem, so they ask for help from the Gestapo headquarters in Iráklio. An SS colonel drives to Míres. He quizzes Kemál extensively. In the end, he feels that Kemál's cover is deep enough to avoid detection, and he leaves in the morning.

The prisoner stands up and looks around. It is the look of a man who knows it is his last. He sits, lowers his head and goes on, almost talking to himself.

"There is some animosity in Cyprus between us and the Greeks. I guess since we are in the minority, we resent anything the Greeks do, even if doesn't bother us. Still, Greeks were also among my friends. We played together, we went to the movies together, and we chased the girls together; we did anything that young people do together. If I…"

He stops there. A bullet had entered his brain. All are taken by surprise. All partisans carried guns in holsters, but Hárris also carried a small pistol in his pocket. Sitting to the prisoner's left, Harris had raised his hand behind Kemál's back, without being noticed, and fires at Kemál's head, with the little gun.

Kóstas isn't happy, and he shows his anger by shouting, "Damn it, Hárris, why didn't you wait? Now we cannot find out a lot things we could have gotten from him."

"It's getting much too late in the afternoon for most of us who need to leave this place," is Hárris' excuse. But Pat has the apropos comment.

"Yes, Kóstas, but it was a kind way of doing it."

Still, for him and Kóstas, the disposing of Kemál's body is crude, vulgar and unsettling. While everyone is getting ready to leave, Demítris and Hárris pick up Kemál's body move it to the edge of the ravine and throw it over, before Kóstas notices.

Kóstas chides them strongly about that. "There is no way that a grave could be dug for him up here," is Demítris' matter-of-fact statement.

It is late in the afternoon, and they are leaving.

Kóstas, Pat, Giórgis, and Bárba Gerothanásis are the last ones. As Giórgis is leaving to report to Petrakoyiórgis, his leader in their present liméri, Gerothanásis approaches Kóstas.

"Kóstas, petháki mou, I am taking the rope, as you won't need it for the katsikáki now."

"Bárba," Kóstas replies, "I really cannot take the dead katsikáki. It will be dark before we get to Lohriá and, as you know, the descent is treacherous."

"Well, I will take it to Grigóri's mitáto, then," Gerothanásis mumbles to himself.

Gerothanásis, carrying the dead katsikáki on his shoulders, wrapped around his neck, leads the way as they are leaving. He looks down in the direction that the corpse had been thrown and murmurs unfeelingly.

"Now, the vultures will have a few meals close to their water."

Pat and Kóstas are the last, following right behind Gerothanásis. Pat, who notices that Kóstas is shaking his head in disapproval, makes the last comment of the day.

"War is unforgiving, Kóstas."

Revenge!

An unforgiving man

When Antónis leaves at the end of the Water of the Vultures meeting, he is going to the liméri of his small partisan army. Before joining that partisan army, Antónis is a member of Advance Force 133. The incident that forces him to leave the spy ring was reported to me as follows.

One night, Antónis' father, a shepherd as most men from his village are, has a small group of his sheep stolen by rustlers. For the shepherds whose livelihood depends on their flock, that loss isn't only significant for the welfare of his family but it's also a moral challenge for the shepherd, as it's an embarrassment for a sheep herder to allow someone to steal his sheep.

Antónis' father, a grizzled old man, is wise to the ways of the men in his village and the surrounding villages. He also knows how to follow evidence left behind by the rustlers who move the stolen animals on foot—which is what they have to do in their area.

The old man knows that he has to act quickly. If the rustlers are from a relatively nearby village, they will move fast to dispose of the stolen animals. Quite often, after such a theft, the sheep are taken to another village, and they are quickly slaughtered, providing the meat for a big celebration after a wedding, engagement, or baptism.

Before leaving, Antónis' father mentions to his family the general area in which he is going to search. It is a village some distance from Antónis' village, and around it is a cluster of a half a dozen of much smaller villages. After a few days when his father doesn't return home, Antónis is notified by Pétros, one of his brothers. The two brothers are afraid that the old man has met with foul play. They suspect certain families in the area to which their father had said he is going for inquiries.

They feel that their father is most likely dead, killed by the rustlers. Because of that assumption, they take along one of their father's old dogs. If their father has been killed, they reason, he would have been buried at some field around the cluster of the villages where he had gone. They concentrate their search in that area. They make several inquiries from the men they know in that area.

For several days no one volunteers any information. Antónis has a lot of friends there, but still no one comes forth. Much of that is from fear. If the rustlers are from a "bad" family, anyone who gives them information will most likely be killed by a member of that family. Finally, late one night, a villager whose brother was associated with Advance Force 133 tells them to search in a certain area.

When they previously were in that area, they didn't notice anything unusual. Now, they spend several hours searching that area but find nothing. As they are getting ready to leave, their father's dog runs into a tomato field and starts digging. They notice that the field hasn't been watered for some time and the ground has cracks.

Nearby farmers tell them which family owns that field. Antónis and Pétros know the family, and they are aware that they have two young sons who have been suspected in the past for rustling sheep and goats. They borrow spades from the farmers and begin digging. They find the bodies of their father and the dog that was with him.

The two brothers shame their friends in the villages into telling them how the murder of their father occurred. The old man had caught the two young men and a cousin of theirs butchering his sheep. When he accosts them, the inexperienced and not-so-bright young men finding themselves in a difficult place, and they instinctively shoot the old man and then his dog. To eliminate evidence of their crime, they take their bodies to that field; they dig a shallow grave and plant tomatoes in the field.

The brothers leave word that the three young men will not live much longer. After that, the three young rustlers stay close to home, venturing into the mountain fields rarely, and only with their fathers. The problem the murderers have, however, is that they are shepherds, and shepherds need to be with their flocks from early in the morning until late in the evening up on the mountainside.

Any other time, in such a situation, they could leave the village and go to a large city on the mainland, away from the island, where they would find work and attempt to hide. But this is war, and Greece is occupied. There is no place to go. They have to stay in their village, and as shepherds, they have to go to the mountainsides to take care of their flocks. This is a big complication for them and their families.

Antónis and Pétros make it a show of faithfully, both or one of them, going every day to the areas in which the young murderers have been taking their flocks. But the only shepherds they could see have been the fathers, brothers, or cousins of the three young men. After a few weeks, the two brothers can't continue. Antónis needs to be with the spy ring, while Pétros has his family and his own sheep to take care of.

The brothers decide they need to develop a long-range plan, and so they do. Initially, instead of going every day, they begin to go sporadically, one of them showing up at some safe distance in the places where they hope to find the murderers. Then, they stop altogether. Pétros admits to the patrons of the local kafenío that they have responsibilities which force them to abandon their quest to avenge their father's death—but they would again take up the effort when they get the time.

The brothers know that a certain one of their fellow villagers will deliver that news to the family of the murderers. The brothers had been told by one of their friends who live in the murderers' village that this fellow had informed the young rustlers that their father's sheep are an easy target for stealing. Antónis and Pétros haven't shown any animosity toward that man. Stealing sheep is almost a sport in the mountain villages, albeit a dangerous one.

Those actions by the two brothers are deliberate. Antónis and Pétros want to use that fellow villager in their effort to avenge the murder of their father. In addition to that, the two brothers know that it is a fair game in the mountain villages for men in one village to finger a relative or friend in another village an easy target for stealing of flocks of sheep, goats, or even other domesticated animals.

When a good many weeks pass and the two brothers aren't observed to be at the places the murderers are normally taking their animals, their families relax a bit, and the young men take back the shepherding of their animals—initially with one of their fathers. Antónis is so advised by his friend in the village of the murderers. It is then that the brothers begin shadowing the murderers again. They do it mostly individually, taking turns.

Before, they allowed their presence to be known going to and being close to where the murderers have their animals. Now, making the mitáto of Pétros as their base, they avoid being seen by their villagers going to the place of the murderers or coming back from it. And when they are at the murderers' places, they stay out of view. Eventually, the fathers stop accompanying the murderers.

One evening Antónis has them in his sights, but another young shepherd is with them. For the next few days it is the same scenario. After that, one of the three murderers is consistently farther away from the other two, and Antónis doesn't feel confident of getting all of them. Finally, one evening the three young men are close together, and Antónis drops them all.

Antónis hurries back to the village and goes straight to the kafenío. He walks in with his rifle. He doesn't sit. The kafenío patrons sense that something happened and are watching him. Antónis, with his matter-of-fact voice and expression announces, "My father, God bless his soul and forgive his sins, has been avenged. All of his murderers are dead." He walks out and leaves the village.

Antónis knows he is now a marked man. The adult male relatives of the three dead young men will come after him—and there are many of them. Now, his own days are going to be short if he stays in his village. To continue with the Advance Force 133 isn't an option either. Not only can't they protect him, but he will become a serious liability to the group.

During his time with the spy ring, he had spent, a few times, several days with a small partisan army, in the western part of the island. Now, he walks down from his mountain, then over a couple of small valleys and up on another mountain where there is the small partisan army. He joins that partisan group, and when their leader is killed in a skirmish with a German patrol, he becomes the leader of the group.

When the partisan armies are disbanded after the occupation, Antónis is arrested by the police for the killing of the three young men. He is a hero for most of the people, but for the police, he is a problem. If they allow him to stay free, he will eventually be assassinated. Thus, it seems that the vendetta between Antónis' family and the families of the dead young men will progress the way all murderous revenge affairs do in some of the mountain villages.

The men who know what is going on are wondering what will occur next, and the unexpected happens. Antónis escapes from jail and disappears. Speculations about his fate abound. They range from his taking off to the mountains and hiding among the shepherds there to the Greek secret service moving him to another place in Greece to the British secret service taking him to one of their colonies.

Because of the war, I hadn't gone to school for five years, so I'm still in high school, and I don't follow what is going on. A few years later, while I'm in Athens, Aristédis fills me on the real saga of Antónis. Both the British and the Greek secret services don't want Antónis in jail, even if it is for his own protection. It isn't too difficult for them to arrange an "escape" from jail, and they keep him under wraps until he is moved to Australia.

Additionally, Aristédis tells me what exactly happened when the three young men are shot. Antónis, in fact, hadn't killed his father's murderers. Antónis had been on a mission for the spy ring at that time. It is his brother, Pétros, who had taken over the shadowing of the murderers. And it is Pétros who had done the deed. Antónis arrives at his brother's mitáto just as his brother is returning from his revenge mission.

Antónis is single. Pétros has a family. Antónis has flexibility in his movements, while his brother is tied down by the needs of his family. Antónis tells his brother that he will claim the killing. So, the only thing Antónis has done is to pick up the rifle and walk to the kafenío to announce the deed as his.

"Dunbabin was aware of all that," Aristédis finishes his story, "and that's why the Brits helped Antónis to conveniently break out of jail and leave Greece."

CHAPTER 31

The Political Climate

Bedfellows of sorts

In the political arena, the Greeks pursue their choices with the same emotional intensity as any other endeavor in their lives. And the war, but especially the occupation, helps to sharpen the difference and intensity of those choices, which has lasted up to the present.

In the early 1900s, the Greek governing regime had been a constitutional monarchy, and the political stage was controlled by the Philéléftheron (love of freedom) Party, and the Laikón (the people's) Party. The Laikón Party holds conservative principles both in governing and in sustaining the society's conduct and strongly supports the monarchy. The Philéléftheron Party bears liberal principles both in governing and in nurturing the society's behavior and favors a republican government. In the bare political arena the Laikón Party is strongly pro-monarchist, while the Philéléftheron Party seeks the abolishment of the monarchy.

Since Venizelos, a Cretan politician, is the leader of the Philéléftheron Party, its supporters have been called Venzelikí. As the years go by the Venzelikí come to include the socialists and republicans. The socialists put priority on the needs of the people, no matter what the state cost is, while the republicans are anti-monarchist but want a constitutional republic—with responsible state finances. As we will see later, this definitive dichotomy affects the political climate on Crete, as well as in the whole country, first during Greece's Nazi occupation and then several years after the war's end.

Close to the mid-1930s, the Venzelikí attempted to remove the king by a coup, but they failed. Then, the communists started making a lot of noise, and apparently, King George II had had enough. He dissolved the parliament and appointed General Metaxás as prime minister. Metaxás was given the charge to contain the communists, and the king bestowed on him enough powers for reaching that goal. Metaxás, supported by the army, used those powers to move not only against the communists but also against the liberals. The communists, however, were the ones who suffered the most abuses by the Metaxás security operatives. Communist leaders were jailed, tortured, and exiled to uninhabited islands.

Metaxás, however, didn't stop there. In order to assure the future of the monarchy, he devised a system of education through which the youth were systematically proselytized into his political philosophy and system of governance. But to do this successfully, he needed to get to the youth well before it forms any political ideas and before it has been politically influenced by parents. Greece is an agricultural country. The country has thousands of villages but only a relatively small number of cities. The villages have elementary schools, but the high schools are mostly in the cities. So, by far, the majority of pre-high school age youth is in the villages.

Metaxás devised the eight-year high school, which included the last two grades of elementary school. This forced the brighter young village children at the age of ten to move into the cities for high school education and away from their parents. At the same time, Metaxás abolished all youth organizations, including the scouts. In their place he established Νεολέα (Neolέa—Youth), a government-sponsored and funded youth organization, and made it mandatory that all high school pupils were automatically members of Neolέa. High school pupils were required to attend all meetings and activities of their respective Neolέa chapters, or they were expelled. And expulsion meant no high school education and therefore no chance to enter a higher education institution.

In the fall of 1937, my parents took me to Iráklio in order to start the first grade of the new eight-year high school in Koraís, a private school. There I'm caught in the Neoléa trap. When I refused to attend my assigned Neoléa Chapter's meetings and activities, I was notified that expulsion proceedings will follow. I was saved by the kindness of an elderly, well-known physician who found out about my predicament from third parties. Even though he didn't know me (I'm told he liked what I had done), he sent Petrákis, the director of Koraís, a letter about my (fictitious) bad health. I hadn't been bothered again. At that time, it seemed to me that both the doctor and Petrákis didn't like what is going on in the country's new secondary school system.

When the Germans conquered Greece, there was no coherent political plan in the country for organizing resistance to the occupiers. Eventually, in the mainland, the leftists (Venzelikí socialists and the communists) worked together and formed an underground national resistance organization. The mostly well-educated communist leaders had learned a thing or two from their suffering under Metaxás and the seeming apathy that the Greek population at large showed toward his actions against them.

The leftist activists organized a resistance organization named National Resistance Front. It is known as EAM, from the acronym of its Greek title. EAM comes to life at a moment that almost everyone wants to fight against the Germans, no matter who his ally is in that effort. In their plenary sessions, the organizers had developed the charter of EAM. That charter was a master work. It included all the proverbial buttons, bells and whistles that any person, under the onus of a tyrannical occupation, from laborer to an intellectual, could understand and love.

And that was fine. What wasn't fine was that the most aggressive leadership in that group came from the communists, who eventually are able to take effective control of that political organization, as well as of ELAS, the strong partisan army EAM has fielded on the mountains of the mainland. In the ensuing years, EAM's social agenda slowly moves toward the East (Soviet Union) and away from the West (the Allies).

The leftists strongly suspect that, after the war, the English, especially Churchill, will support the return of King George. The antipathy, the emotional fever of all the anti-monarchists is so strong that they dismiss, as Western propaganda, what Stalin has done in Russia, and go with the leadership of EAM, which has downplayed or just rejected the information about his atrocities. The poor, and most of us are poor, fall for the slogans that the leftists extract from EAM's charter.

At the same time, some of the educated and intellectuals became attracted to EAM's charter dream of a genteel democratic society that takes into consideration the poor masses and guarantees freedom of expression and movement. But they dismally failed to examine more deeply what the association with the Soviet Union will do to the promises of EAM's charter.

For some time, it seemed that the majority of the people failed to look deeper and find what had been hidden behind the slogans extracted from that charter. By the time some of the leaders of the republicans of the political center and of the monarchists wake up, it is impossible to even come close to EAM's popular appeal, political strength, and the number of armed partisans.

It doesn't help that the right and part of the political center are split between the monarchists and the republicans. The two of them go their own separate ways. The monarchists support the return of the king, who is unpopular, and the republicans support the establishment of a democratic republic. The result is that the masses lump them together and they don't buy the political intent of the republicans.

The left is also split between the communists and the socialists, but they work together. And it is done in such a way that the masses buy the message of the socialists and ignore the threat presented by the communists.

As the war is ending, the differences between the political right and the political left crystallize into a single question. And that question is: "Should Greece fall within the sphere of influence of the West (Britain and America) or within the sphere of influence of the East (the Soviet Union)?" EAM steadfastly supports and promotes the option of going with the Soviet Union, while the political center and right promote the West option.

It is also a question within Dunbabin's group. So, when Dunbabin becomes aware of it, he simply states, "This question will be answered by Churchill and Stalin," and discourages any serious speculation among his co-workers as long as Germans are still on the island. But we Greeks are ... what else but Greeks! We tend to go with our emotions rather than cold rational logic.

EAM emissaries to Crete reach the island sometime in late 1942 to early 1943. First it's hard work for them, but then their message finds traction. For the balance of the occupation, they spend their time and energy in proselytizing.

When I first heard the message of EAM in Vyzári, it had been from Manólis, a young fellow villager who is a civil engineer, and I sympathize with the drift of it. One day, though, sitting with a group of our village elders outside the Makrí Manólis store, the conversation is about that message. The elders don't like it. "It is phony," one of them contends, and the others appear to agree. I had been so shaken by my Neoléa experience in Iráklio that I couldn't stand even the thought of another such possibility. I spend some time with the civil engineer again. The more he talks, the more I begin to buy the arguments of the elementary-school-educated elders in our village, and at some point the elders win.

The various local resistance organizations on Crete known as EOA, which are bound together to form EOK, come to life from the initiative of local folks like Antónis Lítinas, and not by agenda emissaries from the mainland. They spring up from the social ground of common people who have no hidden political agendas, just the desire to find ways to cope with their new oppressor. On the other hand, EAM has been formed on the mainland by leaders who have their own political and social agenda.

While some intellectuals sympathize with EAM's social positions, EAM's slogans feel like music to the ears of the poor masses in the cities, especially in Iráklio—where I witness its influence after the Germans evacuated that city. And the Cretan leaders of EAM spend their

clandestine time in actively spreading EAM's political gospel and proselytizing. After it is clear that Nazis Germany is on its knees, the Cretan
wing of EAM begins to show signs of active life in the resistance.

The leftists now show the same disorganized operational skill against
the Germans as the leaders of the republican armies had shown throughout the occupation. Actually, however, the Cretan leftists, in their haste
to show that they too have fought the Germans, act with gross disregard
for the safety of the villages and the people around their altercations.
Also, since they had come in the resistance so late, and even though their
figurehead on Crete is General Mándakas, they now need someone who,
actively, has been fighting the Germans all those years.

Because of that, they court Badouvás. They hope, according to Cooper, that he will switch sides and take over the leadership of the Cretan
ELAS. Cooper writes that Badouvas appears to be receptive to that idea.
When Leigh Fermor realizes that, he convinces SOE in Egypt to give a
fancy-sounding English title to Badouvás. This pleases Badouvas, and he
stays with the Allies. But his top lieutenant, Yiánnis Podiás, takes over
the leadership of ELAS in Crete.

The public appearance of EAM makes life uneasy for veteran resistance operatives, as well as for the mountain villagers. It is obvious in
Vyzári and in the villages I'm most familiar with that people who we
thought of as allies, or simply trusted observers, begin to develop some
distance from us, to the point that we come to worry about their trust-
worthiness.

In Vyzári, especially, the political schism in the community makes
the relationships even among relatives to be rather tenuous—to say the
least. The majority of the villagers are with us, I know. But some seem
to be changing. I'm especially concerned when I realize that a few are
friends or relatives, and that hurt increases when the leftists in our village turn us over to the Gestapo.

Close to noon one day, while visiting Vyzári, I spied Manólis, the civil engineer, sitting alone on a bench in the village square, and I sat next to
him. We are just the two of us. Since I have noticed his change in attitude
toward me, I start a political conversation—which I normally don't do.

He tells me that I and my family support the British, who are pluto-crats and enemies of the common people. I must admit that I have no strong objections to that line of thinking. Before the war, the British had been heartily disliked by the common people in the poor countries, and Greece isn't as poor as other nations, but poor it is.

Before the war, Britain is pegged as the richest, the most powerful, and the most arrogant nation in the world. Citizens of small or poor countries picture all Brits as rich and arrogant as their country, and they look at them with a mixture of envy and hate. Not much unlike the way today's poor masses and a lot of intellectuals of the world see America and us Americans.

Then, he switches to the argument that we support the British op-eratives on Crete, who really are doing this for the interest of England and not of Greece. I think about that for some time, as I have seen that argument before. It seems a strange argument while a war is still going on, with Russia and the West fighting a common enemy. I realize it is a simplistic argument that finds traction with unsophisticated folks, but not with such people as Manólis. Then it dawns to me that that's an ar-gument he uses with the young people in the village.

"Manolis, suppose that in this war Greece and England reverse roles. We are the superpower and we sent to England such officers with the same mission as the British are here. Wouldn't you expect them to look out for the interests of Greece too?"

"Yes, of course."

"Well, why should it be alright for us, but not for them, now?"

"But that's not the same. That's hypothetical, and this is happening now."

"Well, let me put it in another way. In this war, is Germany our en-emy?"

"Yes."

"Is Germany the enemy of England also?"

"Yes."

"Don't we both strive for the defeat of Germany?"

"Yes, of course. But, so is Russia."

"Yes. Since all three countries work together to defeat Germany, we could have Russians helping us here. If that was so, would that make any difference to you?"

Manolis, I sense, feels uncomfortable. He takes some time, before saying, "No."

"But, if we had Russians, don't you think that they also would work for the interests of Russia?"

But he doesn't want to listen to more of that—it's my impression he is dismissing me because he has the education I don't have, so I'm not as "deep of a thinker" as he is.

"The fact of course is," I'm thinking as I'm going home, "that in a war you fight along with the people who are willing to help you. After all, plutocrat England and capitalist America have welcomed the proletariat Russia in their fight against Germany, and proletariat Russia readily accepts the material help of the capitalist America."

"And why do they help you?" I ask myself. "Because by helping you, they help themselves," I repeat to myself. And that's why they do it—which is much different than the promises from the people who haven't come to share the danger with you.

The saddest part of this political dichotomy is the fact that it eventually leads to a strong distrust among former friends and neighbors, bringing to the surface, at times, even hateful feelings for one another. And it becomes so strong in the mainland that it eventually leads to a most ruinous civil war—a tragedy.

CHAPTER 32

An Apostolí

Adventures at night

W hen I return home from my visit with Manólis, Mother tells me that Uncle Kóstas has stopped a few moments for a quick lunch. He had asked her to let me know that I should be in Aghios Ioánnis by tomorrow noon.

When, the next day, I arrive at Koronákis' house I find out that I'm to be involved in another Apostolí—a nocturnal clandestine rendezvous with a British navy boat to exchange personnel and to bring in supplies from Egypt—it is the most dangerous group activity of the spy ring.

After the operatives of Force 133 arrive on the island, considerable planning and effort go into the preparation for and the actual evacuation of the stranded Anzac soldiers on the island. The evacuation takes place through night runs by the British Navy's fast motor launches.

The preparation and the actual escorting of the stranded soldiers to the secret and changing shoreline points and helping them to be put on sea vessels comes to be known by the code name Αποστολή (Apostolí). Αποστολή literally means the undertaking a certain mission—sending someone to accomplish a defined task, to reach a certain target.

In this case it includes the efforts of putting together a group of stranded soldiers, coordinating, by wireless radio, with the British intelligence and naval forces in Egypt, the selection of the shore place and time the British vessel will pick up the group, choosing the route to that shore point, planning the security and the supervision of the trip there, as well as helping in the embarkation of the men into the sea vessel. It is a complex intertwinement of effort and dangerous action.

After the repatriation of the stranded soldiers, the meaning of the term Apostolí is modified to mean any activity that takes place in moving people and material back and forth, to and from, the island and Egypt.

Following my capture by the Gestapo and my subsequent escape, Kýrios Yiánnis has shown enough confidence in me to occasionally, but rarely, include me in an Apostolí. My guess is that I'm included when the danger isn't great. And now it is close to the end of the war, in favor of the allies, and the Germans don't seem to control the south shore of the island as tightly as before. Nevertheless, I take my inclusion as a great honor.

I'm the last one arriving at Koronákis' house. After I take a seat, Giórgis, the agent in charge, starts the meeting. Giórgis is a captain in the British military intelligence service. The other leader of the group, Yiánnis, is from the village of Aghios Ioánnis. Giórgis simply tells us when we will leave, how we would move, but not where we are going, and that this time we are taking a few donkeys for loading incoming supplies. He names two men who are to walk ahead of the group by about a kilometer and two men who will walk about the same distance behind the group. I am one of the two in the rear group. Giórgis has been on the island, off and on, for over two years. He left for Egypt before the end of the war. I never learned his real name.

Among the assembled men there, there is a beautiful young woman. The really gorgeous young lady is a surprise, as in my experience women are leaving the island with their husbands or fathers. Later, I'm told that she has been a Dunbabin agent, embedded as a secretary into a German sensitive office in Iráklio. Her boss, a colonel, had also been her lover. Her boss was among the military personnel who had been transferred off the island recently. As I had been told, she is warned by another female agent that the Gestapo is asking questions about her. She realizes that her cover is about to be blown and bolts from Iráklio.

We leave after darkness and we arrive at a safe house in Saktoúria while it still is dark. I had been there before. It is a mountain village high up from the water. Waiting for us in the safe house are two Cretan partisan chieftains and three British intelligence operatives. The operatives and the partisan officers, whom I didn't know, are scheduled to also leave for Egypt. As the morning light timidly breaks in, tiganites with warm honey become our breakfast, and Giórgis visits with us.

He tells us about the negotiating of the treacherous downward trip to the shoreline and the German observation stations at some distance on both of our sides. Blankets come to each one of us, and we try sleeping. After eating salted olives and bread that evening, we leave as soon as dusk falls. When we arrive at the shore, a small, well-hidden cove waits for us. The tiny beach is easily approachable only from the east. As I have found out in a previous apostolí, the beach is so small and sort of sunken at the shoreline that, even during the day, it isn't visible from the ground above until one reaches it.

The British Navy's motor launch comes in silently, almost. A rope is thrown from the approaching small rubber dinghy to one of our men, who is already in the water, and he brings it to the shore. The dinghy attached to it brings four men to the sand. The young lady and three men get into the dinghy, which is pulled by another rope from the motor launch. Following the same procedure, we quickly exchange men and get the supplies.

The motor launch leaves as silently as it arrived, amid the darkness of the overcast moonless night. Working silently, all men on land are engrossed in the task at hand. They place in proper order the weapons, ammunition and supplies the motor launch has delivered. About a dozen men had also disembarked on the tiny beach. The task I'm given is to move a few batteries from the edge of the water to the donkey closest to me. My companions, about two dozen of them altogether, are busy getting the weapons, ammunition and supplies ready to be loaded on the donkeys.

It is then that he appears out of the darkness. No one hears him coming. It is as if an order is given to stop what we are doing, as his sudden appearance brings us all to a standstill. He approaches the group as if he knows who we are. When he comes next to us, we notice that he is tall and robust. From where I stand, I can only see his eyes and nose, as he wears the traditional black saríki—a knitted scarf with which mountain Cretans casually cover their heads. His long hair has spilled down from his saríki. He has a profuse black beard covering his face, a thick mustache, and rather ominous-looking thick and bushy eyebrows.

"Who is Captain Giórgis?" the stranger asks in conversational tone, without the traditional Cretan greetings first.

"I am," Giórgis replies, also in conversational tone, as he moves to the front of the group. Yiánnis immediately joins him.

"I want to talk to you privately."

"These are my comrades. If you have anything to say to me, you say it in front of them. And since you seem to know who we are, tell us who you are."

"I am with the heroes of ELAS."

I hear the man next to me, who is among the newcomers, saying, "Heroes? How the hell they are heroes? They haven't been in a real battle yet."

Uncle Kostas tells me later that this fellow is from a village in the Haniá prefecture, and he and his few men had been there because they are visiting an EAM man, in one of the area's villages. Most likely, someone in Saktoúria had given him the name of the captain.

"What do you want?"

"The guns and ammunition."

"Why should we give them to you?"

"We need them to fight the Germans."

"We also need them for the same purpose."

"You can get more at another time."

"What if we don't give them to you?"

"We will take them by force."

"How is that?"

"I have at least twice the men you have. We have been here for over two hours. We have the high ground, we have blocked your way out, and my men's guns are already trained at your direction."

The times I have been involved in an Apostolí our only concern had been the possibility of being entrapped by the Germans, if a traitor has warned them, an accidental encounter with a German patrol, or if German sentries close to our activities detect us. In the past the spy ring has operated hundreds of those missions, and I never had heard that there ever had been any concern about other Cretans getting in the way of an Apostolí. So, this is not only the very first such incident, but also a dangerous unpatriotic action.

Contrary to that, the men and women in the villages close to the rendezvous coves are most helpful in keeping an eye out for German movements, and they have supplied any needed assistance, especially if the navy vessel misses the rendezvous date by a day or two because of the weather. So it is a surprise when the stranger materializes at the location of this Apostolí and demands the weapons that had been brought by the boat.

After the ELAS man tells Giórgis that they will take the weapons by force, Giórgis turns toward our group.

"Pick up your weapons," he orders.

Most of us have already picked them up.

Then, Giórgis turns to the ELAS man.

"If you want to take our guns by force, you will have to fight us."

"You really will fight for these weapons?"

"Yes, we will."

"Really?"

"Yes, really! Now, leave."

"Let's not be so hasty about this, Captain."

"What do you mean?"

"There is really no need to kill each other for these weapons."

"Well?"

"Well, you are in a terribly disadvantageous position."

"So?"

"I may disappoint you, Captain. But we will not kill fellow Cretans for a few guns."

"What do you propose then?"

"How about giving us a dozen of the guns?"

"We will give you six."

"We will take them."

The visitor left for a few minutes and returned with three of his men. His men take the six guns and some ammunition and leave. The guns are like the one I carry, light submachine weapons the British commandos use.

The stranger addresses Giórgis.

"Captain, you are a difficult man. But you are fair."

He disappears in the darkness without another word.

During this interchange, two newcomers stand next to me. One is a Brit second lieutenant, and the other one a Greek-Egyptian agent, whom I had known from his previous duty tour to Crete. I noticed that during the dialogue, the Greek-Egyptian was explaining to the lieutenant what had been going on.

We hurry up to load the donkeys and leave the cove, as we have to clear this area and be away from the village, in the next two hours left before morning, otherwise we would unnecessarily endanger the village. When we are passing through Saktoúria, the leader of the area's EOK chapter, whom we had met in the safe house, waits for us and has a short visit with Giórgis.

The Greek-Egyptian, who is on his second mission to Crete, tells me that among the British newcomers are four noncommissioned officers and the second lieutenant. They all are new to Crete, except that two of the noncommissioned officers have served on mainland Greece and the third one in Yugoslavia. The lieutenant barely speaks Greek—one can easily guess that he has hurriedly taken Greek language lessons.

Soon morning comes. We are in areas without close motor roads, and the men and women in the villages we pass by, and the men in the fields, look out for us. We are in friendly territory, and the group somewhat relaxes—but not by much.

The new lieutenant notices the situation. He approaches Giórgis, who is walking with Níkos. Níkos tells me later what occurred between the new lieutenant and Giórgis.

"One has to admire the stealth by which those forty or more men came right next to us, Captain," the lieutenant begins. "Have you known anything about this fellow and his group before?"

"No. Not specifically this man. We have information that the communists are attempting to organize some force, but no definite details, yet."

"That's a bit late, isn't it, Captain?"

"Yes, it is."

"But, it appears that they have done it. You really took a grave chance down there, Captain."

"Chance? No. Not, actually."

"Really! What do you mean?"

"He didn't want to kill us."

"Is that right?" said the newcomer with a hint of a sarcastic smile.

"He just had taken the possibility that we might be frightened enough to give him the weapons. If he had wanted to kill us, he most likely knows where we are going and he could have set a trap some place in between."

"I don't understand."

"At our position in the cove, there are German sentry stations, about two to three kilometers from each side of the cove. With the first gunshots, the Germans would have come down upon us."

"I'm sorry, but I still don't understand."

"First, the leader of our visitors had been bluffing. I had suspected he most likely has fewer than a dozen men. Then, he must have been informed by the local EAM cell about the German positions. So, they know that if the Germans came down, they not only would not have any guns but they would also be dead."

"And we too!" the newcomer mumbles.

"It also is obvious that our visitor is new to this game. After all, the war is almost over, and he calls his men heroes. Heroes of what? Of daring to come out in the open now that Nazi Germany is just about dead? I also suspect that we most likely have help."

"Really? You must be kidding, Captain."

"When we pass Saktouria, I'm informed that not only our visitor has only six men with him, but he also is aware that a substantial local nationalist force is behind them, for our support."

"If so, why did the nationalist force allow them to pressure us about the weapons?"

"Lieutenant, they will not attack ELAS for the same reason that our visitor settles for just six guns. Don't forget that the Germans are close enough to detect any disturbance. Besides you heard our visitor say that he won't kill Cretans. The nationalist forces feel the same."

"Captain, I am wondering why this operation took place in such a dangerous location. As you already have mentioned there are German sentry stations on both sides of the cove."

"Lieutenant, there are German sentries relatively close to all coves in which we have rendezvous with the boats."

"I didn't realize that."

"It is dangerous in all of them. The island, however, is long, and the length of its south shoreline is even longer, probably over 200 kilometers, because it is highly jagged and has hundreds, if not thousands of coves. If the Germans had attempted to effectively seal the coastline, they would have had to commit several thousands of their forces—forces they need to protect their bases from the Cretan partisan armies, British commando raids, and for intimidating the island's general population, in order to keep it at bay."

"Are some coves less dangerous than others?"

"It depends. Since the Germans cannot effectively seal the shoreline, they have established sentry stations in high positions. From those positions they command some degree of surveillance that can detect suspicious activities."

"So, the coves closer to the sentry stations are more dangerous than the ones farther from them."

"That's correct, Lieutenant, but normally, those are the best coves for our operations. Still, under the cover of a dark night, as last night, we can cautiously move about without detection, and we do."

"Do you trust the villagers who are close to the coves? From what we have been told during our orientation in Egypt, villages from which one or more of their inhabitants are found helping us are destroyed by the Germans."

"Yes, that happens. Still we couldn't perform these activities successfully without the total support and cooperation we receive from the men and women of the villages close to the coves, even though they know how dangerous it is for them to do so."

The newcomer lieutenant has become quiet for more than an hour. Then, he tacitly approaches the captain again. "Captain, during the weeks of training and orientation in Egypt readying us for our assignment here, we never had touched in detail on the things that I saw and what we went through last night, and even right now as we pass these villages."

The lieutenant continues, looking directly at the captain, "Captain, what I realized in these few hours on Crete is that I have a lot to learn."

"We all did, lieutenant," the captain replies without a smile.

The Radio

Clandestine news

After reaching Aghios Ioánnis, I leave the group and walk to Vyzári. The next day is Saturday, and on Saturday evening I listen to Radio Cairo on EOK's clandestine radio.

Before the war, phones and radios are among the items we considered luxury items in our villages. Each village has a communal phone, except for very small settlements, such as Sáta, which doesn't have one. In most of the villages, the phone is located in the kafenío or in a popular store; sometimes in the house of the village's mayor.

Radios not only constitute an expensive luxury, but they also present a serious difficulty in operating them. Since no electricity reaches the villages, radios require batteries, like the ones used in cars. Those batteries have to be charged, and lucky is the village that has the equipment to do that. For most villagers, batteries must be taken by a donkey to the village that has charging facilities—which might be hours of a donkey trip. Like the phone, the only radio in a village usually may be found in the kafenio and normally operates only for news broadcasts. If a village has a doctor, then he might have a radio. And very few villages have a resident doctor.

When the Germans arrive in Crete, they proceed to outlaw the ways by which we can communicate long distance with one another and with the outside world. They confiscate the radios. Telephone lines from cities to villages come down. Possession of a radio means the death penalty, administered on the spot. So, even if a villager has hidden a radio, he finds it almost impossible to secretly operate it.

Colonel Dunbabin and his staff in their visits with the mayors of the villages and EOK leaders do disseminate war news, but they have a rather minuscule audience, besides the fact of unpleasant events in the news. When, however, things start going in favor of the Allies, Dunbabin sees an opportunity to enhance the morale of a larger number of patriots. He and Uncle Kóstas consult with Lítinas and some patriot mayors bordering the Amári Valley and in Ambadiá. Ambadiá is the south area of the éparchy of Amári, extending from the hills rising immediately south of Vyzári and all the way to the Sáta Hill.

The initial decision is that a radio will be installed somewhere in the éparchy, an activist will listen to the evening news broadcast, in Greek, from either Radio Cairo in Egypt or Radio London. That person will summarize the news and make available the summaries to runners from other parts of the éparchy. Dispersion of the summaries extends to trusted patriot leaders in villages in the Messará Plain, and villages both north and west of Amári.

They decide to have the radio in Vyzári, and I have been assigned to be the person operating it. The plan is both ingenious and straightforward, as Uncle Kóstas explains it to me. I'm to listen to the news broadcast and take notes, then develop a summary of the news and using carbon paper make six copies of that summary. My uncle tells me that whatever I need will be supplied.

Back at their villages, each of the six runners makes six more copies of my summary. Runners from six other villages pick up those copies. I never had known why six copies. I simply had assumed that 36 bulletins covered pretty much all the settlements in Amári. And that's how it started. Much later, however, I find out that the area covered by the scenario of the six bulletins had been extended, covering also a few villages in the Messará Plain, and villages west and north of Amári.

All runners, all the way to the end, must not divulge to the recipients from where they receive the bulletin. In each village the man receiving the bulletin may decide not to make new copies if, in his judgement, there are potential security concerns.

Since I must share my time between Sáta and Vyzári, I decide that I will be doing this once a week. And because Uncle Kóstas remarks that on each early Saturday evening Radio Cairo broadcasts, in Greek, a summary of the week's news, I decide to listen to that broadcast. Later that evening runners from six villages are to come and pick up the copies of my summary of the news. My uncle also tells me that before the radio is brought to me, I must solve two problems: charging the batteries and security.

Nikolís Aggelidákis, a first cousin of my father, is the operator of the small factory that mills the olives and grain in Vyzári. He readily agrees to charge the batteries, as long as I take them to the factory late at night and pick them up again also late at night. If the factory doesn't work for lack of diesel, Nikolís also operates a water-powered grain mill, in Páno Helonés by the Liyiotis River, and he has fixed facilities there for charging batteries, while milling grain.

The security problem proves to be difficult. I have to find a place in which I could hide the radio and batteries and also operate the radio. Hiding it in our house or our stables is out of the question. If I'm fingered, the Gestapo will demolish everything in their efforts to recover the radio. And in such a case, I will be sending my mother and my siblings to death or to a work camp in Germany. For the same reason, I can't hide it in someone else's house or, for that matter, anyplace in the village.

I take to the fields. Caves are well-known and used at times by children and adults during foul weather or for clandestine meetings of lovers. Small shelters built away from the village by farmers are too far, too open, too public and have no place to hide the radio and batteries. In that process, I examine the four small churches in the fields around our village, and I also reject them for the very same reasons. That leaves me with the four creeks in our immediate area. They are threatening in the winter, but they have little or no water in the summer.

The creek going through the village I eliminate from consideration—too naked in the village and too public above and below the village. The one skirting the village's the north side offers considerable protection from roving eyes, but the area around it is much too busy. Desperate, I begin looking at the two creeks a few hundred yards south of the village. They aren't next to village, and thus they offer better privacy in entering and leaving them than the other two possibilities.

Because of the thick and tall bushes at their banks, those two creeks also offer the best privacy once one is in their beds. After checking both of them, I dismiss the one closest to the village because it offers little protection in approaching and leaving it. I end up with the creek about two hundred yards to its south. That creek, possibly because it is the largest creek in the area and has water year-round, it has been baptized as "river." It is the Πίσω Ποταμός (Back River).

It is difficult getting on its bed because of the wild vegetation growing on its deep and sharp banks—small wild trees of fig, pear, and other trees, tall and thick myrtle and oleander bushes and a proliferation of thick menacing thorny bushes. Walking on its watery bed, I'm looking to find a location that may provide privacy, and isn't covered by water in the rain season. The more I look the more I'm disappointed. No little caves are available, and I can't find adequate recesses above the winter water levels that can be available or approachable when the rains come.

One day, walking slowly on the creek bed, I spy what I think may be a good place, just above the north bank of the creek—because of the area's topography all these creeks have an east-to-west orientation. I climb out of the creek and walk up to that place.

Yes, it's a promising place. It is several hundred yards from the donkey road, and because of the topography and the thick trees, it is hidden from all sides, except from across the creek, where a high hill rises almost vertically from the creek's south bank. Other than goats scaling that steep side, the possibility of anyone, even hunters, walking there is remote. I'm satisfied that I can feel reasonably secure there.

I'm aware that the owner of that area is the elderly Panayiótis Vlastós, a respected old gentleman, dedicated bachelor, and a very private person.

In the village and the area he is known as Makrí (Long) Panayiótis, because he is tall—that is, taller than most of us. When young, he had cut into the gently rising ground, from just above the edge of the creek's north bank. He had made a large level area for a vegetable garden, which had been watered by partially damming the creek upstream.

The condition of the large garden lot indicates that Makri Panayiótis must have given up its maintenance for a long time—several years, I guess. That surprises me, as he is a very meticulous gentleman, someone who is known to be tight with his money and looks after his interests most carefully.

At the time he started the garden or shortly after that, he must also have planted climbing jasmine clematis. That jasmine had grown huge by now. Using tree logs, he had constructed a large, high and relatively extensive support system for the ever-growing jasmine. Through the years, the jasmine overgrew the support assembly. Its branches eventually grew beyond the top and spilled down all the way to the ground from all the sides of the supporting assembly.

Looking at it, I fail to see what is under the jasmine. Then I tentatively part the hanging branches. There are layers upon layers, some dry, of the hanging jasmine branches. Enough but not much light penetrates the layers of the hanging jasmine branches, except from the north. I walk under the jasmine assembly. I'm surprised. Up to six people, if not more, could comfortably seat under that structure. Another surprise is that once I'm inside it, I can hardly see things outside, except from the north side where the layer jasmine branches aren't as thick.

The west side of the garden is the side most exposed to domestic animals. Makrí Panayiótis had built a thick and high τράφος (tráphos) on that side. A tráphos is a thick, four or more feet high, fence built from rocks without mortar to bind them. Such construction in Crete dates since the time of the Minoan civilization, more than five thousand years ago, someone has told me.

A small section of that rock fence encloses the jasmine area from the west. Just outside that short part of the tráphos, there also is a thick and fairly tall stand of prýnos trees (wild acorn trees, with firm little leaves having menacing tiny prickles). That tree stand shades the jasmine from the west in afternoons. On that side, the lightest layers of jasmine branches had fallen between the outside part of the tráphos and the prýnos tree stand, because the top of the assembly extends over the tráphos. But because of the prýnos tree stand, no one could approach the jasmine area from the west.

When I walk outside from the north side, I'm pleased to see that even from that side, with the fewer layers of jasmine branches than the east and south sides, one can't see what is in the interior of the jasmine enclosure. It is then that I decide to use that place for the radio.

That evening I walk to Makrí-Panayiótis' house at the northwest edge of the village. After the greeting niceties, I talk to him.

"Bárba Panayiótis, I'd like to talk to you about the potamída (garden place by the river) you have at Píso Potamós."

"What about it?"

"Are you aware, sir, of our family's involvement in the resistance?"

"Of course, Mihalákis, I am. I live here, you know!"

"Sorry, but I wanted to make sure."

"That's alright. What do you want?"

"I'm going to be in possession of a radio. I need to hide it in a private place where I can use it when necessary."

I was expecting a surprised reaction from the old gentleman but it didn't materialize. He just looks at me with a steady cold stare.

"What do you mean by using it?"

"I'll listen to news broadcast of the Cairo Radio station."

Now, his stare changes to what I read curiosity.

"What for?"

"It's in Greek."

"I didn't know that Cairo gave the news in Greek."

"It does."

His eyes come close together—expressing doubt, I read.

"How do you know?"

"The people who are bringing the radio told me. Cairo Radio also broadcasts Greek music for a half hour every day."

He stays quiet, while watching me, and he seems to have relaxed.

"That's nice, Mihalákis. But why do you to listen to the news?"

"Well," I thought, "if I want to use the place, I have to take the risk of coming clean with him." So, I answer, "I will write summaries of the news, those summaries will be distributed to patriots in our area."

He stares at me, as something must be wrong. After some apparent hesitation, he asks, "Who asked you to do this?"

"My Uncle Kóstas and the people who are with him."

"They must be good people, Mihalákis."

"They are."

"That's good. You said you will distribute the news. How are you going to do that?"

It's time for me to hesitate, and I do. Sill, I'm deep enough by now, so I go ahead.

"It has been arranged that after I write a summary of the news, I'll make copies. Runners from other villages will pick up those copies and take them to their villages."

"My gosh, Mihalákis, did you develop this plan?"

He is smiling now, while continuing, "It's magnificent. We need this. You have your grandfather's name. He and I had been good friends before he left for America. He would have been proud of you. "

"Thank you, Sir, but I didn't develop the plan. I was asked to do this by the people who will bring me the radio." Then, "Have you been at your potamida lately?"

"Let's see now. It has probably been five or so years since I was there last. I cannot take care of a garden as large as that one, anymore, and no one else seems interested in using it."

"Maybe we should go there together tomorrow."

His face shows surprise.

"Why?"

"It will be easier for me to explain what I plan to do."

"Now, wait a minute. You are going a bit too fast for me. Does anyone know that you are planning to use the potamída?"

"Yes, my uncle Kóstas and, I imagine, my father," I lie.

He looks at me, as if it were the first time he has seen me. I'm uneasy. He realizes it.

"Mihalakis, I'll help you. As you suggested, I'll come to the potamída, but let's go separately. I'll meet you there about an hour after daybreak.

"The location, Mihalakis, is almost perfect," he tells me the next morning. "It is out of the way. No vineyards or fruit trees are close by or in the general area, and since the area around it belongs to me, no one takes his sheep or goats here for foraging."

He looks at me, smiling.

"And, you know what else?" he continues. "There is no reason for the agrofílakas (agricultural policeman) to come here, so the leftists will not know about it."

The agrofílakas is not a trusted person for many in the village, and he also is a close relative of one of the leftist leaders in the village.

"You know, Mihalákis, when I was younger, I liked to come here and spend hours under the jasmine, especially in the summers, when I took my noon nap here. It is such a peaceful and calming location."

This reminds me of the gossip I had heard in the village, some time past. According to it, he had used the place for meeting a certain married woman. Thinking about that, I almost didn't hear when he asked, "Now tell me how you plan on using this place?" And I do.

He agrees with me that the space under the jasmine would be almost perfect for operating the radio. Even though the place is known in the village, it has been abandoned for many years and no one has an interest in it. And the jasmine offers the needed privacy, even if a casual hunter comes close to it. That last thought brings to my mind the possibility of other clandestine lovers using the jasmine enclosure, now. But even so, I decide, they wouldn't be here in the evening.

The ground on its north side creek has a gentle slope toward the creek. Still, the cut on the ground that created the large level area just above the river resulted in a fairly high earth wall on the north side of the garden patch. That cut earth-wall is now covered with dead vegetation. We think of digging into that wall and making a large-enough hole to hide the radio. We start digging the next day, but it isn't easy. Besides that, we are making some noise and we are changing the looks of that wall—if anyone happens to pass by would see the disturbance. Eventually, Makri Panayiótis has a better solution.

Sitting in the jasmine-covered area, we are visiting about the radio. Suddenly, he almost shouts, "I know where it would be much better!" and pointing at the thick tráphos, he says, "In there."

"How?" I ask.

"I worked with the laborers who built it," he answers, "and I know how it has been done. We can easily form areas into the tráphos that are large enough to hide the radio and the batteries, and then we can easily rebuild around them."

"How about the rain?"

"Let's think about that later. This is perfect. I don't understand why I didn't think about it before. Let me show you." And he proceeds to do just that. Most of the rocks are large. Almost all of them had been unearthed when the laborers leveled that side of the hill to make room for the garden plot. As someone who is part of the crew that built the tráphos, Makri Panayiótis knows exactly which rocks could be moved and how to do it, in a way that it didn't disturb the overall structure and appearance of the tráphos in that section. It takes less than a half hour to make, in two separate locations, room for the radio, battery, and cables in one and for the reserve battery in the other.

Makrí Panayiótis shows me how to add the rocks he chose to cover the first space, and then he has me do the same for the second space. Then he asks me if I want to do it again, to make sure I can do it. I thank him but I say no. Both places look as though the rocks had never been touched since the construction of the tráphos.

As we talk about the rainy season, we debate how we can protect the radio from the rain. We feel that we don't need to worry about the batteries. Again, Makri Panayiotis comes up with the best solution. He has a number of askiá (plural of aski). Aski is a relatively large container made from goat's skin, and it is used for the temporary and normally short-distance transportation of olive oil. Makrí Panayiótis splits open three large askiá and cleans them up. They are just fine for the protection of the radio, battery, and cables.

Meanwhile, Ippokrátis from Fourfourás, an EOK leader and one of Dunbabin's men, passes through Vyzári in the middle of that week. I show him where I will operate the radio. Two days later, Uncle Kóstas and Dunbabin have their staff bring me a radio, two batteries, a lot of tablets and pencils, and plenty of carbon paper. Since we have had no radio before, Giórgis, one of Dunbabin's operatives, shows me how to connect the cables to the battery and radio, turn the radio on and off, control the sound, and how to dial to Radio Cairo.

The note paper, carbon paper, and pencils are in a large old leather case. After I take out enough paper, pencils, and carbon paper to last me for an estimated longer than a two-month period, we put the leather case with the reserve battery and cover it with one of the askia. Makrí Panayiótis is pleased. "Can I sit with you," he almost timidly asks, "and listen to Radio Cairo?"

"You don't have to ask, Bárba Panayiótis. You can listen anytime you would like to do so. Maybe sometime we can even listen to Greek music, too, for a short time."

"Does Cairo have Greek music too?"

"I'm told that it does."

Once we complete all preparations, I leave for Sáta. But before that, I go to Fourfourás and visit with Ippokrátis. I tell him to send a message to Uncle Kóstas that I will have my first news bulletin on the second weekend after that day.

After dark, one late Saturday evening, two weeks hence, six runners come to our house, one by one. I don't know any one of them, and we have no conversation. I just tell them, though, that on the next Saturday I will not have a bulletin, and that whenever I will not have a bulletin again, I will forewarn them the week before. Each one listens, moves his head to signal that he understands, makes a 180-degree turn and leaves without a word. This goes on for month after month after month after …

I also make extra copies for Dr. Iákovos, Giórgis Saounátsos, the kafetzís, and Makrí Manólis, the mayor. Makri Panayiótis often listens to radio Cairo, sitting on the rock next to my rock. When he isn't with me, I make a copy for him, too.

Dunbabin conceives the idea and provides the hardware, while Antónis Lítinas, who heads the Amari section of EOK, as well as Uncle Kóstas, work out the mechanism for the dissemination of the news bulletins and the list of the men who receive the bulletins—I have no idea who they are. And the plan those three men conceive works beautifully.

Most Saturdays, I'm sitting under the jasmine, sometimes with Bárba Panayiótis, listening to Radio Cairo and taking notes. I take what I need with me, I go home, summarize what I have heard, make the six single-page copies I need, and then wait for the runners. Right on schedule six quiet young men come, one at a time, and leave as silently as they have come.

The recipients of the bulletins may use them as they please. It is something that we can't control. And that's where the danger enters. So, why do Dunbabin, Lítinas and Kóstas take such a great chance? The answer is simple. They do it because they care. We have suffered all this time under the thumb of a brutal occupier. We are going from despair to despair to despair. We can't see an end of the war. We have been scared that Germany will win the war. And most of us in the villages are in the dark. We are depressed and don't exactly know how this miserable war is going.

And now things are changing. Germany is stalled in Russia; signs are that the Nazis' string of victories has come to an end. And then rumors come that the Americans and British finally move into Europe. There is tangible hope now that our oppressors will be forced to leave us. There is real hope that our suffering, our fears, our misery, our humiliation will soon end. The people start sensing the aroma of liberty coming their way. But we still don't know how fast, how soon. What is really happening, is the villagers question. Enter Dunbabin, Kóstas and Litinas—and then the bulletin. Those three men love their fellow villagers. They care for the people around them.

Everything goes well until sometime in early 1944.

By that time, the interest of the local population has shifted from the progress of the events of the war to what will happen to Greece after the war. The EOK leaders and EOK-leaning villagers, as well as their EAM counterparts, especially the few communists around, are anxious to hear what will politically happen after Germany's surrender.

My news bulletins reflect the fact that there is speculation that Stalin and Churchill will divide Europe into what euphemistically call "spheres of influence." Our people, both nationalists (republicans and royalists) and Eamítes (communists and socialists), wonder and worry where they will put Greece.

The nationalists prefer the West (England and America), while the leftists hope for the East (Soviet Union). On the left side, the communists love Russia, while the socialists don't trust the capitalist West, and like most Cretans, most of the people in our area are concerned about the possible return of King George—whom they don't want.

It seems from the news that Stalin argues that Russia has suffered enough from Germany's invasion, so the Soviet Union needs and demands a large buffer zone between Germany and Russia proper. Stalin's real agenda is somewhat hidden in that argument. Stalin actually feels that by keeping the Eastern European countries under Russian influence, they will eventually adopt communism and become Russia's natural allies.

In my case, the formerly silent runners are now talkative when they come for the news bulletins. They ask me, time after time after time, as the Allies are moving toward Germany from both the east and west, if there is news or indications about Greece's lot after the war. While before I hardly had exchanged even greetings with them, now they linger around, hoping that some news I heard would indicate the decision of the Great Powers' position on that development. It seems to me that each one of the young man feels that he has the right questions or manner that would dislodge that information from me.

It is sort of annoying to me, but their insistence in talking allows me to realize that two of the runners are leftists. When I mention it to Uncle Kóstas, he tells me that he personally knows the men to whom the bulletins go. They are leftist, he tells me, but they are patriots. They are fully trustworthy, he assures me. Still, I'm somewhat apprehensive because of what the leftists in Vyzári had done to us, and now those two make it no secret that they prefer Greece to go with the Soviet Union.

The main argument of the leftist runners is that the Russians are mostly Eastern Orthodox Christians as we Greeks. They feel that since Greece is a southeastern European country, it is natural for Greece to stay with the Eastern European bloc of nations. They also earnestly believe that Germany is being defeated by the Russians, readily dismissing the more than five-year tenacity of England, totally ignoring the material and weapons America gave to Russians in helping them to regroup and eventually stop and then push back the Germans, and downplaying the opening, by the Americans and British, the second front from on the west, in order to ease the pressure on the Russian armies in the east.

From my own experience with the leftists in Vyzári, it is mostly ignorance by the common people, and naïve idealism and misplaced ideology for the educated ones. It's the case of pure ideology trumping realistic and practical reasoning. This intense interest of the runners awakens my own curiosity about the fate of Greece after the war. So I pay special attention to the broadcasts for any hint about the division of Europe. But there are no such hints. There are reports about the meetings of the leaders of the Great Powers, but that's all. Each time I disappoint the runners. I follow Colonel Dunbabin's orders that I should write about what I hear on the radio and nothing else.

From the attitude of the runners, especially the two leftists, it appears to me that they suspect that I know what is happening, but I keep it to myself. It is a natural suspicion, of course, as my family is close to the British agents. Sill, that bothers me. I again visit with Uncle Kóstas, but he still feels that the men those two leftist runners report to are steadfast patriots. He knows them well and he is sure that there is no danger from the leftists to whom those two runners report.

One day, I happen to be in Aghios Ioánnis when a group of important British and Cretan operatives have just arrived from Egypt. General Kelaidís is among them. They are jubilant. General Kelaidís and Dunbabin report to the operatives and agents there that Churchill had given the Balkans to Stalin, after Stalin had agreed to allow Greece to stay within the British sphere of influence. Dunbabin emphasizes that only the intelligence community is privy to that development, but it is a done deal.

The thirst of the runners for information about Greece's fate must mirror, I think, the interest of area's general population. ... I know the information I have is important to the runners and to the people receiving the news bulletin. So in the following week's bulletin, I tweak Colonel Dunbabin's dictate a bit—a lot, my Uncle Kóstas tells me, not kindly, later—by deciding to include the Churchill-Stalin agreement as part of the news I heard on the radio. I feel that I'm doing a service to the people who are asking about the fate of Greece, for several months now.

The runners come and pick up the bulletins. The next day I go to Sáta. There, I find that I have to stay for two weeks. When I return, the individuals in Vyzári who have received the bulletin quiz me about what I wrote. I tell them the truth, which pleases them, and they keep quiet.

That Saturday evening, however, with the coming of the first runner, I know I'm in trouble—big trouble. He begins questioning me about the Churchill-Stalin agreement, and I have a hard time keeping him calm. He refuses to leave, and so it is with the rest of the runners. My mother, who knows what I have done, attempts to calm them down, but she fails.

I'm bombarded with intense, searching, and pointed questions.

"Did you really hear this?"

"How was it worded?"

"When was this decided?"

"Are you sure that it was said that way?"

"Are you sure that you heard it?"

"Which day did you hear it?"

"Was there any clarification about that development?"

I'm absolutely speechless. I hadn't expected that reaction. In retrospect, I should have expected it, but I hadn't. Runners from both political wings have been equally angry when I can't truthfully say that I heard it on the radio, and I also can't say where I had heard it, as I'm not authorized to talk about that.

By the time they all leave, I'm depressed. I think that their anger is justified and now I am terribly sorry that I have included that information in the news bulletin. I unnecessarily have angered the runners, especially the two leftists. Before, they suspected I am not giving them all the news. Now, they know that I'm manufacturing the news.

Any credibility I have until that time evaporates. From then on, only three nationalist and one leftist runner continue coming. And I regret my action even further when Uncle Kóstas severely chides me for breaking the security rules of the spy ring. He also feels that the danger for a leak is now real. Because of that, he recommends to Dunbabin that we stop the news bulletins. And it is done.

As I understand it later, my action has serious consequences within the EOK's leadership in Amári. Lítinas and his colleagues, not knowing how I came up with that information and my refusal to provide to the runners its source, are angered, and that anger increases when Uncle Kóstas terminates the news bulletins without first advising so Lítinas. Apparently, Lítinas then asks a few of his colleagues who have radios to start operating them, but without much success, as Ippocrátis tells me.

This becomes even more serious with Lítinas, when it becomes public that, indeed, what I wrote is correct. Lítinas now feels that both Dunbabin and Kóstas failed him by not letting him know about it right after they had known about it. When I ask Uncle Kóstas about that, he tells me that right now Dunbabin is concerned about more serious matters than worrying about personal feelings.

That development, however, intensifies my feelings of guilt. Feeling terrible for disappointing both my uncle and Dunbabin, I visit with my mother. She says little, but I sense that she is relieved. She probably feels that not working with the radio now is one less thing for her to worry about me.[16]

---

16 A few years back, reading Lítinas' book Χρέος στην Ιστορία, I notice that he hardly mentions his work with Dunbabin and Uncle Kóstas. He even has the military rank of my uncle as lieutenant, when he had known that he had been promoted to major. And he never mentions the existence and contribution of the radio he had helped to come to life.

As my mother had told me once, "Anger brings thick fog into our reasoning." Still, even into my old age, I consider this incident as one of the bitter lessons in my life.

Mother and the SS Colonel
An unusual situation

A few months before the collapse of my radio project, our front door opens with violent force near midnight. Mother and I are sitting in the kitchen by the weak light of a lýchnos. Before we have a chance to react, we hear hurried, heavy boots marching in the family room, and almost instantly we face four black uniforms. Their leading officer has drawn his sidearm, while three submachine guns are trained in our direction.

My mother, a perennially calm woman in her middle forties, looks up when they enter the kitchen. She doesn't move from her seat. She just looks up. It is as if she isn't surprised by the unpleasant visit. It's like she has been expecting it. We both have been, but we somehow have been hoping that it will not happen. But it is happening, and we face the front end of their weapons.

It is the second time during the Nazi occupation of my island that I face this scenario.[17]

---

17 I must have felt some fear, but to this day I don't recall if I had done so. This is strange, as in the Sáta episode I had been dealing with Gestapo officers, while now we are facing the even more dreaded SS officers. Fear must have visited me in both episodes, but I have been unable to presently recollect it—this, even though I clearly remember the other details of both encounters. I most likely do feel fear, but subsequently fear somehow buries itself deep into my head, refusing to surface

I had left Sáta late that day, so when I arrived home in Vyzári, it was dark. My mother and siblings were eating, and I ate with them. After my siblings had gone to bed, I reported on my Sáta responsibilities, while Mother brought me up to date on any new developments among my siblings and in our holdings in Vyzári and Aghios Ioánnis. One of Mother's concerns that evening is that apparently the Advance Force 133 base is presently on Mount Psiloritis, just above Fourfourás. If Uncle Kóstas, Dunbabin, or my father are there, they will probably bring down their staff members for a meal one of these days. She wonders if they will let her know beforehand so she would be prepared for them.

In some cases only my father, Uncle Kóstas and Dunbabin come down for a meal, but occasionally they will bring along several of their men—and every year they seem to be different men. When that happens their food is taken to Livadákia. Livadákia is a rather pleasant place south of the village. From there, one could monitor the village and the highway for a possible Gestapo visit. Livadákia, besides being a more secure location than being in the house, and away from prying eyes, has a cool small spring, grassy ground, and large plane trees that make the place, especially from spring through fall, conducive to relaxation—and operatives on the move need that and a good home-cooked meal with some wine. This time, however, I'm sure that they will not come down, as this weather isn't for Livadákia.

No matter how cautious we are, there is no way that we can hide all that from our fellow villagers. It is such a small village that anyone's and everyone's business is pretty much known to all. They don't know details of what we do, but they observe our behavior and movements, and that's enough for guessing the rest.

Through the last few months, my mother and I have been discussing and evaluating the risk of someone bringing us to the attention of the Gestapo. Up to now, I feel that our fellow villagers are patriots enough to

---

in my conscious. Yet, after the Sáta episode, every time I walk behind the loaded donkey from Sáta to Vyzári, I feel fear anytime I can't see ahead because of blind curves and the ups and downs of the road in the hilly countryside. I'm always concerned about the possibility of a German patrol being ahead on the part of the road I can't see.

keep their mouths shut, while Mother feels that even if there is a traitor among our villagers, Jehovah would protect her and her children.

When it openly surfaces that a few of our villagers have become members of EAM, however, and knowing how strongly the leftists hate the British, I start to seriously worry for our family in Vyzári. I voiced that concern to Uncle Kóstas, but he feels that the members of EAM in Vyzári won't stoop that low. He tells me that he has friends in other villages who are members of EAM, and he knows that they are strong patriots. Normally, Uncle Kóstas is correct in his evaluation of current situations, but this time he errs. Or, I should say, our village's EAM members betrayed his confidence on them.

Our house is located on the south edge of the village, between one of the village's main streets to our north and a small creek kissing our house on our south. A fairly gentle hill rises quickly from the south bank of the creek.

We own the banks and bed of the creek, as they are within the bounds of our property, as we also own the hill property adjacent to the south bank of the creek. The complex of our stables, to the north, is across the street from our house, while our property to the east borders the properties of the village's main church and elementary school. To our west is a tiny square, with a small factory for milling olives and grain next to it.

The house is an L-form structure, with an ample courtyard and an adjacent garden with a well on its north side, between the house-structure and the street, and a small yard just above the creek on the house's south side. The short leg of the L is a one-story structure with east-to-west orientation, containing the reception/family room and the kitchen; both are extra-large rooms. The long leg of the L is a two-story structure with north-south orientation, which contains the bedrooms on the second floor and, again, two extra-large storage rooms on the first floor.

Besides cooking and baking our bread, the kitchen, a rectangular room, also serves as the dining room. And since it is the only room with heat, it also often serves as the family/reception room during the cold winter months. The hearth, the built-in oven, and the pantry are on the west wall. The sink is on the south wall, with the excess water of it going into the creek, and next to the hearth, as we have to warm the water for washing dishes.

It's normal for hearths in village homes to be located just a foot or so above the floor, so that people could sit close to them in the winter for warmth, and this is the case at our farmhouse in Sáta. My father, however, had built the hearth in our Vyzári home at chest height. Because of that, during cold evenings, we had to take embers from the hearth, put them in a metal container and sit around that container for some warmth.

When the SS barges in, my mother and I are sitting on chairs near to a such metal container filled with dying embers. It is a cool evening, and that is the only heat in the house. The lead officer, I notice, is a youthful colonel. My mother, still sitting, looks at the colonel and calmly addresses him.

"What is the reason for this visit?"

The officer holds his advance, his eyes get larger and looks at my mother sort of puzzled, then he answers in perfect Greek.

"We are seeking your husband."

"So, you are," says she. "I wish you good luck." She stops for second or two and then, "As he doesn't seem to stay long in the same place."

Mother follows that with a disapproving frown, and continues, "Would you please tell me why you behaved in such a rude manner in coming into my house?" Then, "I have children sleeping and your noisy entrance could have disturbed them."

Having undergone the experience of a relatively cruel interrogation by the Gestapo, I'm amazed by what follows.

The colonel, still standing at the place he had stopped, looks at her for a few seconds then he lowers his pistol and puts it back into its holster. He addresses, in German, the rest of the men who have entered the kitchen with him, and they withdraw into the family room. Then, he asks Mother if he can take a seat. Of course he may, she tells him.

The colonel pulls a chair away from the large kitchen table and sits facing my mother.

"Where is your husband?" the SS colonel asks Mother in a conversational tone after he sits down.

"I don't know."

"You tell me that he is your husband and you don't know where he is?"

"That's exactly what I am telling you, κύριε αξιοματικέ (officer, sir), because that is the way it is."

"We have information that he is occasionally here."

"That's correct."

I notice that my mother is looking directly at the officer, but her gaze toward him is rather mellow—not submissive but not antagonistic either. She answers directly, with staccato answers, but her demeanor shows no fear or even undue concern—it is as she is telling him, "I understand that it is your job to ask me these questions."

"Then, how come you don't know where he is?"

"In order for you to find this house and to know what time to call on us, you must have an informer in this village. Since he is from here, you should not trust him, as he hasn't told you the whole story."

Mother's reference of the timing of the SS visit has village security implications. The village has developed a security plan for an early warning about German night raids, as well as for protection from marauding sheep and goat rustlers. All male villagers, from early teens to elders, are divided into one- or two-man sentinel teams.

They take turns in being posted at night, for two to three or so hours each team, on two hills—Patela, a hill in the midst of the village, and Aghios Nikólaos (Saint Nicholas), a higher hill on the northern fringes of the village. When I visit Vyzári for more than two days, I serve on one of those teams.

From Aghios Nikólaos, one has a commanding view of the Amári Valley to the north and the single narrow winding motorway leading to the village from Rethymno, the closest German base. Consequently, one can see the lights of vehicles for almost ten kilometers ahead—during the night only German transports travel. For some reason, as Mother tells me later, the Aghios Nikólaos sentry had been terminated about a week before the SS visit. Thus the SS group comes to the village without any early warning.

"What is the whole story?" the colonel asks.

"My husband and I never got along well. Even before your army had come to Crete, he rarely had stayed home for long."

"Why?"

"Several reasons."

"What are those reasons?"

"He doesn't like farming and village life, so he lived in the cities before your arrival. He has been a shareholder and an officer of the Syngelákis Transportation Company. That company had served the cities of Haniá, Réthymno and Iráklio, as you must know already. So, he had been staying in hotels in these cities and rarely had been coming to Vyzári."

"What about after that, after our arrival to Crete?"

"When the Greek-Italian war broke out, the buses and other vehicles of the Syngelákis Company were taken over by the government. They had been given to the armed forces. My husband then had moved here and had been spending his time between here and Sáta, a hamlet south of here, where the family's farmhouse is. After your armies arrive, he basically had moved there. He did come here occasionally but only for a few days at a time, mostly to get his clothes washed. Lately, however, his visits are rare."

"Our information is that he is with foreigners."

"Do, please, let me finish what I was saying."

"Go ahead."

"All of a sudden, I hear that he and his brothers have left the farmhouse, and they are up in the mountains. As you have mentioned, the rumor is that they are with some strange men. I have had a hard time believing it, and especially now that you say that they are foreigners, as he doesn't speak any foreign language.

"You see, here in the mountain villages, social intercourse is sparse, and the news doesn't reach us quickly, and when it does, it is colored with a lot of gossip. In order to pass the time people do gravitate to suppositions, which are often based on misunderstood facts or false reports.

"Nevertheless, the next time I see my husband, I ask him if it is true that he has left the farmhouse. I notice that he doesn't like the question. However, he admits that much. And when I ask him how his family would get the necessary wheat and other food supplies, he dismisses me. He doesn't want to talk about it. And it isn't strange as he has shown in the past the same negligent attitude about me and his children."

"Who takes care of your properties in Sáta now?"

"We have hired a family from a nearby village."

I can't but marvel at the way my mother answers the questions—firmly and comfortably. She isn't taking time to ponder each question, and there isn't even a hint in her voice or in her body language of strain or concern. I'm especially thankful of the way she had answered the last one. We do have a hired family to help with chores in Sáta, but I'm in charge of our holdings there, and I spend a lot of time there. She answers the question in such a way that the officer will not associate me with Sáta.

"Please, continue the story about your husband."

"As you probably know from your informant, my husband is a philandering animal. He has also been a very poor provider for his family. Up until the last few years, he truly had shown only sporadic interest in his children. Instead, he had open and rumored liaisons with several women in cities and villages around the island."

"Does he have one here, in Vyzári?"

"I don't know, but I am sure he mustn't. The village is small, and it would have become public knowledge. And even though I have very little interaction with the rest of the villagers, someone would have told me—people, you know, like gossiping and some like to delve into the misery of others. He had a lover, however, before our marriage."

"Is that woman still in the village?"

"Yes, she is. I am sure that since you have found this house, you can find her name and house too."

"Any other reasons?"

"My husband is an agnostic, an atheist most likely. He doesn't believe in God the way I do. This has produced a constant friction between us."

That hasn't been quite true. Yes, my parents have been in constant friction about the family's economy and finances, but not religion—my father didn't care about religion. Mother, I realize, had said that in order to put more distance between the two of them.

"Please continue," the colonel says.

"His insistence in living in the cities, staying away from his family for protracted periods of time, sometimes for months, his womanizing, his tendency to lose his temper, the ruinous ways in which he has handled the financial affairs of our family, and our religious differences forced me to a point where I begin to contemplate to renew my efforts in divorcing him."

"Did you go ahead with it?"

"As you probably have been told, ours is an arranged marriage, as virtually all marriages are in this part of the country. I hadn't known my husband before our marriage."

"How then had the arrangement been made for your marriage?"

"My husband has an aunt in Aghios Ioánnis, my village, which is south of here. She and my mother had been close friends, so it had been easy for the two of them to put us together. They did this, even though I'm five years older than he, which is an anomaly here as almost always the husband is much older than his wife."

My mother stops there for a few moments before she continues.

"But, I haven't yet answered your question about the divorce. Divorces in the mountain villages are frowned upon and they are practically nonexistent. Yet, I had started divorce proceedings a few years back, and that's where we are now. Divorces here take a long, long time. Even in the cities, it can take several years before they are finalized because the Church doesn't allow them, and the Church is powerful in Greece."

"So, you are going to divorce your husband?"

"Yes, up to now, I hadn't activated the proceedings because of the children, but I'm planning to try again at the end of the war. Incidentally, our papers are filed in the regional court in Réthymno. You may retrieve them from there."

"Yes, I will do that."

I know that my mother has, however, neglected to mention that the divorce papers had been there since 1929. She hasn't pursued the divorce after filing it because of strong family pressure initially, and then for the sake of us—her children.

"You said that you have had religious differences with your husband. How is that, since I understand that all Cretans are Orthodox Christians?"

"Yes. We both had been baptized at birth as Christian Orthodox. But since then, we have changed."

"How is that?"

"Well, my husband makes fun of my religious beliefs. Still, he never goes to church unless there is a baptism, wedding, or funeral, and he has had a strong condescending attitude toward regular churchgoers, and he covertly ridicules the ignorance of the clergy."

"What about you?"

Mother stands up and retrieves one of her books and her copy of the Bible. She hands them to the SS officer and sits down.

The officer's surprise is evident in his face. He looks at my mother, and then he looks at the book that has come with the Bible. And again he looks at my mother as though he really is seeing her for the very first time. Now, he keeps his eyesight on her for sometime before he asks.

"Are you a Jehovah's Witness?"

"Yes, I am."

"Really?"

"Yes. Really. And I'm surprised that you haven't been told so by your informant."

"That's strange. Up to now, I haven't heard of the existence of Jehovah's Witnesses in Cretan villages."

"We aren't many. Actually, I don't know how many. Being a woman and in a mountain village has kept me isolated from the rest of them. Your armies have terrified the mountain population here, so I imagine that those Witnesses are keeping quiet because of your presence on the island and the reputation your country has regarding our religion."

"How did it happen that you became one of them?"

"My father died fairly young. At that time, my four older siblings are either married or have left the household, leaving my mother with her three youngest children. I'm the oldest of the three. My mother, a very intelligent woman, always seemed to be annoyed and disappointed by the sparse and shallow religious knowledge of the priests in our village and the surrounding villages. She also had been offended by the social behavior of some of them.

"One time, a cousin of my mother's, who is a Jehovah's Witness, had come to our house for a long visit with my mother. Other Witnesses followed, and my mother turned. And, of course, we did too."

"Do you really believe in the Second Coming?"

"Yes."

"And the resurrection of the dead?"

"Surely."

"Do you really believe that if you die now, you will be resurrected during the Second Coming?"

"Yes, I absolutely, do."

"And then you will live forever?"

"Yes, of course."

"What about your children?"

"I hope they will follow the right road as they grow up. It will be a most difficult burden for me to carry on if I lose them forever. The only worry I have now is the thought that they might not follow the path of life."

I now notice that any apparent shade of tension on the sitting SS officer has disappeared. The stiffness in his body is gone, both body and face are now very relaxed. He even adjusts his position on his chair to a more comfortable pose. Having gone through a Gestapo interrogation and having heard from British officers about some of the terrifying interrogation tactics of the SS, I can't understand the behavior of this high SS officer.

Before this night, I would have had strong difficulty in accepting that there are SS officers who can sit down and talk with the person they are interrogating in such a civilized manner. Yet, even though not as tense as before, I still wonder. "The hard time will come later," I fleetingly think.

Still, my mother's calmness is infectious. Even if I had been afraid before, I'm not afraid now—though still somewhat skeptical how this session is to end. After all, there are officers in the next room and, I imagine, men all around our house.

In Sáta, I didn't have the time to think and to fear how that session would end, as I was the recipient of the questioning. This time, I'm the observer, and again I'm not terribly alarmed. I'm just amazed at my mother's performance.

My mother is an avid reader. She has read the Bible over and over and over again, as well as all the books and periodicals supplied to her by the Jehovah's Witnesses sect before the war. She had supplemented that reading with nonreligious literature books, including some of the classics that she had been able to get her hands on. I never have caught her reading light books for just entertainment or to pass the time, and she doesn't approve of my reading romance and mystery novels, which I personally like.

Because of her religion and her reading habits, she has been continuously ridiculed and harshly criticized by local priests and by some of the men and most of the women in Vyzári and the surrounding villages. I once overheard my great-aunt Argyró, one of my paternal grandmother's sisters, asking rhetorically, "Who ever heard of a woman reading books?" in discussing Mother's preoccupation.

Since my father was home rarely during my younger years, from the time I am in grade school, my mother starts visiting with me about the family's business. Normally, my siblings (all younger than I) go to bed earlier. After they do, Mother and I often sit by the kitchen table or around the dying embers, and she talks about the family's business. During those times, Mother had never brought up my father's philandering ways or the treatment she receives by the villagers because of her religion.

It must be more than two hours that Mother and the SS officer leisurely discuss the Jehovah's Witnesses' dogmatic beliefs and proselytizing practices. Then they switch to the ways the Jehovah's Witnesses look upon the world, including the Orthodox and other Christian Churches and their hierarchies, religious and national holidays, religious and patriotic symbols as crosses, icons and sculptures, national hymns and flags, government laws and edicts, wars and warlike behavior, and finally the reasons some national governments are persecuting the Jehovah's Witnesses.

I'm surprised at how much the SS officer knows about the way the Jehovah's Witnesses react and interact in those matters. I have read a few of my mother's books, but I'm totally unaware of most of the points that the SS officer brings up.

My biggest surprise, however, is Mother's ability to hold her own in that debate—and it's sort of a debate now. She counteracts point by point everything thrown at her. And she does it knowledgeably, calmly, and at times with enough humor to make the Colonel laugh.

At one point, the German asks my mother how much education she has.

"I never attended school," is Mother's answer.

"I am sorry, but you must be lying to me now."

"No, I am not! I do not lie!"

"Then?"

"When I was growing up, my father sent only my brothers to school."

"To be so knowledgeable you must be a good reader. How did you learn to read?"

"I continuously pestered my brother Agesílaos to read to me from the schoolbooks that he was reading. Eventually, he decided to teach me how to read, so I may leave him alone. After that, I read his books and any books that other boys in our village have. I even had borrowed books from adults."

"And that's all the education that you have had?"

"Yes."

"Amazing! You are surprising, Mrs. Paradisanós."

It isn't difficult to detect the astonishment in the German officer's face.

A pause follows. Both of them remain silent for some time. The officer seems to be thinking. Then, he continues the interrogation, which has actually become sort of a dialogue.

"As you said, the report that your husband comes here once in a while is correct. Since you are estranged, why does he come?"

"We aren't totally estranged. Because of our children—our relationship isn't warm and amicable, but we still behave as a proper family. In this case, however, he knows that I don't approve of the war and anything associated with it. I do this not only because of my beliefs as a Jehovah's Witness, but also because of the death of my most dear brother, Agesílaos. He had been killed in Asia Minor during the Greek-Turkish war that had taken place just after the First World War.

"As far as I know, my husband visits the village rarely, and it is rarer still when he visits me because of our children. I cannot bring myself to the point of stopping him from seeing his own children. And that is for the sake of the children."

"Is he armed when he comes to the village?"

"I don't know about the village, but he knows that I do not approve of arms, and I will not allow him to see our children if he comes to the house with weapons." At that point, I feel a bit guilty, as in Sáta, Aghios

Ioánnis, at times, and always in an Apostolí, I do carry a light submachine gun, but Mother hadn't been aware of it.

"When he comes, are other people with him?"

"Once he is with another man. I do tell him then that I don't want
him to come to the house with one of his cohorts. He hasn't brought
anyone since, but I have heard once that he went through the village with
another person."

"Do you know the names of those persons?"

"No."

"Would you please describe the person that your husband brought
to the house?"

"I actually can't. He is much taller than my husband, has a full, long
beard, he hasn't cut his hair for a long time, his clothes don't fit him well,
and they have been soiled, much more than my husband's clothes."

"Has he ever told you from where he comes or where he is going?"

"No. He knows I wouldn't have liked that."

"Why?"

"Because it must have something to do with whatever he is involved
in, and since I don't believe in activities related to violence and especially
war, I'm not interested in what he is doing."

"Do you know who he visits in the village?"

"From what I have heard, he just passes through and at times he
stops at the kafenío for coffee. Besides, I doubt that he can visit anyone.
He isn't liked by our villagers because of his womanizing."

Another pause follows—this is a long one. The SS officer seems to be
in silent contemplation, while Mother waits patiently. Then, he proceeds.

"May I look over the rest of the house, please?"

"Of course, you may."

"Mihalákis," Mother addresses me, "show the officer the other
rooms."

I light another lýchnos, and moving to the next room, the SS officer dismisses the men waiting in that room—which must have been welcome for them, after being in a dark room for such a long time. They walk into the courtyard and then through the courtyard's large and heavy door into the street. Leading the officer, I proceed to the rest of the house.

The smaller of the storage rooms contains several large and small wine wooden barrels, and a number of large glass containers of raki. The wine and raki are from our grapes. There also are a few medium-sized ceramic pots with honey—my father's avocation and genuine love is raising honeybees. I simply report to the officer that all the barrels and the containers of rakí and honey were full before they came to Crete, but not now—he almost smiles.

The much larger storeroom is filled with dozens of large ceramic containers, most of them as tall as me. For most of the years before the war, the majority of them were full of olive oil, while the rest contained wheat, barley, oats, and various legumes. Now, however, they are empty, except for three that contain olive oil. The officer looks at them and asks what they contain. He doesn't bother looking inside of any of them.

After that, we move into the courtyard. In order to get to the second story, we must use an outside concrete stairway.

Mother had transformed one small bedroom into her salah—drawing room or parlor, which she had used in receiving her more important guests. All of my siblings are sleeping in the largest bedroom. When I take the SS colonel to the salah, his interest zeroes on the two dozen or so framed pictures that are hanging on the walls.

In the late 1800s and early 1900s, my father's parents and three older brothers, as well as several other relatives and friends from other villages of Amári, had immigrated to the United States. Through the years, those immigrants have sent us numerous formally posed pictures of themselves. Mother has used many of them to "decorate" her salah's walls.

While the colonel is viewing each picture, he asks me who the people in each picture are. After I tell him the names, he follows with, "Where are they now?" And my consistent answer is "America."

Finally, after he went through a dozen or so pictures and my answer is America every time, he turns to me and smiling says, "We will go to America, too!" The moment he says it, however, he seems to realize that he shouldn't have done that, as he stops smiling and looks embarrassed. And, of course, I know the reason for his embarrassment. It is obvious by then that Germany is losing the Russian campaign. The mystery for me is how he has guessed that I know that.

The last room to be checked is the large bedroom. As I'm going to open the door, he asks "What's inside?" "My younger brothers and sisters sleep here," I reply. He stops me by putting his hand over my hand that is holding the doorknob, and in low voice he tells me not to open the door.

Instead, he moves out of the second floor, and we go downstairs. Now, I am following him. With the colonel leading, we go back to the kitchen. Mother is there and still seated. The colonel goes directly to her.

Staying at attention, the colonel knocks his heels together.

Addressing my mother he says, "Χαίρεται Κυρία μου" ("Goodbye my Lady").

Then, he picks her hand and kisses it. He salutes her, knocks his heels again, and makes a perfect 180-degree turn, and then he smartly marches out.

Without saying anything to each other, Mother and I go to bed, as if nothing has happened.

In the morning Manousoyiánnis, our closest neighbor from across the street, appears surprised to see us. But he says nothing until the Germans leave the island. Then he visits with my mother. During the night, he had taken careful looks, spying on the comings and goings of the black uniforms. He had been amazed when he had seen us coming out of the second floor in the morning. Our house, which stands alone, had been tightly encircled by the German soldiers, he reports. He had assumed that they had taken all of us with them.

Even though our fellow villagers are aware of the German visit to our house—the only house in Vyzári to ever be visited by the Germans—no one ever admits it or asks us what has happened during that visit. And stranger yet, no one ever has showed that they are aware of that visit.

Mother and I had occasionally wondered if this behavior comes from politeness or respect from among our friends and the good people of the village, and because of fear or regrets from the rest. And we wonder, is it a collective guilt or guilt of one? And all of them must be wondering how and why the murderous Germans spared us? What's next, they may think? In contemplating that, it's sort of fun for me, and Mother shows a timid smile.

We do understand, of course, that the person or persons who fingered us might now wonder and even fear that we might know how it happened for the Germans to know about us. And, yes, it is a mystery to them that we are still in the village, safe and free. A mystery we have kept to ourselves. But the other mystery is solved after the war, when we find out for sure that members of EAM in Vyzári had turned in my father's name.

Sometime after the SS visit, my mother and I have a session with Colonel Dunbabin. His interest isn't only because the Paradisanós brothers are part of his staff, it is also because of the way the visit has ended.

Normally, such a visit by the SS isn't a kind one for the targeted family. In the past, it always has resulted in the whole family being liquidated or taken prisoner and shipped to a concentration work camp and slave labor in Germany. So, Dunbabin listens to my mother describing the SS visit and then talks to us. He basically summarizes what he and his agents feel.

Reports from the field agents in Haniá indicate that the colonel reports directly to the top commandant of the German forces in Crete, and apparently at this time he is the top SS officer on the island. Now, however, Dunbabin's staff had only assumptions.

One, considering the way that Jehovah's Witnesses were persecuted in Germany by the Nazis, the SS colonel must have had intimate experience with Jehovah's Witnesses, probably in his own family, colleagues, close friends, or a lover. Two, our family had not been targeted for outright liquidation. Instead, we were to be sent to a concentration work camp in Germany, and the colonel is able to spare us, as he must have had another family to substitute for us.

Finally, the intelligence operatives feel that the Gestapo major, who had caught me and supervised my interrogation in Sáta, must have neglected, or purposely avoided (because of his failure to grab Papadoyiánnis) reporting the incident to his Gestapo superiors in Iráklio, and that's why the Gestapo top brass on the island and the SS headquarters aren't aware of my involvement in that episode.

Still, it is apparent that Dunbabin and his shop have only suppositions, and no hard facts.[18]

In addressing Dunbabin, Mother's calm assessment of both episodes, mine in Sáta and hers with the SS colonel, is that "Jehovah came to her family's side and protected us."

And, in a way she is right about the Vyzári episode, I feel. Her deep faith helps her face the SS officer without a hint of fear. So, I don't want, nor do I need, to dispute my mother's conclusion. However, my personal conviction has always been that even if the SS colonel had some previous experience with or about Jehovah's Witnesses, Mother's inborn courage and intelligence, and the deftness with which she had handled the situation, saved us all.

And I realize that I have been lucky again. But this time, I am lucky because I am the son of Maria—my mother, the Jehovah's Witness.

---

18 It is confirmed only after the war, when Dunbabin finds out that the initial information about my father and his family had come to Gestapo's attention from a source associated with the Vyzári leftists.

CHAPTER
35

The Abduction
The impossible becomes possible

D unbabin is in the early to middle thirties, a calm and solid man; a contemplative and deliberate academician. He is an Australian. Leigh Fermor is in his middle twenties, an exceptionally intelligent, freewheeling traveler and writer; an exciting and risk-taking man. He is a Briton. It isn't a surprise then that the two men diverge in their perception as to the way Advance Force 133 is to operate on the island. And this is vividly shown in this chapter, which summarizes Leigh Fermor's abduction of a German general.

Originally, the agent Xan Fielding is assigned to the western part of Crete, which includes Haniá, the political capital of the island, and the seat of the commandant of the German forces on the island. Dunbabin is given the eastern part of the island, which includes Iráklio. In addition, Dunbabin's assignment includes the overall supervision of the British intelligence activities on the island—but still the odd agents on the island have the freedom to communicate with SOE in Cairo. When the SOE reassigns Xan to a mission in another part of the occupied Europe, Leigh Fermor is sent to take his place.

As the years go by, the Iráklio prefecture becomes the most important prefecture for the Germans. It includes by far the largest city of the island, more military bases than the rest of the island, and the general in command of the German forces in that prefecture also has the responsibility of keeping an eye on the Lasíthi prefecture occupied by the Italians. It follows that the commandant of the German forces in the Iráklio prefecture becomes a divisional commandant and the most important general on the island after the overall commandant of Fortress Crete in Haniá.

When Dunbabin and Kóstas take a fairly long time resting and regenerating, they leave for Egypt. At that time, Dunbabin gives the responsibility for the eastern part of the island to Leigh Fermor. Apparently, Paddy had always eyed that assignment, as during the Battle of Crete he had been among a small British intelligence team stationed in Iráklio. So, Leigh Fermor makes his base in the Iráklio prefecture. At that time, I think it is a natural move for him.

Years later after coming to America, however, during one of my trips to Crete, while visiting a nephew of mine living in Tavronítis, a town just west of Haniá, I'm introduced to Psyhoundákis, one of Leigh Fermor's close associates.[19] Since we hadn't met during the occupation, we spend a lot of time visiting about our respective experiences.

During our long conversation, he states that Leigh Fermor had wanted to break away from Dunbabin's way of doing things. Besides that, he tells me, Leigh Fermor hadn't trusted the Amariótes, so he wanted to get rid of Dunbabin's Amári associates (Psyhoundákis isn't from Amari, of course). Even though Psyhoundákis had been boastful during our whole conversation, what he said bothers me a lot, as Uncle Kóstas is Dunbabin's top lieutenant, and I know how Dunbabin loved and trusted the Amariótes.

Leigh Fermor had developed a friendship with Capetan Badouvás, the troublesome leader of one of the Cretan partisan armies. According to reports, Paddy is instrumental in the move of Badouvás and his army from Mount Psilorítis to the mountain formations in the Italian-occupied Lasíthi prefecture. It appears, or so thought my uncle and George Tyrákis, the restive Leigh Fermor is using the Badouvás army to create

---

19 He's also the author of the book Cretan Runner.

some trouble for the Germans in the Iráklio prefecture, especially in places close to the Viánnos area. At that time, General Müller is the divisional commander of the German forces in Iráklio.

Müller apparently has had enough and proceeds to send a large number of troops to the Viánnos area, destroying and looting more than a dozen villages and killing well over 500 people—people who had nothing to do with what Badouvás had done. This is a strong indication of the difference in the way Dunbabin and Leigh Fermor approach their jobs as military intelligence operatives. Dunbabin, with his measured attitude, is acting in a way of not unnecessarily hurting the innocent Cretan population, as opposed to Leigh Fermor's attitude of acting aggressively against the enemy no matter how unnecessary and pointless the action and what happens after that for the civilians close to the action. In this aspect, by the way, Dunbabin thought Badouvás to be a "loose cannon," while Leigh Fermor liked Badouvás' bravado.

Following the Viánnos catastrophe, Leigh Fermor, while in Egypt, comes up with the idea of abducting General Müller and recruits for that another agent, Captain Stanley Moss. The apparent motivation is revenge for what Müller had done in the Viánnos tragic affair and as an attempt to improve the morale of the people affected in that area. He presented his plan to the director of SOE, Bickham Sweet-Escott, reportedly the most experienced SOE executive, who objects to Fermor's plan. Sweet-Escott objections are centered on two points. One, there is no strategic value in abducting Müller. Two, the result of the abduction would be "heavy in Cretan lives."[20]

Eventually, Leigh Fermor's proposal is approved.

As it happens, by the time Leigh Fermor secured the approval and is ready to return to Crete, General Müller is moved to Haniá, as the overall commandant of Fortress Crete. He is replaced in Iráklio by General Heinrich Kreipe. It is said by some of Leigh Fermor's friends that Paddy

---

20 This was described in the book *Patrick Leigh Fermor*, a memoir on Leigh Fermor's life written by Artemis Cooper. I'm surprised reading that in Cooper's book, as Dunbabin had also been against it for exactly similar reasons. Still Cooper doesn't bring up Dunbabin's objections, as she avoids writing about Dunbabin unless it is absolutely necessary.

wasn't aware of that development, but that seems highly unlikely. And, apparently, the SOE office agreed to still go ahead with the abduction, but now Kreipe is the target. That is strange, as Kreipe is new on Crete, so he isn't tied to the atrocities in Viánnos. But as Cooper writes, one general is as good as another in Leigh Fermor's mind.

By this time, Dunbabin and Kóstas are back from Egypt. Dunbabin is now the official political British representative on the island, a diplomatic appointment. Nazi Germany is going down in defeat, the German troops on Crete are trapped, but they continue to be powerful enough to raise havoc, as the Cretans don't have the forces and the heavy armaments needed to fight back and protect themselves. So the situation calls for a diplomatic solution, and that notion has already started secretly.

Dunbabin's people feel that if Leigh Fermor wanted to punish Müller, he should have moved to Haniá, an area he knows well, and attempted to abduct Müller there. But he doesn't. He simply substitutes General Kreipe for Müller. After the war, Leigh Fermor meets General Müller, who is in jail in Athens, and Müller tells him that he wouldn't have been as easy to abduct as Kreipe had been.

Leigh Fermor proceeds to put together a small group of agents, including my friend Giórgis Tyrákis. Cretan operatives living in the vicinity of the German military headquarters are asked to detail the movements of General Kreipe. The general is staying in the Villa Ariádne, near the ruins of the ancient city of Knossós. Knossós had been the capital of the Minoans. The Minoans had developed the first major European civilization more than fifteen hundred years before the advent of the classical Greek civilization. In Greek mythology, Knossós is associated with the Labyrinth, Minotaur, and the first humans to fly. Knossós is about five kilometers south of Iráklio.

General Kreipe's office is in Arhánes, a pleasant town just south of Knossós. He is in the habit of traveling by car twice a day for fewer than five kilometers from the villa to his headquarters and back with a chauffeur and a bodyguard. Leigh Fermor's plan is to intercept the general's vehicle. He chooses the location, the time they would intercept the general's car, and the route of their escape.

One evening in late April 1944, Leigh Fermor's group, dressed in SS uniforms, waits at the chosen location, close to the village of Skaláni. The general's car is stopped at dusk by two British agents. Both agents look like genuine Gestapo officers, and Leigh Fermor speaks German like a native. The chauffeur and the bodyguard are swiftly neutralized.

The agents force Kreipe onto the floor of his car and then drive off, using the general's car as the getaway vehicle. The agents drive through Iráklio, a city that is well-fortified and tightly guarded. They pass through several checkpoints manned by unsuspecting German soldiers, who, seeing the general's car, freeze at attention and salute—still they have a few tense moments a couple of times. After their dangerous ride through Iráklio, they drive onto the northeastern side of Mount Psilorítis. The car stops, and the General and his captors get out. Leigh Fermor proceeds to drive the car on. Eventually, he ditches the car and begins walking toward, Anóyia, a village high on the north-northeast slopes of Mount Psilorítis, in the eparchy of Mylopótamos of the Réthymno prefecture. The men with the general also walk toward Anóyia, as does the rest of the party that had been with them at the ambush site.

The route through Iráklio is necessary. It is the quickest way that the abduction party, with their captive General Kreipe, can reach the rugged and massive mountain terrain before the German forces realize that their commandant is missing. That terrain offers not only a myriad of ways to hide but also the friendliest population on the island to both the resistance and to the Allied intelligence group.

It takes three weeks on foot going in a general southwest direction, through the éparchies of Mylopótamos, Amári, and Ághios Vasílis of the Rethymno prefecture, to reach the area of the Rodákino village on the south shore of the island, where they are picked up at night by a British Navy vessel. On their way there, they are hosted and protected by the villagers they passed in those eparchies, and especially the shepherds on the slopes of Mount Psiloritis and Mount Kéndros.

Coming down to the Amári Valley from the west slope of Psiloritis, they face their greatest danger of being captured. German intelligence had either figured out that the abductors would have to go through there, or informers have told them so. The Amári area is filled with German soldiers who move through the villages and the fields loudly calling Kreipe's name.

The people in two villages, Apodoúlou and Aghía Paraskeví, hide them, and their valiant actions save the abductors. When the Germans are unable to find their general and retreat, the Kreipe party moves to the east side of mountain Kéndros by the villages of Ano Meros and Gerakari, and through it the west side of Kéndros in the eparchy of Aghios Vasílis, eventually reaching the Rodákino area.

That's how Leigh Fermor and his companions are able to accomplish what is thought to be impossible—the successful abduction of the commandant of the island's German forces in the east part of Fortress Crete. The action is perpetrated close to his headquarters and almost next to his living quarters. And it is committed with finesse and apparent ease, and then continues to unfold with a raw and daring boldness as the abductors drive into and out of the largest and one of the most highly fortified and guarded cities on the island.

It is a most dramatic feat, clever—brilliant in planning and brave in its execution. It is a feat that leads to a unique episode in World War II and a story that one reads only in spy and adventure novels. All in all, it is a valiant and brazen act, elegantly executed.

Later, Leigh Fermor's action is criticized in some quarters, but one cannot question the high level of intelligence that went into the planning of the abduction and the cleverness and bravery with which it had been performed. Two episodes in the Kreipe party trek through the mountains deserve to be mentioned.

In the first days of the trek, General Kreipe asks Leigh Fermor not to leave him alone with the team's mountain Cretan members. They are such "uncivilized brutes," he reportedly tells the major. That remark of General Kreipe reflects the notion held by the top German military leaders about the Cretan mountain villagers since the attack of the paratroopers four years before. Their closed mind couldn't accept that villagers, far way from the battlefields, would come to fight for their freedom, bringing with them the weapons they had—even if homemade.

The other episode occurs their first morning on the west slopes of Mount Psilorítis. When they wake up, below them lies the Amári Valley. Across the valley, Mount Kéndros rises, facing Psilorítis. As the sun rises, the rays of the sun begin escaping Mount Psilorítis and start illuminating the east face of Mount Kéndros, with its village of Ano Méros, the highest village of the Amari area. The lighting up of the east side of Kéndros starts at its top and moves slowly but steadily downward. The sun's rays seem to stop for a moment or two before moving farther down, and they do it at their own lazy speed.

The scene in front of the group is stunning. At their feet lies the Amári Valley with its thousands of olive tree groves. Well over a dozen villages are dotting the area like giant white pearls. The sun is steadily walking ever so slowly down from the top of Mount Kéndros before reaching the valley. And in the middle of the valley, the Liyiótis River crawls much faster than the sun coming to meet it. While General Kreipe observes this, he audibly quotes a stanza or two from Horace. To the surprise of the General, Leigh Fermor completes the following stanzas. That's the beginning of a steady friendship between the two men.

Since I have been in Leigh Fermor's presence only a few times, I only learned of his great magnetism from others who described his intelligence, fearless exploits, and his strong inclination for good times. His reputation and popularity are further enhanced by the abduction of General Kreipe. On that score, however, he is also seriously criticized, especially by the left-leaning political constituency of the island, as well privately by some of the Cretan intelligence operatives. That criticism intensifies when the Germans, as a punishment for the abduction of Kreipe, loot and destroy a good number of villages and indiscriminately execute their men.

Even though supporters of Leigh Fermor attempt to dispute this, the fact is that the dozen or more villages, especially in the eparchies of Amári, Aghios Vasílis, and Mylopótamos, paid dearly for Leigh Fermor's glory. Even one of the abductors, my friend Giórgis Tyrákis, has so admitted that to me, more than forty years later.

During the abduction and the following days, when the Kreipe party goes through the Amari region, Colonel Dunbabin is nowhere to be found. The official explanation is that Dunbabin has the flu.[21]

Dunbabin has come to deeply care for the people of Crete, and he knows that they would suffer dearly from Leigh Fermor's action at this point of the war, so he isn't in favor of the abduction. Dunbabin doesn't verbally criticize the abduction. But others aren't so restrained. The criticism is centered on three points.

First, substituting General Kreipe for General Müller is a mistake. Kreipe is new to the garrison of the island. He isn't responsible for the acts of Müller. Sure, Müller would have felt shame if he had allowed himself to fall into the hands of the British and Cretans, and he would have deserved it. But there is no moral reason for abducting Kreipe. Second, the timing is all wrong. Germany has been defeated. It is only a matter of months before the war would end. Movements had been initiated to have representatives of the International Red Cross come and negotiate a truce between the German garrison, and the Cretans and England through the British agents—it is secret but Leigh Fermor is cognizant of it.

Third, Leigh Fermor's judgment is questioned for leaving a note in General Kreipe's car that states that the abduction of the General has been carried entirely by British agents. Leigh Fermor must have strongly suspected that the Germans will not buy that, first as such an action can only be successful with local support, and then informers will so advise the Gestapo. Paddy may have left the note in an attempt to absolve himself, in the Cretan eyes, of any responsibility in what will follow. The final judgment of Leigh Fermor's critics is that since he is so intelligent and has become so knowledgeable of the wartime island, he is aware of, and has most likely considered, all these objections to his action. So the only explanation that makes sense to his critics is a suspicion. And that suspicion is that the rush of excitement in undertaking such a dangerous task moves an enlightened but still vagabond and cavalier secret agent, as

---

21 Stanley Moss includes this fact in his book about the abduction, as a slap at Colonel Dunbabin's character, as Dunbabin's close associates feel. Captain Moss, however, has no feelings for the suffering of the Cretans, but Dunbabin does.

Leigh Fermor is, to ignore all the above reasons for not undertaking the mission. Such reasons, they feel, would have stopped a man who truly loves and appreciates the people of the island. And those are the reasons that made Dunbabin oppose the abduction.[22]

---

22 In the book *The First Victory,* author George Blytas seems surprised at Leigh Fermor's action that late in the war. He is of the opinion that both the abduction of General Kreipe and the whisking to Egypt of General Carta, the commandant of the Italian forces on Crete's easternmost Lassithi prefecture, also done by Leigh Fermor, were done for propaganda purposes.

But propaganda for what reason? Nazi Germany was on its deathbed at that point of the war. And the Allies don't need any such propaganda anymore. What he had done mirrored his attitude in growing up and facing life almost alone.

Leigh Fermor was born in 1915. As a young man, he was uneasy and bothersome to the point that had changed schools several times. But he was self-disciplined in his studies and brilliant enough to easily absorb new and complex information. He effortlessly mastered languages, which led to his study, on his own, of Greek and Latin classic literary works in the original language.

When he was eighteen, he left England for Holland. His vague plan was to walk through Europe until he reached Constantinople (Istanbul). Because of his age, his handsome looks, and his exceptional intelligence, he had little problem in being taken care of by older couples, poor or rich, especially women, as well as British expatriates and officials. While walking throughout a country, he not only learned its language but also studied its social life. He walked through Holland, Germany, Austria, Czechoslovakia, Hungary, Romania and Bulgaria, and a little over a year after he began, he reached Istanbul.

His travels continued to the monasteries of Aghios Oros (Holy Mountain)—Mount Athos, in northern Greece. The tranquil life of the monks fascinated him, and he stayed there for some time studying in the library of the monasteries. Later, using Athens as a base, he traveled to Crete and other parts of Greece. In Athens, he met Balasha, a Romanian princess. Balasha was older than Leigh Fermor. She was an extraordinarily beautiful woman—by Leigh Fermor's own admission.

The two of them lived together in Kardamíli, a tranquil coastal town in the Máni peninsula of Pelopónnisos (Peloponnese), the southernmost province of mainland Greece, spending their time traveling in Greece and Romania. Leigh Fermor had already begun writing, but now his writing became a serious calling. When war broke out, they were in Romania. He said goodbye to Balasha and left for England. He enlisted in the army. His experience during his pre-war walks through Europe and the languages he had mastered come to the attention of the War Office in London, and he ended up in military intelligence.

Bringing Down Ano Méros
A village is destroyed

Unfortunately, Bickham Sweet-Escott and Dunbabin are proven to be right. Müller, the commandant of Fortress Crete in Haniá, reacts to the abduction of General Kreipe with as fiery a zeal as he has done in the Viánnos area, resulting in the destruction of several villages, including Ano Méros.

But let me fast forward.

One summer, forty or so years after the end of the war, I'm vacationing in Vyzári, at the same time my friend Giórgis Tyrákis is vacationing in Fourfourás. Giórgis, at the end of the war, had been helped by the British intelligence corps to immigrate to South Africa and settle there. After that summer coincidence of both of us vacationing in Crete, we begin to occasionally have at least part of our trips there be at the same time.

When he and I are growing up on Crete, there are motor roads for only a few villages in each area. Now, however, there are highways for all the several hundreds of Cretan villages and hamlets, no matter how small they are or how high on the mountains they are located. The roads vary in quality and upkeep, but motor roads they are. With a car, it takes us only minutes to visit some villages that had taken us hours of walking during our youths.

During those visits, we are reminiscing about the war. He talks about his experiences as one of Leigh Fermor's men, and I about Sáta, Ághios Ioánnis, and as one of Dunbabin's occasional runners.

The first time we drive to Ano Méros, I notice that Giórgis is uneasy. He is worried about the reception from the surviving villagers. In Ano Méros, however, there is no noticeable objection to his presence.

As we have seen, Ano Méros is one of the villages the Kreipe group had gone through. And, of course, since Giórgis had been part of that group, he does feel that he might not be welcome in the village now. He, as I and others had felt then and still feel, think that the visit of the Kreipe group contributed to the destruction of Ano Méros, Gerakári, and the several other Kéndros smaller settlements.

So let's go back to those days.

In August of 1944, Kýrios Yiánnis (Dunbabin), my father, and Uncle Kóstas visit our home in Vyzári. My mother and I are surprised. Not a single one of the three had stayed overnight at our house after Sáta had been compromised. And now, all three of them are in our house for three consecutive days. It is also strange how open their visit is. They take no precautions. They don't seem to have any concerns if the villagers see them. It all seems unreal, even though we know that we are at the end of the war, and the German forces are looking for ways to disengage from the island. What we don't know, however, but Dunbabin and both my father and uncle know but don't tell us, is that negotiations with the German garrison have been going well for the German forces to withdraw to the Haniá area.

Besides being relaxed, Dunbabin is very deferential to my mother, showing his high respect for her. He takes any opportunity that comes along to ask her about her religion, and they often debate the religious and social positions of the Jehovah's Witnesses. I never had seen him so animated and smiling so much. Initially, I think that he is looking for clues for the reasons that the SS colonel didn't take us to be shipped to labor camps in Germany, but then I settle on the thought that this is an intellectual exercise for the professor in him.

The morning of the second day with us, Dunbabin summons me. He gives me a sealed envelope and orders me to deliver it to the mayor of the village Ano Méros. Ano Méros—high place, the place above—is appropriately named. The village literally holds fast at the steep and almost sheer eastern face of Mount Kéndros—the mountain rising on the west side of the Amári Valley. The treeless area of the mountain begins almost above Ano Méros. It is a daunting trip by foot—the only way to get there, unless using a donkey or mule.

On that journey, I cross the Liyiotis River flowing from north to its south meeting with the Libyan Sea. No bridge, but in late summer the water has receded enough that I could cross it without getting wet. I jump from the bank of the river to a large, flat boulder in the water and then to a series of other flat boulders. After the water recedes in the summer, each boulder is strategically placed on the riverbed by farmers. The Liyiotis flows southward on its trip to the Libyan Sea, while some of the creeks that supply its waters flow from east to west and the rest from west to east, depending from which mountain formation they come. In the winter, Liyiótis growls like a temperamental and dangerous tiger, but in late summer, it purrs like a friendly pussycat.

Immediately after leaving the river, I have to tackle the sharp, steep eastern slope of the mountain. The climb requires some serious effort, but I don't feel it much. Mainly shepherds live in Ano Méros, a relatively small village of friendly people. I readily find the mayor's house, and walking into the courtyard of the house, a beautiful young girl, possibly my age, or about a year my junior, welcomes me.

Her name is Aleksándra, says she, and I guess that she must be the daughter of the mayor, but friend Giórgis Tzitzikas, who is a native of Ano Méros, later expresses doubts about the girl being the mayor's daughter. Yes, the mayor is home, but he has guests upstairs, and we should wait until her mother comes home, the girl tells me. The mother has gone to their vegetable garden and should be back at any moment now, she adds. So we wait and visit.

I don't know why, but I instantly fall for a beautiful girl, and that's what happens with this one. I'm totally fascinated by the beauty of

Aleksándra, her smile, and the timid way she moves around. Aleksándra is almost as captivating as Agápe. I'm, however, attracted to Aleksándra even more, as she appears to be much more innocent than Agápe.

Apparently, Aleksándra reads that on my face, as she blushes, becomes much more animated, moves around awkwardly, and a few minutes later comes closer to me. It seems to me that I'm with her for just a few minutes, but when her mother arrives, she estimates that I had waited longer than an hour and apologizes.

The mother is aware of my family's involvement in the resistance, and she says that the mayor is in an important meeting upstairs, but as soon as she clears my appearance with him, I can go up. When she ushers me upstairs and closes the door behind me, I'm surprised by what I witness.

There must be more than a dozen resistance leaders assembled there. Among them I see Manólis Papadoyiánnis, who had just come from Egypt, courtesy of the British navy's clandestine nocturnal trips to the island. Papadoyiánnis, a former governor of Crete and, as we have already seen a prominent resistance leader, sports a full beard and a mustache, both well-trimmed, and he is going by the moniker "papoú"—grandfather.

The mayor welcomes me; my father and he are good friends, he states. He puts the envelope on the table in front of him, but he doesn't open it. I'm waiting for the possibility that the mayor might have a message for Kyrios Yiannis, but he states that he doesn't. As I'm leaving, Papadoyiánnis stops me. He turns to the other men and says, "I want you to know that this young man saved my life and the lives of my wife and son." This is in reference to the episode we have seen, which had happened when I had run from Sáta to Aghios Ioánnis, to alert the spy ring operatives and Papadoyiánnis of the approaching Gestapo detachment.

Aleksándra waits for me at the bottom of the stairs. She looks at me while saying, "Mihális, the day after tomorrow some of us will have a big party. It will be a nice one. Why don't you stay with us, and we will go together." Her mother hears her. She joins us and says, "We will be happy to have you here tonight and until you will be ready to go back to Vyzári.

Please, stay." The girl pleads, "Mihalis, please stay, please stay, please!" I stand there like a moron. I don't know what to do. Those beautiful eyes, that sweet mouth seem to be begging. How can I refuse, when my heart is jumping and my total body aches for her? An overwhelming emotion paralyzes me.

But I also know that I have a job to do. It has become an inexplicable part of my psyche. That is, the maintenance of security in the intelligence service is paramount. That notion has become second nature to me. Dunbabin has to know that the envelope has been safely delivered. I also feel that he should know about the individuals who saw me delivering it. My high respect for Dunbabin just doesn't allow me to disappoint him—especially after the radio debacle. Still, all the way to Vyzári I curse myself for leaving the girl. Eventually, the thought occurs to me that I can go back the next day and surprise Aleksándra.

After our guests leave the following day, however, my mother tells me, "Mihalákis, our vegetable garden at Páno Helonés hasn't been watered for a week and it needs water badly." She continues by asking me to water it that evening. The garden is adjacent to Liyiótis River and some distance from Vyzári. My father's first cousin Stéllios, who is about five years my senior, and I decide to spend that night together, watering both of our families' vegetable gardens there—"I'll go to Ano Méros tomorrow," I decide.

In that location, watering our gardens during the night is easy. Because of the German night curfew, not many people, besides the resistance fighters and the sheep and goat rustlers, venture out at the middle of the night, unless a villager has something important to do. Our gardens are adjacent to each other and next to the east bank of the Liyiótis River.

On the west side of the river the small Mount Sámitos rises. At the feet of Sámitos, and across from our gardens, on the west side of the River, are the villages of Petrohóri and Lambiótes. A donkey road, adjacent to the west river bank, begins at the lone highway in the middle of the Amári Valley, passes Lambiótes and Petrohóri, and then continues on to meet Mount Kéndros and escalates to Ano Méros.

The Liyiótis River has been partly dammed upstream, and a large water channel serves the gardens downstream, and at the end powers a water mill for grain. So once we reach Páno Helonés, we do as we have done before. We divert a small portion of the water from the main channel into the small ditch leading to our gardens. Then, we set the water at several strategic points for each of our adjoining gardens; we visit for a while, and then fall asleep under an olive tree.

Almost always, we awaken about an hour or so before daybreak, a bit before other villagers from surrounding villages begin coming to take care of their gardens. We reroute the water back to the main irrigation channel, and our gardens, along with some of the ones around them, have had all the water they need for a week.

Sometime past midnight, we estimate later, we awaken. A strange noise is coming from the donkey road on the other side of the river. Even though we can't see across the river because of the night's darkness and the thick cover of plane trees and bushes growing on the riverbanks, we soon realize that German soldiers are marching along the donkey path. Our initial concern increases when it becomes apparent that it isn't just a patrol—as we initially think—it's a large body of soldiers. We stay put for what seems to be like hours. Speaking in low voices, we surmise that since the soldiers are going south, they are going to Petrohóri, a bit over a kilometer southwest of us.

When the noise passes, we slowly and carefully divert the water back to the main channel. Without even thinking, we walk toward Pýrgos instead of Vyzári. Pýrgos is a large and high hill at a short distance south of Vyzári. There, we hide in our vineyard, which is part of the massive expanse of vineyards of the village's folk. We sleep under the vines, which in turn are under a huge and tall pear tree, whose pears aren't edible, but we use them to feed our pig.

It is August 24 in 1944, when enough morning light arrives. We venture a look at Vyzári. What we see are German soldiers manning machine guns on the flat clay roof of a large house located at a commanding position in the village. At the same time, we can just barely see another group of soldiers on top of the Pátela Hill, which splits the village into north and south sections. Later, we find out that the Germans had also occupied Petrohóri and Lambiótes. "It is a wise action," Stéllios and I tell each other, "that last night we had come to the vineyards instead of going home." We hadn't even discussed the choice. Because of our experience during the years of occupation, our brains instinctively made that choice for us. The Germans always go to defined settlements and not outside them.

Later, we find out that all the citizens of Vyzári have been herded into the schoolhouse, and they had kept them there, after their names have been taken. In that process, they kill one of our fellow villagers who, evidently, hadn't completely comprehended their directions. In the evening, they allow the villagers to go to their homes, but they have to stay there until they are told otherwise.

Assuming that the German forces will use binoculars to scout the area, we decide to stay under the vines and to move as little as possible. We are high enough on the hill to allow us to have a good view of several villages, including Ano Méros. In the early afternoon, we think we hear explosions from that direction. When we decide to chance a careful look that way, we notice pillars of what we think is smoke coming from the village. We realize then that one of the destinations of the Germans passing by the river includes Ano Méros. Now, we assume, the Germans are destroying the village and possibly killing its inhabitants, as they have done in numerous other villages on the island in the course of the past four years.

While I'm thinking of Aleksándra, the thought comes to me that I would have been in Ano Méros as I planned, and if the Germans have executed the men who can carry a rifle, I would be dead. So, I silently thank Mother for asking me to water the Páno Helonés garden. As I'm thinking about all this, Stéllios becomes terribly agitated and begins to cry because he assumes the same lot as Ano Méros is awaiting our own village. But, of course, there is nothing we can do. So we eat fruit, sleep, and sneak to a nearby spring for water. The next day, when we notice that the machine guns are gone and the military transports have left the village, we carefully venture returning to our homes.

The Germans have indeed destroyed Ano Méros. They allow the women and the young children to leave and hold all males who are able to carry a rifle. After that, they massacre those male villagers. Next, they loot the houses. At the end, they put the bodies in the houses, and they dynamite and burn the homes.

Now I realize that, indeed, I must very, very much thank my dear mother. I'm lucky again, as Mother saves my life for the second time by keeping me from going to Ano Méros as I had planned to do. "And for what, I ask myself?" "To be with a pretty girl," I answer my own question. It's the first time I realize that pretty girls can get me in deep trouble. Yet, I totally forget about that when I meet the next one.

Not all male citizens of Áno Meros who are able to carry a rifle perish that day. A few men are taking care of their sheep or goat flocks on the mountain slopes and sleep close to them. A few have joined the Allied intelligence service or one of the resistance partisan armies. Among them is George Tzítzikas, a good friend, who is serving in the Petrakoyiórgis partisan army.

A man, whose name I'm told is Spýros, had been injured and left for dead. He manages to crawl into bushes just outside the village. He is able to reach Petrohóri, the closest village. It takes a few days under the care of Dr. Iákovos Stavroulákis, the senior of the two doctors in Vyzári to bring him to a state in which he could relate what has happened. And he does have a story to tell, even though it turns out that it is similar to what we already have heard from accounts of two men who had served as interpreters for the Germans, when they had destroyed other villages. But still, this man's account deserves to be repeated.

After the Germans encircled the village, the soldiers at daybreak went from door to door and awakened all villagers. The Greek interpreter told them to go to the village square. After that, the officer in charge, who was a Gestapo or SS captain, ordered the soldiers to go back and carefully check all houses to make sure that no villagers were still in their homes. They found two, a father and his son hiding in their stable. They shot them both right there. After the sun came up, they proceeded to separate the villagers. They selected the women, the young children and the very old men—the males that they most likely feel are unable to carry a rifle—and tell them to leave the village. If any of them were close to the village in half an hour, they would be shot. The group of men remaining in the square varied from teenagers up to their seventies.

Next, the officers wearing Gestapo uniforms began interrogating them. They asked to provide them any information they have about the time the group that had abducted General Kreipe passed through the village. Then the colonel used his sidearm to kill the first two men who had been questioned by him and who had answered that they don't know the answers to his questions. The questioning went on for some time, with two other men shot in the square by the colonel. The great majority of the villagers have no idea about what is asked of them. It is correct that the party that abducted General Kreipe passed through the area, but fewer than a half a dozen men know about Kreipe's party passing through.

Sometime in midmorning they dismissed them and told them to go back to their homes. As Spýros was turning onto the street of his house, he heard weapons being discharged. He looked back and saw one of the villagers fall. He started to run. As he was reaching his house, he was shot and fell, passing out apparently for a few minutes, as when he came out of it, a dead neighbor was laying on top of him. Hearing gunfire, he stayed still.

Some anguished cries from men who had fallen could be heard. He noticed that close by, two such pain cries were silenced by two gunshots. Eventually the gunfire stops. He heard soldiers walking on his street. When one of them comes where he is lying, the soldier kicked the man above him hard. After some time passed and he heard no one on his street, he crawled on his belly to the end of the street and out of the village at a patch of bushes.

It should be noted here that men who are close to Leigh Fermor feel that the island's German garrison used that murderous distraction as a warning to the Cretans that even though Germany was being defeated, German forces would not leave unpunished any challenge to their power.

That view simply absolves Leigh Fermor from that tragedy.[23] Listening to my good friend Giórgis Tyrákis, one of the abductors of Kreipe, and having heard some of Dunbabin's men, I am convinced that it is the Kreipe affair that had sealed the lot of the villages of Ano Méros and Gerakári and the half a dozen smaller settlements in that area of Mount Kéndros, as well as villages in the Aghios Vasílis and Mylopótamos eparchies.[24]

---

23 My old friend, Giórgis Tzitzikas, feels that way even today.

24 Apparently, according to Cooper, after Leigh Fermor had taken General Kreipe to Cairo, he had been either traveling or had been sent to other intelligence assignments, as he hadn't returned to Crete until the Germans had been in the Haniá area for months. And it was then that he had first learned of the destruction of the Kéndros' villages, which, as Cooper writes, saddened him deeply.

That, however, doesn't stop him for leading some villagers in an attempt to provoke the Germans in the Haniá area, thus creating some problems for Dunbabin, who is still monitoring the conditions of the truce with the Germans.

The Battle That Wasn't

Destroying valor's claim
by a shameful act

I t's about two weeks after the destruction of Ano Méros, Gerakári, and the rest of the Mount Kéndros villages when, on Sep-
tember 9, a rabble group of members of EAM moves against
the Asómatos Station, about five kilometers north of Vyzári,
near the center of the Amari Valley. Before the war, it served as an
agricultural institute, and during the Greek-Italian war, it had been a
POW camp for Italian prisoners from the Albanian war front.

Originally, the place used to be a monastery, hence its name "Asómatos," which means a body devoid of flesh, bones, and blood—devoid of
what makes a human body.

When the government had taken over the Asómatos' considerable
and elaborate monastery facilities and properties, as judged by local
standards, the plan had been to transform the place into an agricultural
research and scientific training institute.

In taking over the monastery and metamorphosing it into a working
farming establishment, the government plans to provide teaching, training, and research for the benefit of the island's farming community. A
brother-in-law of mine, who as an agronomist had served as the director
of the institute before the war, told me that Asómatos never had ful-
filled the charge given to it, due to interfering government regulations,

directions from the top, the failure of the government to provide adequate funding, and the channeling of the station's products to government agencies, instead of being sold on the open market and using the proceeds for the improvement of its programs.

After the Germans realized that the institute could help them improve the quality of their officers' mess halls, they took over Asómatos. They placed there three of their own agricultural technicians, and they employed a few villagers for the cultivation of the fields, the care of the animals and the olive and fruit trees. So, the institute changed to an agricultural station for the benefit of the meals of the senior German officers in Haniá, Réthymno, and Iráklio.

Capetan Petrakoyiórgis' resistance army has, most of the time, its main clandestine base on the Amári part of Mount Psilorítis. Bourdelis, a Petrakoyiórgis local chieftain from Fourfourás, has his team of partisans stationed in the area of Psilorítis close to Fourfourás and Vyzári. Colonel Dunbabin, Capetan Petrakoyiórgis, and Antónis Lítinas have discussed the presence of the Germans in the heart of the Amári Valley.

They evaluate the danger the Germans' presence poses to their respective organizations, after studying the movements and overall behavior of the German technicians. For that purpose, Litinas had recruited, as an agent for EOK, one of the villagers working for the Germans in Asómatos. Lítinas also has members of EOK from key villages around the institute observing the station for any unusual developments in and around Asómatos.

All reports indicate that the three Germans are indeed agricultural specialists, and according to EOK's spy inside the station, the Germans don't even wear their sidearms while working. They have a wireless radio but they don't seem to use it. They also treat the local men working in the station well.

This behavior of the German technicians is even milder than the behavior of a short-lived German outpost in Fourfourás. After a few months of the assessment of the contributing danger meted out to the area by the presence of these men, they find out that it hasn't harmed the effectiveness of the Amari area as one of the main, if not the main, clandestine resistance center on the island.

Petrakoyiórgis and Lítinas had considered the removal of the German technicians. But for what reason and, most importantly yet, what would be the consequences of such an action? Instead, the EOK observers of the station are asked to immediately report to Lítinas and Bourdelis anything out of the ordinary at the station.

Additionally, Petrakoyiórgis gives more partisans to Bourdelís, and Bourdelís is asked to be ready for any anomaly at Asómatos, as he had been when the Germans had the station in Fourfourás. The continuing reports from all those sources consistently indicate that those three Germans in Asómatos show no indication that they are involved in spying on the locals. They keep all their activities within the compound.

The German forces, of course, use Asómatos for their benefit. Still, what they take from the place isn't critical for them, except possibly olive oil, as they have stashed enough food supplies for their men. Eliminating the Asómatos food source will put a little dent in the quality of the meals for their officers, but that's all. The products of Asómatos aren't critical for the Amariótes either.

True, during the winter of 1941-42, many families in Amári had gone hungry, including my parents' family. But by 1944, there is no hunger in the area. For sure, there aren't plentiful food supplies, but there are enough for all, even for the poorest. So what the Germans are taking doesn't affect the Amariótes, critically. Besides, even when the Greek government had control of Asómatos, the products from Asómatos hadn't been given or sold to Amariótes.

The men who care about the people of the area feel that the most benign reaction of the Germans to the forcible removal of their Asómatos technicians would be the Germans bringing a new group of technicians and a sizable number of soldiers and equipment to guard them. But they know, from the way the Germans react when their authority is challenged, this was unlikely to happen.

The Germans rule from sheer, naked strength. They aggressively react to any perception indicating challenge to their authority, and their answer is definitive and cruel punishment. The concern then is that the Germans would also use that challenge as an excuse to destroy some villages close to Asómatos and then possibly establish a military station in Amari at the Asómatos location.

Things with the Asómatos station go along peacefully until late 1944, when the leftists decide to act. Information coming to local EOK officials from areas outside Amári, especially the Messará Plain in the Iráklio prefecture, indicates a strong concern among the EAM leaders, including Podiás, the leader of ELAS, for their coming into the active resistance so late.

Podiás, aware that confidential negotiations for a truce between the German garrison on the island and the British and the Cretan nationalist partisans have begun, becomes concerned that soon a truce will be worked out. Some think that Podias hadn't expected the International Red Cross to intercede and the negotiations to take place so quickly. Now the Germans will be out of reach for ELAS to engage them and develop some sort of resistance history.

Podias and his area EAM leaders agree that before the truce agreement is signed and becomes public, some dramatic and high-profile actions must take place to get ELAS on the map of the resistance to Germans, with concrete accomplishments. In those deliberations, the Amári area comes up. And if one doesn't care what happens to the Amári villages, the choice is excellent.

It has the primary elements needed for such an operation; that is, the bait and the most convenient location for an easy and safe trap. And on top of that, the justification of revenge for the Kéndros calamity.

Podiás needs a way to provoke the ire and fury of the Germans, seeks locations in which to trap and ambush them for an easy win, and find a convenient way to disappear after the altercation. And Amári has exactly what they need. Taking over the Asómatos station will provide the provocation and the Potamoús location is the easy trap and then a convenient retreat up on Mount Psilorítis.

The name of the Potamoús (River's) location comes from the dozens of small creeks fed by tiny springs that proliferate there. It is my favorite location on my back-and-forth trips between Réthymno and Vyzári. It is one of the rare places on Crete that stays green all summer long. I love the feeling of the sea of green on the steep sides of that area's ravines.

The Potamoús topography provides an ideal location for an ambush. Going south from Réthymno to Amari in the mountainous center of the island, the German transports have to use the narrow, unpaved, and unmaintained motor road. As soon as they leave the city, the transports must scale, by zigzagging, a high hill (a small mountain, really). Once reaching the top of that hill, the transports move down, by zigzagging again on the backside of that hill. At a much shorter distance now the transports reach a tiny valley that is at a much higher elevation than Réthymno.

Passing that little valley, the road begins to climb again. This time, the climb is on an even higher and just as steep mountain-hill. The negotiating of that mountain-hill is again by zigzagging, just as difficult as before, if not ever more so. The Amári Valley lies several hundred feet higher than the mini-valley. To access the valley, the transports must reach the top of that hill, pass the village of Apostólous, reach the small settlement of Fotiní and then climb down just a bit to reach the valley.

To reach the top of that hill, however, the German transports have to conquer dozens of sharp and difficult-to-negotiate hairpin curves, and the narrowness of the unpaved road makes the effort even more difficult. The transports have to move maddeningly slowly, and the thick and tall bushes make it impossible to effectively see what is beyond the road, not only ahead, but also both uphill and downhill.

Once Podiás and his men realize that, they put together a working plan, but they need to approach the Amári leftists. The Messará Pain leftists provide that. And it is then that Uncle Kóstas is informed, by patriots from the Messará Plain, that the Amari area is targeted by Iráklio's EAM leaders, but no details are known. Capetan Petrakoyiórgis is apprised of the possibility of a potential situation developing in Amári and alerts Bourdelís.

The ELAS plan is to recruit local Eamítes (members of EAM) and have them attack the Asómatos station so that it appears the whole thing is done by locals only. This would force the Germans to send military transports to take back Asómatos. In doing so, the Germans had to go through Potamoús, where the difficult terrain and the anomalous topography will allow a small group of ELAS fighters to set a trap for them.

When the plan is put into action, local leftists, who haven't been apprised by Amári leaders of either the Red Cross negotiations or to the Potamoús plan, put together an amorphous ELAS group and, following ad hoc procedures, move to Asómatos. Taking over the place is child's play. Still, later, not only do they brag about it, but grossly exaggerate their actions. Bourdelís is alerted. With little effort, Bourdelís rescues the three Germans and orders the apparently disorganized ELAS group to leave. The three German technicians are taken by the Lítinas group.

Unbeknownst to Bourdelis and Lítinas, however, what appears to them disorganized and an ad hoc action, is part of the more significant Potamoús plan. Thus a group of ELAS men have already moved to Potamoús, while the Germans are sending forces to rescue their men in Asómatos, as the Iráklio EAM planners have hoped.

Meanwhile, the Red Cross-sponsored negotiations have just about been completed, and Dunbabin is instructed by the British Middle East Command in Egypt to hold in check the Cretan partisans. In case the Cretans break the negotiated agreement co-signed by the British, representing the Allies, the Cretans shouldn't expect to be helped by a British armed intervention.

Dunbabin is alerted about the Asómatos incident and sends word to Lítinas to advise the leftist Amariótes to avoid an altercation with the Germans. Lítinas does so, and the local leftists agree, but they break that agreement by sending a few men to Potamoús. When Dunbabin finds that out, he sends a hurried message that the truce has been agreed upon and will be signed, so the leftists shouldn't engage the German forces. Now the leftists listen and send one of their men to Potamoús with that message. He, however, doesn't make it all the way there, as the altercation has already started.

At Potamoús, a simple but ingenious trap has been set up for the Germans. Coming to one of the interior hairpin turns, the grade of the road is gentler than at the point the hairpin turn starts. There the elevation of the road changes, requiring that the troop transports slow even more in order to change gears. That point is the most vulnerable area for military transports going uphill, as they face fire from uphill, not only in front but also from the sides of the narrow ravine that forms the curve.

Apparently, the Germans, lulled by the truce negotiations, don't take the Asómatos action seriously. So they don't go on high alert. They send two troop transports and fail to alert them of any danger on their way to Asómatos. Thus, now, the ragtag ELAS members enter the main phase of their leaders' plan—an armed altercation with the Germans. A group of possibly around fifty, as someone reports, ELAS partisans have been manning the location of the trap at Potamoús. At the chosen hairpin curve location, the ELAS group attacks and destroys the two transports, killing most of the men and picking up a few prisoners.

The German commanders in Réthymno, for some reason (after all, negotiations have just been completed for a truce), still don't realize the difficulty of their situation and send four more transports, which are destroyed in the same manner. Because of the previous incident, however, the Germans are alert enough to take necessary precautions so most of them avoid captivity by using the thick vegetation, but the ELAS men take some more prisoners.

Now the Germans become serious.

They start shelling the area around Asómatos with artillery rounds. More than a dozen German military transports head toward Amári. But after reaching the tiny valley, their men leave the transports and begin moving up the hill on foot. Hundreds of soldiers methodically examine the ground at the sides of the road, as well as some distance on the uphill area, before the transports continue. It takes long hours, but they find no resistance, and eventually they arrive on the top of the hill, at the village of Apostólous.

Meanwhile, what has happened in Asómatos during that time is both serious and comical. The three Germans thank their liberators and agree to be with Lítinas and his group when they face the incoming German forces. The three German technicians consent to say that they have been taken prisoners by a group of men who don't seem to be from the area and that local partisans had freed them.

One of the EOK officials there takes the Germans to his village, with the ostensible reason of protecting the Germans from further attacks by ELAS to Asómatos. When the EOK men face the fact that the Potamoús altercation is going on and are surprised by the German artillery bombardment, they know that the area is under serious threat from the anger of the Germans. So, their anxiety and worries are intensified. Now they must re-examine and study their options.

They finally realize that, strategically, they must come face to face with the German officer leading the troops on their way to the Amári Valley, and they must have the three German technicians with them. So they ask the official who took the German technicians to his village to return them.

He, however, refuses to do so. He wants to keep them in his village and in his house. He expects the German forces to level the villages around Asómatos. So, having the freed Germans, he figures, would help him in saving himself, his family, and his village. Now the rest of the local EOK officials have to start negotiations with one of their own men for the return of the three Germans, a comedy fraught with potentially grave possibilities.

The small settlement of Fotiní stands next to the village of Apostólous. At that point the road begins to go downhill into the Amári Valley, and just a couple or three kilometers from there is Asómatos. Lítinas, with the local EOK officials, moves to Fotiní. With them are the three Germans of the Asómatos station, and Dr. Iákovos Stavroulákis, who carries the Red Cross emblem, as he is the Red Cross representative in the area.

The German officer in charge has an interpreter along, and Lítinas advises the officer in charge that the attackers are from outside our area. The three German technicians verify that the attackers of the Asómatos station didn't seem to be from Amári and that partisans from the area had freed them. By implication that means that the Potamoús attack has been done by the same ELAS group. The Germans calm somehow, but they say that a decision would be made about the fate of the area after the arrival of an officer, who is coming from Haniá.

Meantime, the brave Eamítes have disappeared. Instead of facing the incoming German troops for a real battle, they choose to take their captives and retreat on Mount Psilorítis, leaving the Amári villagers to fend for themselves. Reportedly, in those ambushes the Germans lost 26 men dead, and ELAS has taken 12 captives.

According to "carefully told whispers," the ELAS men take the captives to a place on Psilorítis, where it's convenient to hide dead bodies. They proceed then to execute the twelve prisoners, one at a time. Those brave Eamítes could have instead turned them over to Dunbabin's associated groups to be taken to Egypt as POWs.[25]

The killing of these captive soldiers, and the way it is done, brought us Cretans down to the same level as the Nazis. Yet, when the leftists come to power several years after the war, the city of Réthymno has named one of its streets in honor of the Potamoús altercation. One wonders how much research had been done by the then-political leaders of the city before doing that. But, most likely, this indicates again politics at work.

As I understood it then, information from their sources in the Iráklio prefecture has the leaders of EAM discussing the possibility that the Germans would aggressively react against the villages of the Amári Valley. In the end they decide to go ahead anyway, after one of the group reportedly stated, "Such a punishment in that area is deserved as they have for far too long protected the plutocrat English."

---

25 The book Το Αμάρι στις Φλόγες (*Amári Is Burning*), written by Μανόλις Παντινάκης (Manólis Pantinákis), appears to substantiate the "careful whispers." The author quotes one of those brave EAM fighters who, proudly, boasts that he killed a big SS man while another German soldier watched him do it—what a terribly sick boast!

Doctor Iákovos

A brave physician

In all this, there are a few local men who act with sanity in protecting the Amári Valley's villages and its people. Among them are Antónis Lítinas and the local EOK officials, and a few doctors, including Dr. Iákovos Stavroulákis. They are the protagonists of that day. I don't remember if I ever met Lítinas, but I do know Dr. Iákovos personally. He is the senior of the two doctors in our village.

As it happens, he had once visited the Asómatos station when one of the German technicians was ill. As the area's official representative of the International Red Cross and because he is familiar with the station, when the shelling of that area starts, he mounts his horse and goes there. He is among the first two doctors arriving at the scene and taking care of the injured from the shelling. I recollect that the other doctor is killed. Following that, he becomes involved with the efforts of Lítinas and his colleagues in trying to save Amári from the anger of the Germans. When the local EOK group decides that, strategically, it will be better to meet the Germans before reaching Asómatos than awaiting them in the station, he volunteers to accompany the EOK officials to Fotiní.

Dr. Iákovos holding the International Red Cross emblem, and the three German men of the Asómatos station face the incoming German military transports at Fotiní. The three technicians tell their story, about how they had been saved by local partisans from the ones who are not from Amári, and the anger of the German officer in charge subsides a bit. However, he tells the apprehensive members of the "welcome" committee that any discussions on this situation will have to be with an officer who is coming from Haniá.

When finally that officer from Haniá arrives in Asómatos, he is accompanied by another officer who speaks Greek. Both officers wear uniforms that don't indicate the branch of the army to which they belong, as well as no insignia for their ranks. As Dr. Iákovos reports, the behavior of those two officers isn't the behavior of angry German officers. They are serious and unsmiling, alright, but the usual Teutonic coldness is absent, and they seem to be acting in a conciliatory manner. This a mystery. "Maybe, General Müller isn't the top commandant of the island anymore," Dr. Iákovos thinks, "or even if he is, he finally has gotten the message that the war is just about over, and Nazi Germany is dead."

By the end of the long proceedings, it becomes apparent that the Haniá officer is aware that Dr. Iákovos is fluent in French, as he asks the doctor to stay in French. After the rest of the participants leave, Dr. Iákovos is ushered into a small room where the two German officers are.

During the ensuing conversation, it turns out that the officer in charge is a general, while the other officer is an SS colonel. The General tells Dr. Iákovos, "The colonel is well familiar with your village, doctor." In Dr. Iákovos' mind comes the SS midnight visit to our house.

Now, I'll move ahead by well over a year in order to include Dr. Iákovos' visit with the two German officers, as told in late summer of 1946 in French when Tom Dunbabin and Paddy Leigh Fermor visit us in Vyzári (Chapter 43). Dunbabin, Leigh Fermor, Dr. Iákovos, and the three Paradisanós brothers have a conversation after dinner. My mother and I are sitting with them.

At one point during that conversation, the Asómatos and Potamoús incidents comes up. The doctor is asked by Leigh Fermor to relay what happened during his visit with the German general in Asómatos. I am surprised, and apparently my father is too. It is the first time that we both have heard of that. Dr. Iákovos seems to hesitate, but he obliges.

"You are right, major, he is a general," the doctor admits. The doctor then tells his story, which goes something like this.

At the beginning, during their amicable conversation, they found out that both of them had attended the same French university, the general for only a few years—I believe two. So they spend considerable time talking and reminiscing about life in France, and especially life at a French university. Then they drifted into their family situations.

After those niceties, the general asks what the doctor knows about the ELAS group, which had invaded Asómatos and attacked their transports. If they weren't Amariótes, as he has been told, the general wants to know who they are and from where they had come. Dr. Iákovos affirms his information, but he doesn't think the general believes him. He then decides to go further by making the following points.

The people of Amári are mostly nationalist patriots, with a few mostly young men and naïve adults, who are leftist and therefore like Russia rather than the West. The technicians in Asómatos have been there for some time. If the Amariótes wanted them out, they could have done so any time during their tenure at that station. And if local leftists wanted to attack Asómatos, they didn't do it because they know how most of the Amariótes feel. If locals were part of the attack, it is because of ignorance and naiveté in following the men who came from other parts of Crete—most possibly from the Messará Plain of the Iráklio prefecture.

He completes his statement with, "I imagine you know that, General, as I feel that your intelligence service must have already briefed you on the situation around here."

At that point, the general smiles and says that the Asómatos technicians told him how Dr. Iákovos had helped one of them when he was ill. Then, the general asks the doctor if he knows the man who brought his partisans to free the three men from the leftists.

The doctor's answer is, "I had known him as a young man before the war because he is from Fourfourás, which is very close to Vyzári."

The doctor guesses, from the general's reaction, that the general already knows that.

The general stays silent for a few seconds and then asks the doctor to relay to Bourdelís his appreciation for saving the technicians. To this, the doctor replies, "I doubt that I will cross paths with him now, but if I ever do in the future, I will do as you requested." Then they shake hands, and the colonel escorts the doctor out.

Dr. Iákovos stops there and looks at my mother. Still looking at her he says, "Maria, the colonel didn't tell me what happened here, but he told me how deeply you impressed him."

Mother has no reaction besides a thin smile.

Colonel Dunbabin smiles at my mother and addresses the doctor.

"Γιατρέ (Doctor), I imagine you haven't as yet realized what you and the officials of EOK have done. When the German forces were bottled up in Haniá, I was able to have visits with their top officers. I found out the Gestapo planned to destroy about a dozen or so villages in the Amári Valley.

"The German command, because of the signed truce agreement, stopped the Gestapo from executing their plan. Instead, they chose to first investigate what had happened and then decide what to do. So, they sent your general, doctor."

"And that had been entirely different from the way the Germans had reacted other times," Leigh Fermor adds.

Dunbabin continues, "The bravery and the intelligent way by which the EOK officials handled the situation and your good luck that your general, Doctor, having attended the same French university as you, helped to persuade your general to recommend stopping the Gestapo from punishing the Amári Valley and, worse yet, break the truce agreement."

To which Leigh Fermor adds, "The people of the Amári Valley owe you and Antónis a lot, doctor."

Now, I'm returning back to the events of 1944.

Having walked from Sáta to Vyzári two days before the Asómatos and Potamoús debacles, I witness a few of the leftists in our village getting into a truck going to Asómatos. Later that evening, my father also had walked to Vyzári from the Perdíkis Metóhi, where a skeleton crew of Colonel Dunbabin's staff is staying. The colonel and Uncle Kóstas had not been around for more than two weeks, my father reports.

Because of the worsening situation, especially the shelling of Asómatos, men in or bordering the Amári Valley begin taking their families out of their villages. Most take their wives, children and older parents up on the mountains, while others move them to villages outside the Amári Valley. Since I mention to my father about some of our village's leftists going to Asomatos, my father begins to be concerned about our village's vulnerability. He walks to Fourfourás to find where Bourdelis is, but he fails to make contact. He notices, though, that many of the villagers have left Fourfourás. He is also told that families from other villages have also left their homes.

Coming back to Vyzári, he asks me to walk to a number of villages close to us and check out if their people have also done so. Nikolís Portálios, one of my friends, and I start walking early the next morning. We have spent the whole day visiting Petrohóri, Lambiótes, Amári, Opsygiá, Monastiráki, Vystagí, and Platánia.

They all appear abandoned, either partially or almost totally. Here and there we speak to one or two people who are still in their homes. Everyone seems concerned, but they have decided to take their chances. They are staying in their homes for various reasons—illness, old age, concern about their domestic animals. The ones who can move around say that they spend the nights outside their villages.

Coming back, my father and the few remaining villagers in Vyzári, even the families of the leftists, decide to move out the next morning. My father is among the last ones to take my mother and my siblings to the side of Mount Psiloritis, in an area between Fourfourás and Platánia.

Nikolís Portálios, his cousin Spyráki, Giórgis Koufákis, and I move up on Pýrgos Hill. We spend a few days there enjoying fruits, especially grapes and pears. For more substantive food, we descend to the village, which is now silent, and pick up chickens from any stable in which we could corner them more easily. We take the birds up on the hill, clean, and cook them, with skewers made from tree branches, over burning coals in open fire.

The Germans finally let the local EOK leaders know that they wouldn't punish the area. The EOK leaders, in turn, pass that information around, and the people begin returning to their villages.

Considerable German forces, armed vehicles, and equipment come and stay in Asómatos for the short balance of time till they follow the rest of the German forces to the Haniá area.

CHAPTER 39

The Nightmare Ends

Breathing again

As the Americans and British from the west and the Russians from the east continue moving toward Germany, the German garrison on Crete is abandoned by the Motherland. The soldiers find themselves trapped and alone. The fact that Germany is losing the war, however, has heightened their sense of safety, and the abduction of General Kreipe has hardened their will to fight to the end. But for what end? Yes, they still have the troop numbers, the arms and the heavy armaments to effectively defend themselves from the partisans and the general population, but for how long and for what purpose?

They can, of course, put down their arms and surrender to the Cretan partisans. But they don't trust them. Their leaders have such a picture of the Cretan mountain men as uncivilized, crazy, and wild beasts, and they know they are hated by the population. And the British are busy, so they are not going to send any forces to accept their surrender and protect them from the Cretans.

Their decision is to assert their authority even more than before by punishing the Cretans as brutally as before, while they are making plans for a long stay on the island. The circumstances force them to stay and wait until the end of the war, when the British will be able to come and take them as prisoners.

The Cretan nationalist partisans have suspected that, for safety reasons, the Germans must move all their forces to a single location. The most strategically logical place for that is in Hania, and Dunbabin verifies it. Hania is manageable in size and, as the political seat of the island and of the seat of the overall commandant of the German forces, it is already well-fortified.

The Germans choose an area around the city of Haniá and the neighboring Souda Bay, a large natural harbor, on the west part of Crete, and secretly begin moving arms, ammunition, and supplies there. It is a good plan, but moving the large number of men from the city of Iráklio and their bases in the Iráklio prefecture is the problem.

The highway from Iraklio to Haniá is a narrow road that passes through several villages, towns and the city of Réthymno. The toughest part of the route, which is also the longest, is the section from Iráklio to Réthymno. That section goes through the north side of Mount Psilorítis. It is a wild ride, up and down steep grades, in and out of deep ravines, with hundreds of hairpin curves. It would be difficult to defend a retreating force using that route. A defense could be undertaken but with large losses of men.

Because of that, even if the Germans had paid minimal attention to the partisans in previous years, they now have to consider them a serious threat. Their Gestapo informants report that the partisans plan to attack them during the withdrawal from their bases. And, indeed, the leaders of the partisans in the center part of the island had met in Pandanássa, a mountain village in Amári and close to the city of Réthymno.

Capetan Petrakoyiórgis and Colonel Dunbabin had called a meeting. Most of the leaders of EOK in the central part of the island are there. Dunbabin has with him Uncle Kóstas and Petrakoyiórgis and his top lieutenant, George Tzítzikas. Among the others are General Kelaidís and Papadoyiánnis.

But the partisans are aware that they lack both the men and the heavy arms to effectively stop the Germans from moving there. Dunbabin is worried. He wants to avoid a bloodbath so late in the war and so close to the end. So, he consults with the headquarters of the British Mideast Command. The International Red Cross intervenes. They propose negotiations, and that proposal is accepted by both sides. The German forces retreat to Haniá and the area around it. They are to wait there until British sea transports come to Souda Bay to take them as war prisoners.

Initially, the mountain Cretans feel that they have been robbed of a redress, from avenging the barbaric deportment of the Germans toward the island's population. In reality, however, they don't. The previously powerful and arrogant Huns are now enclosed in an area from which they cannot move. "They are like rats fallen in oil and hiding in a hole," my great-aunt Koronákena tells me.

And not only that. The time they spend there gives them time to reflect on what they have done, as each one sitting idly wonders what is happening in their city, neighborhood, and with their families back in Germany. And glancing beyond their area, they see a countryside of which they had been masters, but now it is free and beyond their reach. And then they will be wondering who would be their master and how that master treats their loved ones. And when they finally go back home, how will that master treat them?

"That's not enough," my Great Uncle Koronákis says, joining his wife. I imagine that feeling is so for most Cretans, especially the thousands who have lost one or more members of their family during the nasty occupation.

It is only when, finally, the Germans are taken off our island that we start breathing again normally, but the saliva in our mouths is still bitter.

PART FOUR

CONSEQUENCES

CHAPTER 40

Iráklio

Returning to school

When word comes that the negotiations have been completed and that the Germans are to withdraw to Haniá, Dunbabin and Uncle Kostas are already in Iráklio. A group of more than a half dozen men, including my father and me, is sent to Aghía Galéne—a fishing harbor village on the south shore of the island, some distance southwest of Sáta.

Aghía Galéne has a small harbor, and our mission is to wait for the British navy ships bringing personnel and supplies.

After a few days, however, that mission is canceled because of foul weather, and we are moved to Iráklio. My father and all others leave for Haniá. I'm taken to the British compound. I don't know the British officers there, but they behave like they already know me. And these new officers work for Dunbabin, the now official chief British diplomat on the island. The new men don't appear to be hardened soldiers like the ones coming during the occupation.

The city officials have made available to the Brits the multistory building I'm in. The British use the building for their offices and sleeping quarters (which includes me). The building is in one of the most pleasant parts of the city, facing the city's largest square. The municipal garden lies in the middle of that large square.

It has been several weeks before my father comes from Haniá. A few days later, my father tells me that he has visited with Petrákis, who has just returned from Egypt and is again taking over the reins of Koraís, the private school I had attended before the war. He and Petrákis, my father tells me, have made plans to get me back to school. A few days later, as my father is leaving for Haniá again, he tells me to go and see Petrákis.

This—going back to school—plan of my father's is a surprise. I'm so well-situated in the British compound and I feel so very comfortable being there that I hadn't thought to make any plans for anything else, including going back to school. When in 1940 the schools had closed because of the Italian invasion of Greece, I went to Vyzári. So I haven't gone to school since then, and it now is 1945. If, in all those years, I had continued going to school, I would be graduating from high school this coming June.

Apparently, when the Greek-Italian war started going in our favor, schools in Iráklio and the other cities reopened. So, I'm thinking that pupils in the cities who have continued going to school will be graduating in June, while I'll be in the second high school grade with classmates who could be four to five years my junior. On top of that, almost half of the current school year is already gone.

Now, thinking about all that, I have a serious problem with my father's school initiative. "How could I cope with school again after all these years away from it?" I wonder. Also, starting school after close to three months after it started is a big problem for me. I feel more concerned about my well-being now than I have had during the days and nights I'm walking the road between Vyzári to Sáta and back. Then, if a German squad is around the next blind bend of the road, it is only my life, but now I fear failure and shame. I'm frightened—totally!

And then, staying in the British "diplomatic" headquarters is extremely enjoyable. I listen to their reports about the Haniá situation and what is happening in the rest of the world, and a few times a day I take walks throughout the city with some of the agents. Even though I'm not in the army, I'm wearing a Greek military uniform. When people see me, most of then look at me as if they recognize me, and I always get a friendly and warm smile. I feel that I'm an important person. At times I go to the municipal garden and just sit somewhere and read newspapers or mystery and romantic novels.

Thus, avoiding seeing Petrákis is easy.

When my father returns from Haniá almost a month later, he isn't pleased; he is angry. It is the first time I have seen him looking at me with genuine disappointment. From the time I unexpectedly pass, at the end of my fourth grade the high school entrance examinations, to my hard and at times dangerous life and work in Sáta, to my service for the spy ring, I feel he looks at me with pride for my actions and the way I handle myself. He has never verbalized anything, but his eyes say what he is feeling. Now his eyes don't look at me in the same way.

My father's disappointment helps me to review what kind of a future I want. I definitely don't care to go back to Vyzári and work as a subsistence farmer. I don't remember ever having such thoughts, but even if I had, my Sáta experience has cured me from any such thought. Before the war, I dreamed of becoming a doctor or a civil engineer. Now, I review that possibility and I still like it. But to enter the university for such studies, I must have a high a school diploma!

"My father is right," I decide. Ever since 1940, when the Italians invaded Greece, I have had the freedom to pretty much act as I please. It has been a lifestyle which, at times, is dangerous, but it has been managed mostly by my own will. And, boy, how I have loved that freedom! But now it is 1945, and that freedom is no more—it is gone. My father's directive and my own decision to go back to school eliminate that way of life.

I sure don't like it, but I must accept it. And I do.

Now, I know, I have to see Petrákis.

A bit over a month before my eighteenth birthday, I walk to school. The school building has been partially bombed. Half of it lies in ruins, but there is enough room for the sparse pupils who are there now. It is easy to find the office. I stand facing the door a few moments before knocking—when I cross the threshold of that door I will have to shed the personal freedom I have had for almost five years. I raise my fist, but I hold it back for a few moments, and then I knock. Petrákis seems to be expecting me.

As I walk in, he looks up from his desk. He seems to recognize me and smiles—something that he hadn't done when he and his son were looking for a way to escape the Gestapo by going to Egypt. This time, however, he doesn't mention that experience, and I in turn keep quiet. Even though he has smiled, I know that he holds the keys for a serious part of my future. He welcomes me, compliments me on deciding to return to my studies, and attempts to assure me that I will be able to catch up with the rest of the pupils in my grade. But that scares me. "I'm not smart enough," I silently tell myself.

Petrákis tells me that the octatáxion (eight-year) high school, established by the dictator Metaxás, had been abolished and the old exatáxion (six-year) high school has been reinstated. In 1940, when schools had closed, I was thirteen and just starting the fourth grade of the octatáxion high school, which corresponds now to the second grade (sophomore year) in the regular six-year high school.

Now, sometime in late January or early February 1945, if I remember correctly, at the age of almost eighteen, instead of being a high school senior, I find myself re-enrolling into the high school sophomore grade again, and I think, "What a drag!" Petrákis must have read on my face my predicament.

To ease my pain, I think later, he tells me that he is sure I will be able to catch up with the pupils in my classes even though almost half of the school year is gone by—normally school years start in October and go through most of June. As he is talking, I suspect that he and my father have visited about my hesitation to go back to school.

And then he drops another bomb on me. "I have such faith in you," he continues, "that I'm sure you will not only catch up with the pupils in the second grade, but by June you will also be able to pass the exams for the third grade." Hearing that, I now know that Petrákis and my father have conspired to have me complete the work for two high school grades, both second and third, by the middle of June. I just don't remember my exact reaction to that in front of Petrákis, but I do remember that after leaving him, I'm running more scared than ever before. Two years of schooling in just less than six months! Now I'm doubly sure that I will fail and bring shame to my parents.

Petrákis has already put together the books used for both grades. They are tied together for each grade, and he hands them to me—they are heavy. Walking back to the compound, I realize that I won't have time anymore for going to the park, reading romantic novels, or walking around the city. I put the books on a free shelf at the British headquarters.

I start classes. And I'm right. I'm, by far, the oldest pupil there, and it shows in the manner the other pupils play, the way they look at me, and how much book material I don't know. I'm often, much too often, embarrassed and, continuously, a very unhappy student—but I stay. After a few weeks, I begin to do passable—just—work in mathematics, science, and history, but I'm in deep trouble in ancient Greek language and classic literature, and even deeper yet in Latin.

Petrákis seeks my father. His report to him is that I'm being helped by the teachers in all subjects, except Latin and in classical Greek literature. I have sensed that the classical Greek teacher doesn't like me; possibly, I think, because I wear a military uniform, which signals nationalistic political allegiance—at that time, politics is my least worry, but the fact is that I'm associated with people who aren't leftists. I don't vocalize that to my father, however, as I know I have huge difficulty in both subjects. Still, my father tells me, Petrákis feels that, even though I'm behind, I would make it in the classical Greek literature.

Petrákis is worried mostly about my Latin class. With my father's consent to foot the bill, Petrákis arranges to have the teacher of Latin tutoring me for the balance of the school year. My father pays the teacher with two cans of olive oil, which I deliver. I can see the pleasure on my elderly teacher's face when he sees the cans. Even though Crete produces plenty of olive oil, during the occupation and immediately after it, city families have a difficult time getting olive oil, if they have limited income or they don't have direct connections to the villages producing olive oil.

I don't know how well—or terribly—I have done in the subjects in which I have problems with, or for that matter in all the other subjects, in the final examinations for both grades. But coming back that fall, the fall of 1945, I find myself enrolled in the fourth high school grade.

For years, I'm wondering how Petrákis is able to get me through two grades in less than six months of schooling, but I feel indebted to him. I'm still far behind the pupils of my age who have been able to go to school during some of the war years, but Petrákis saved me two years of schooling—and somewhat has mitigated the embarrassment I'm continuously feeling of still going to high school past the age of eighteen and then twenty.

But I have gotten ahead of myself here. Suddenly, I have jumped several months ahead. So, now let's get back to my first few days in Koraís, sometime in the 1945 winter.

During the second full week I'm in school, all hell breaks loose at the center of the city. We hear rifle and automatic weapons being discharged. At first, I think that partisans are celebrating—back in the village, I had done that, by repeatedly discharging my submachine gun in the air when I found out that the Germans had withdrawn from Iráklio. When the shooting goes on for some time, I pay more attention. The tempo of the shootings resembles a battle more than a celebration.

When the teachers herd all of the pupils into the basement of the building, I am sure that it is a serious entanglement. As we hide in the basement, I become uneasy. During the occupation, danger was constantly around the corner for me, but I never had hid in a basement. Of course, we don't have basements in the villages, but still the basement doesn't seem to be safe.

The basement feels like a trap. It's like a grave, I think. The gunshots continue. Because I'd heard about the friction in Athens between the EAM partisans and the government forces, I surmise that the conflict here is between ELAS, the partisan army of EAM, and the republican nationalist partisan armies. I theorize that since Petrákis, as far as I know, follows the nationalist political persuasion in the city, the school might be a convenient target for the EAM partisans, in case they are winning. I decide that I don't want to be trapped in that basement.

I leave the basement over the teachers' objections. Because I'm older than the other students and I'm wearing a military uniform, the teachers appear reluctant to stop me. I know I will feel much more secure at the British delegation's headquarters, which is close to the school. I begin walking that way, staying close to the walls that line the narrow streets. When I come to the square, where the Brits' headquarters is located, I glance carefully around but I don't detect any movement. The gunfire on my right is still going on.

I wait for some time from my vantage point. The gunfire seems to be less intense. I again survey the square, the part of the streets leading to the square that I could see, as well the buildings I could see around the square. There is no sign of life, save the building of the British delegation, which has a machine gun manned on its roof. Petrakoyiórgis had sent a group of his men with that machine gun to defend the British headquarters, as I'm eventually advised by George Tzítzikas, the top lieutenant of Petrakoyiórgis.

After a while the gunfire has become sporadic. To reach the British headquarters building, I have to cross the width of the square or walk close to buildings around the square. I choose to go through the square. Meanwhile, the gunfire seems to be dying and then stops.

After all that noise, an eerie silence pervades the area. No motion, no noise coming from any direction. Indeed, the whole city lies silent. It is as if no one is left alive, except for me and the men above the British building. But even they appear to have been frozen in place. It gives me a funny feeling, as if I'm the only one alive in the city. A feeling of being in a vacuum takes over my body.

Having decided to take the direct route, I finally come out of my place of safety and begin walking fast but not running. Passing by the edge of the gardens, I fleetingly notice a body just inside the garden. I don't stop. The door of the building opens at the moment I reach it, and I run in.

The British in their building almost have an apoplexy when they see me appear and then take my time walking through the square. Stanley, a captain, opens the door. He appears relieved when I walk in. But he isn't kind at all when he chides me for showing such a "gross stupidity" (his words) in going out into the open, instead of walking very close to the building walls. I try to justify my action, but he doesn't care to listen— after a while, though, we become able to again converse amicably. "Who killed the man in the garden?" is my first question directed to the group. It is a surprise to them that there is a dead man there.

After some time, a Petrakoyiórgis partisan comes and visits with the men protecting the building. Two soldiers who man the gun and a few other well-armed men partisans also on the roof and the building but out of sight leave us. Before leaving, the partisan who takes away our protectors tells us that there has been an armed altercation between the nationalist and leftist partisans. They attempted to take over the city, he states, and Podiás and his men were thrown out of the city, but he refuses to say more.

Later, I find out that there is another version of the altercation. The reason, I'm told, for it is Podiás. According to that version, Podiás had taken to bed the very young virgin daughter of another chieftain. The girl's father and Podiás found themselves in the same place in the middle of the city, and somehow the altercation started. That version, however, doesn't fit in with the length of the altercation, the involvement of Podiás partisans, the dead man at the municipal gardens, the apparent serious concern of Capetán Petrakoyiórgis for the safety of the British delegation, and the dramatic banishment of Podiás and his partisans from the city.

During the long lull following the gun skirmish, some of us sit by the windows observing the square. It is quiet and empty for a long time, for hours. While we wait, Captain Stanley is asking questions from two operatives whom I don't know. The questions vary, but the visiting starts with the question about the apparently large number of partisans in the city. I have noticed that too, so I listen.

During the occupation, both the Badouvás and Petrakoyiórgis armies have been relatively small tactical collections, initially numbering dozens and then hundreds of men. When it becomes apparent that an agreement will be reached for the withdrawal of the German forces from the Iráklio prefecture and the city itself, the Petrakoyiórgis and Badouvas men start marching toward Iráklio. During that march toward the city, villagers who had a rifle hidden, pick it up and join the marchers. One of the operatives say that by the time Badouvás and Petrakoyiórgis reach the city, several hundred men follow each one of them. In any event, the city folks are properly impressed.

Petrakoyiórgis reaches Iráklio first. It is said also that the Germans had agreed to Dunbabin's request that they leave the city proper to Petrakoyiórgis, and so they do. Badouvas then takes the responsibility for the suburbs and the area adjacent to the city.

Another partisan comes to our building. Podiás, EAM's leader of ELAS, attempts to take over the city by a surprise attack on the nationalist forces. It is in vain, however, as it is an unequal fight, in both numbers and firepower. Podiás and his partisans are easily defeated, and Podiás and his surviving men leave the city and the area.

By this time, we notice a few men coming into the square. They look around, pick up the body I had seen, clean up the place, and leave. One of them seems to be a partisan, and we guess that the others must be city workers. Eventually, some partisans show up. Then a few people start appearing in the square—one, two, or three at a time. They start sort of timidly to begin with, and then a few more, followed by others. It is getting to be early evening.

We all are surprised to see more and more locals filter into the square. Some mingle around visiting, while others seem to take their usual early evening constitutional walk, strolling about the area the same as they have done every evening before. It's a slow and orderly walk around the square, then through Justice Street to the small square at the center of the city, and back.

As we have noticed other days, this is the time of the day that a good number of the people living in the core part of Iraklio use to take their evening social walk before dinner. Now, battle or no battle, they decide that they shouldn't waste a nice early evening.

The British agents are surprised. Just a few hours ago people were dying around here, and now these people are taking their usual late afternoon to early evening walk, as if nothing has happened. For the new Brits, this doesn't quite compute.

Captain Stanley, who speaks fluent Greek, has recently arrived on Crete. Like the other newcomers, he seems to be more of a diplomat than an army tough guy. During his very short time on the island, he has been serving as one of Dunbabin's assistants. He's itching to see what's going on, so he decides to go and mingle with the people. Two British agents who speak some Greek and I go along with him.

Knowing what happened just a few hours earlier in the place we are now walking, it feels kind of odd for me, yet not really strange. But for these Brits observing what seems to them to be an almost low festive behavior of the locals, it's a surrealistic, out of body, Kafkaesque experience. It just couldn't be real, they feel. It's strange for all of us, including me, but especially for the British fellows. It just doesn't fit in with what they feel the situation should be.

While still in the square, a young partisan approaches Stanley. The captain introduces him to us. Let's say his name is Sífis, as I don't remember it. Stanley later notes that Sífis is one of the newest "instant recruits" in the Petrakoyiórgis partisan army. He stays with us as we turn to walk toward the center of the city.

Soon after that, a partisan carrying a rifle on his shoulder walks briskly past us, after he has pushed me to get out of his way. Sífis, noticing that, remarks that he must be a Badouvas man as he had seen him the day before with a few of the Badouvás men he knows. About halfway to the center, two young ladies are walking toward the municipal garden. The pretty one knows Sífis, she signals him to join them, and, of course, he leaves us.

Nearing the center square, we notice that people have stopped walking. Making our way through, we find the alleged Badouvás partisan kneeling on the pavement in the middle of the street. He is holding the rifle as if he is going to use it and looking in a certain direction. Well over two hundred yards or more ahead, past the square, a man is on the flat roof of a multistory building—possibly three or four floors.

He is slowly inspecting the sides of the buildings across the street. He seems to be extra careful in examining them. I guess that he is looking for possible damage from the armed altercation. Walking toward the partisan, we see him lift his rifle and train it toward the man on that roof.

At first just a small number of people, and then almost all of the few dozen people around the man with the gun, begin shouting at the guy on the roof, telling him to get out of there. The man on the roof, however, either doesn't hear the shouts or, most likely, he doesn't understand that they are directed at him.

By that time, we are next to the partisan, and we stop a few steps ahead of him. The partisan takes the time to look around him. He shows surprise that the people are shouting for the man to get off the roof, then I see lines of frowning on his face that I interpret as anger. As the four of us stand there, we notice that the shouting has now made the partisan visibly uncomfortable. For no apparent reason, he moves his knee a bit on the pavement, and then again and again.

Finally, he takes his time sighting his target again. His target moves around, a bit faster now. All people around the partisan, including us move a bit away from him and start shouting. As I begin to move, we hear a click. He had pressed the trigger, but the cartridge refused to respond, and after a moment or two, the rifle comes down. I and the people close to us stop shouting, and everyone calms down. But no one moves. New people coming into the square don't advance, they just stay behind the ones already there or fill the sides of the square.

For all the people there, this partisan has become an object of high interest. Either because of the shouting or because he feels shamed by his misfired weapon, this partisan is now visibly upset. He seems to be confused. His hands are shaking as he awkwardly tries to pull from his rifle the misfired cartridge. He picks a new cartridge, but it falls on the pavement and he is now fishing for it—and he is angry again, as the shouting has started.

Now it's much louder than before, as a lot more people have joined us. With so many people around now, the whole city should have heard the shouting. A pandemonium of shouts rings out from what I think to be nearly 200 hundred people. People shout with all the loudness they could muster—their voices warning the man in the roof to take cover. Even though there is no synchronized warning in the shouts, the strength of so many voices carry much louder than before. The partisan, a villager by appearance, apparently about in his middle fifties or older, is really shaken up now. The trembling hand is worse, and cartridge after cartridge is falling on the pavement. He finally is able to put one in his rifle.

He raises his rifle again. All of us, even the newcomers start to shout even louder, and the people in front of him, including us, stop watching him, and turn around to look at the man on the roof.

At that moment the shouting stops, there is no one there!

Now, the partisan is really angry. He stands up, makes no effort to pick up his scattered cartridges. He looks contemptuously at all of us around him. At that moment he hates us all. He does a clumsy 180-degree turn, while looking at us around, with hate, I feel. I think about that look later, and I feel that if he had an automatic weapon, he might have been tempted to mow down all of us. But he doesn't have one, so he leaves angrily, with his rifle on his shoulder, his body erect and straight, his head up, and in a hurry.

Later, I wonder why all of the men around the partisan, including myself, had observed him instead of attacking him. I visit with Stanley about our failure to act. We come to the conclusion that the man is a partisan, and partisans are supposed to be the law enforcers in the city. "We could have shouted," Stanley says, "but we wouldn't even have thought of attacking him, as we couldn't have attacked a policeman in a similar situation."

At some point we turn back. Stanley remarks that the city has, in just few hours, done an excellent job of cleaning the area as there is no blood or other sign on the square and the streets leading to it of a battle—just the hurried repairs of the damage by stray bullets on the buildings.

Walking back to the large square, we notice that the kafenía (coffee shops) by the square are filling up just as they have done on the days before. Since dinner is served around ten in the evening, the walkers fill up the time between their walk and supper by coming to a kafenío and have one or two ouzos, a gazóza (local soft drink), or coffee. It is a time to visit with friends, talk politics, romance a lady, or just relax and meditate.

The captain invites us to take a table and have something. It is his treat. We all have ouzo. The conversation at the tables around us is on that morning's clash between the partisans. Some seem to feel comfortable that Podiás has been thrown out of the city, while a few others strongly disagree.

Much later, I find out that Podiás had been killed. Apparently, Podias moved to the Amári side of Mount Psilorítis, where he was attempting to recruit men to form a substantial group of fighters, with the apparent purpose of attacking the nationalist forces. Podiás and his followers were chased by villagers up on the mountain slopes of Psiloritis. He was found and executed—or murdered, depending on one's political color.

For some reason, the stories of both the battle in the center of Iráklio and Podiás' last hours had been explained in confusing different ways, depending on whom one was visiting with, as Giórgis Tzitzikas who had been in Iráklio at that time as the second in command of the Petrakoyiórgis army, and was a friend of Podiás, stated to me. Later, speculation is that since Podiás had been in Amári a few times, he must have been impressed by the fighting spirit of the Amariótes. Then, because of the easy way by which several Amariótes answer his call for the Potamoús entanglement, he apparently had felt that Amári was a good place to recruit fighters.

A few days after the altercation in Iráklio, my father and Uncle Kóstas come back from Haniá. Meanwhile, Papadoyiánnis had been installed, without any fanfare, as the governor of Eastern Crete—but only a few people noticed. His office is in the building housing the offices of the Prefect—the top civil officer of the prefecture. It's the same building from whose second floor veranda Dunbabin had spoken to the citizens of Iráklio, following the German withdrawal from the city.

The city officials, I'm told, are now placing Dunbabin's people in homes of wealthy citizens of Iráklio. During the occupation, those households had developed close friendly and social relationships with German officers. There are no criminal charges of collaboration against them. They are simply being punished for socially cozying up to German officers. Uncle Kóstas said that he, Uncle Yiánnis, and I are scheduled to be assigned to such a home. That punishment is mild, I'm told, and it is part of a number of other punishments inflicted upon those who showed what is considered unpatriotic behavior.

Uncle Yiánnis has come from Egypt. He looks good, and I'm so glad seeing him again. He had made it back to Crete, even though he had doubts when he came to Sáta to tell me that he was leaving for Egypt, about three years back. He is going to take my place at the British compound, so my father, who is leaving for Vyzári, takes me to stay, temporarily, at the home of a second cousin of his. Her name is Alýki, and she is from Ághios Ioánnis, married to a barber in Iráklio.

Her neighborhood is mostly blue-collar workers and low-echelon professionals and small storekeepers. The houses are modest, mostly one-story structures and attached to each other by common walls, with a little garden in a few of them. Here and there, I notice two-story houses with small courtyards, enclosed by high walls. Even though I stay with Alýki and her family for only a short few weeks, I have during that time one of the most unforgettable episodes of my young life.

CHAPTER 41

Days of Reckoning

Heroes and antiheroes

It is comical to watch the partisans, even the ones who hadn't ever spent a night up on the mountains, strut around in the city. Their leaders and their lieutenants move around the city as if they own it. Stories of their heroism and how they had fought the Germans increase by the day, and they become more and more dramatic.

Initially, the partisans are the absolute law in Iráklio. To a great degree, they control the life of the city, especially in passing judgment on people accused of collaborating with the Germans. Punishment is administered according to the judgment of the judging—who are the partisans. This is unfortunate, as some decisions are suspect in that they are based mostly on questionable motives and on only personal judgment.

Under the circumstances, however, such procedures can't be avoided as the police and the courts have been left in disarray by the Germans. It takes quite a while for the police and the justice system to start operating effectively. Besides that, no citizen dares to interfere with the partisans who are heroes in the eyes of the city people.

And, of course, the partisans are the only ones who have tucked under their belt the terrifying big knife, wear the intimidating sidearms, carry the threatening rifle, or have casually hanging from their shoulders those frightening-looking submachine guns. Even people who consider some punishments unduly cruel, if not barbaric, keep it to themselves.

When the partisans enter Iraklio they and the like-minded city citizens seek to punish people who had shown what their judges consider unpatriotic behavior during the occupation. The partisans especially zero in on women who are known to have been lovers of German officers, and on men and women who are known or suspected to be traitors.

They don't wait for the courts, for the regular legal procedures, for a civilized process to punish suspected traitors—that is, men and women who had become, or suspected to have become, informers for the Germans. The partisans act on their own in punishing them.

Their first and easiest victims had been women, and the retribution to them appears to be simple but vicious, at times barbaric. Besides the women known to have been lovers of German officers, the locals also turn over to the partisans women who have been working in German offices and projects, no matter the reason they had done so—even if a widow had done this because it had been the only way she is able to feed her children.

The punishing of those women becomes a sadistic orgy. If a woman is fingered by someone, the partisans apprehend her—and not gently. With no investigation or research, she is put in jail. The hair of all those women is cut, and their heads are shaved.

And this high-minded judgment and action includes all ages, young and old alike. There is no distinction in the perceived importance of their actions—actually no proof is demanded; just the accuser's information. At certain prescribed times, day after day, the women are paraded up and down through designated city streets. Bystanders swear at the women, taunt them with sexual remarks, spit at them, and throw objects at them.

In time, the police and the courts begin to regain their authority. Eventually, serious allegations about cooperation with the Germans that had resulted in the death or deportation to concentration work or death camps in Germany are brought to regular courts. But until then, the partisans, both left and right, have had a heyday. Reportedly, partisans had acted on their own, silencing people they considered to be traitors—quite often, on just the word of one person. Rumors surface that some men and women had gotten rid of their true or perceived enemies, and social or business antagonists.

Because of that unhealthy social climate, the leaders of the nationalist partisan groups move quickly to protect an easily targeted special group of men and especially women who, working for the Germans, have provided them information or other important services. A good number of young women had worked in German offices and installations in order to spy on the occupation forces. Some of Dunbabin's agents had even become lovers of important German officers.

The partisan leaders who entered Iráklio made sure that their forces would move fast to protect the women and men who had worked for them. Also, Advance Force 133 had advised Badouvas and Petrakoyiorgis to protect their undercover agents, too. In most cases, this protection is carried out successfully. In a few others, the leftists in Iráklio have gotten to the undercover agents a bit too quickly—it is tragic.

These protection efforts brought loud and insistent complaints from a few quarters, but especially from EAM. The leftists had come in the resistance effort much too late to appreciate what it had taken to spy on the Germans. Because of that, the leftists can't bring themselves to accept that all of these people have worked for the nationalist partisans or the spy ring. Their suspicion is that both the nationalist partisans and the British agents protect their friends. And that's simultaneously funny and sad.

A small number of women, however, who actually are guilty of collaborating with the Germans avoid severe punishment, even the prolonged public ridicule. Some partisan chieftains, mostly on the nationalist side, feel that the people of the island owe them more than gratitude for fighting the Germans—if that actually had happened. So, they protect some of the most beautiful young women who actually have been lovers of German officers. They take and hold them as their own lovers—a few even openly.

Over a year later, I observe such a couple. She is very young and one of the most beautiful young women I have seen. He is a minor nationalist chieftain, one of the most intolerant and feared partisans, even among his own comrades. And he is one of the ugliest men I have ever known. The young woman he chooses is more than thirty years his junior. He has her by his side every time he is out in public, strutting around, proud that he has such a trophy. Looking at her, however, it's readily apparent that she is afraid of him. She always has a sad face. I have never observed her revealing the faintest smile. As she is making any movement, she looks at him to see if he approves. I can't help but wonder if she, belatedly, might have preferred the punishment that the other women went through.

In other cases, I'm advised, young women who have worked for the resistance and have been protected by the partisans still suffer the contempt of the population, especially in their neighborhoods. I witness such a case during an unforgettable experience I have in Alýki's neighborhood.

Living in Alýki's house is a pleasant interlude for me. I like her, her husband, and their small children. Unlike the busy British building, I find the house and neighborhood quiet. I can study much better, something I need to do. The house is a small, two-level structure located on the south side of a quaint little neighborhood square, which has a few narrow streets leading in and out of it.

The streets around the square are like spokes of a wheel, connecting the square with other neighborhoods, the church of that area, and with the rest of the city. At a side of the square is the communal water faucet that accesses the city water supply for the neighborhood. The city water comes twice a week, according to my recollection, and runs for some time, I believe an hour. In Alýki's house, however, the city water comes in her small courtyard by extension of the water pipes. The courtyard has been enclosed by a rock-and-mortar wall, which must have been higher than twelve feet. A huge, thick wall-door opens to access the square from the courtyard. When I ask Alýki how come she has a private city water faucet, she avoids answering me by talking to me about the square.

"In the good old days, before the war," Alýki tells me, "the square had been used for the neighborhood's βενγγέρα (venggéra)." Βενγγέρα is a pleasant evening social gathering of the neighborhood women. "We all were friends then," she says with emphasis. "We would bring chairs or stools, sit for an hour or two knitting, mending, exchanging ideas for meals, talking about our children or just visiting." After short pause she continues, "We had good times those years," she closes, with a sigh.

Nearly all of the houses in the neighborhood, including Alýki's, are old. And so, too, are all the houses around the square, except one, which is the other two-story house. That two-story house is an oddity in the neighborhood. It's new and by far the largest and best-maintained house in the area, with a very high wall enclosing what appears to be a large courtyard. I ask, "Aunt Alýki, who lives there?" She seems to think for a few moments before saying, "An elderly widow lady who is a friend of mine."

"Is she rich?"

"No."

"How can she afford such a nice house?"

"It's a long story."

Besides telling me that the widow lives alone, Alýki mentions that the woman has a beautiful young daughter, Alýcia, who is a nurse and lives at the hospital. Alýki appears hesitant to say more, and I drop the questioning.

On the morning of my third or fourth Saturday at Alýki's, I hear the neighborhood women talking at the square, as they normally have done before during each "water day." They come, fill their buckets or other containers, and take the water to their homes. All of them make several such trips, as they fill their home water containers for the days the city water doesn't come.

On that morning, at some point, bedlam breaks loose in the square. After a while, my curiosity propels me to open the courtyard door. But I find that Alýki, using a deadbolt, has secured the courtyard's door.

"What is going on?' I ask.

"Neighborhood women are fighting," Alýki informs me.

"Why?"

"It is a long story."

"I want to see what is happening. May I please, Aunt Alýki?"

After a few pleas, she says, "All right, but be very careful and do not step outside."

I promise, and Alýki disengages the deadbolt and opens the door, just slightly ajar. Since the house is at a corner of the square, I have an unobstructed view of almost the whole square and no one appears to check on or cares about me, if they actually have seen me. I had never before seen women fighting other women. But here it is. Women fighting each other, and I am surprised by the ferocity of the fight. They viciously pull each other's hair; stronger women are ripping off their opponents' flimsy clothes, while some women are on the ground punching and biting each other. Some women with torn clothes and exposed breasts are fighting other women whose breasts are also exposed—they don't wear bras.

That's amazing. Alýki is busy, so she doesn't monitor me closely, and I open the door a just a little more. Two women appear, they look around and then they attack a smaller and a much younger woman who is filling her second bucket. As one woman holds the young woman, the other beats her and tears her clothes off. She spits at the face of the young woman and throws the girl's clothing under the running faucet. The young woman has only her panties on, and she is fighting back, but she is losing.

While the two women are laughing, they put the young girl's head under the faucet. At that point, an older, tall, and large woman arrives with two large buckets. The two laughing women don't notice the large woman until she grabs their hair and almost effortlessly tosses them on the ground. The large woman stays over them, and they don't appear to dare to move. Meanwhile, the rest of the fighting women take notice, and the fighting is tempered down. The presence of the big woman seems to defuse the situation.

Alýki notices that I had opened the door a bit more than she had done. She is angry now. She closes the door and engages the deadbolt.

Then, she asks me to follow her inside the house. After we sit down, I describe to her what I had seen. I admit that I'm dumbfounded and a bit frightened. If the women do this here, I wonder, how a fight among men will be in this neighborhood.

"Now, what terrible thing causes all this?" I ask Alýki.

"The reason for the fight is the problems war brings, even after there is no longer a war," Alýki answers, and then says, "This doesn't happen often, but when it does, it is a mess, a nasty bedlam." Alýki then takes the time to tell me the whole story. When Alýki and her husband moved there, as newlyweds, Alýcia's mother befriended Alýki, and they had become good friends. Alýcia's father had died in an accident at work, and her mother works as a cleaning lady for businesses and rich citizens to support her daughter.

While Alýcia was growing up to be a beautiful young lady, she worked in the hospital, and she was being trained as a nurse. When her training was completed, she was hired by the hospital, lived there, and began supporting her mother.

"Before the war, their house looked like most of the houses in their neighborhood, but it had been destroyed when the Italians bombed the city," Alýki continues with her story.

When the Germans came, they took over the hospital. In time, one of the German doctors and Alýcia became lovers. What follows is that the Germans had contractors build this beautiful house where the old one had been. In addition, the Germans had the city water extended inside the new courtyard.

Because her mother and Alýki are close friends, Alýsia has the Germans also extend the water pipes into Alýki's courtyard. "It was a surprise for us," Alýki says, "and we sure like it, but because of that, we have also attracted strong animosity from a few of our neighbors, so we stay put when a fight like this breaks out, and we make sure our door is well-locked."

All their neighbors had been wondering why Alýcia has such an influence with the Germans, when the parents of other young women who have German boyfriends don't get such benefits. Eventually, they find out that Alýcia's boyfriend is a general, who is in charge of all German medical services on Crete. The new house is now, by far, the best house not just in the square but in their neighborhood and even further, and it generates envy among its poor neighbors. When the Germans are around, no one dares to say anything or accost the girl or her mother. "Privately, almost all our neighbors," Alýki states, "are waiting for the day that Alýcia won't have the protection of the Germans."

"Now, I am puzzled, Aunt Alýki. I have seen the girl coming to the house, and she is beautiful, indeed. But I noticed that she still has her hair. Why, since the women who cooperated with the Germans, had their heads shaved by the partisans?"

"Apparently, Alýcia had some ties with the nationalist partisans, as well as the Allied intelligence service, some say," Alýki tells me. She continues by saying that her husband has heard downtown that she provided badly needed medicines and medical supplies to the partisans, and that her general is an Austrian. It appears that she helped the partisans with the consent of her lover. "They really must have been in love, those two. Her mother told me that when the general left, he told Alýcia that he will return for her."

The moment the Germans left, Alýcia was apprehended by a local leftist group, and another such group had taken over her mother's house. Soon, however, some of the Petrakoyiórgis men had marched into the hospital and freed her and two other nurses. After that, they had come to her mother's house and thrown out the locals who had taken it over. They then told the bystanders that Alýcia had helped them, and now, she and her mother are under their protection.

At that point I ask, "What does that have to do with the fight outside?"

"You cannot imagine the depth of the feelings of the people in the neighborhood," Alýki replies, "All of them had been waiting to see Alýcia punished and shamed, even executed. Instead, the partisans come, and she continues visiting her mother, walking with her head up and as sure of herself as she had been when she had an important German boyfriend. They all had been, and some continue to be, puzzled and suspicious.

"When the reason for that turn of events becomes known, the neighborhood splits. Before that, pretty much all had been against the girl. When they find out that she had given herself to the general to help the partisans, a good number of the neighbors change the hate to adoration, and that includes even a few of the leftists, but not the communists."

"Yes, but that doesn't explain the fight."

"Most men here are laborers. My husband and about two to three dozen others are skilled, or they run small shops, so they aren't laboring in menial work from one day to the next. The majority of our neighbors are leftists, with a number of them, especially the poorest ones, communists."

"So?"

"The communists and the rest of the members of EAM who didn't accept the information for the girl's behavior have come to believe that that explanation had been manufactured. Because of that, their hate for the girl has actually increased as they see her coming to visit her mother as sure of herself as when she had an important German lover. It seems to us that the communists are the ones who start those fights."

"I still don't understand the ferocity of their emotions."

"As I have said, the suffering the war brings doesn't stop when the war ends. When Alýcia comes to visit her mother, some women always accost her. They call her a whore, a Nazi-lover, traitor and so forth. Alýcia still walks among them with her head up, erect and with steady step." As Alýki continues, it appears that Alýcia's detractors become progressively more aggressive, pushing and hitting her, at which point the rest of the women come to defend her. This enrages the women whose husbands are communists and makes things worse, as former friends are now fighting each other.

The young woman who had her clothes torn off is Alýcia's closest friend. Her husband had been taken to a labor camp in Germany more than two years ago, and they haven't heard anything from him since. The powerful woman is the mother-in-law of Alýcia's friend. She isn't only powerful, but she also is a leftist, and not even the most hateful communist will touch her. Not only is her son in a German slave camp, but also her husband had been executed by the Germans.

"Since she is a leftist," I ask, "why do she and her daughter-in-law protect Alýcia?"

"They are among the leftists who have accepted the reason for Alýcia's entanglement with the German doctor."

"Why doesn't the girl ask for protection from her friends among the partisans?"

"A neighbor has told me, and my husband has heard it downtown as well, that such protection has been suggested to her by partisan leaders, but she had refused the offer, saying to them, 'I can take care of myself.' That's another reason some women here and the people who know her in the rest of the city are proud of her, and they are willing to fight for her."

That makes me think that Alýcia is a real Cretan woman—a brave, sure-footed, and self-assured lass.

"Why don't the men get involved and stop the fighting?"

"The men, I think, lack the needed bravado to get entangled with the women. But I also suspect that they enjoy hearing about what takes place from their women. The other thing is that if men had been involved, it can become much more dangerous—and both sides know that."

"What is the history behind all this?"

According to Alýki, before the war they all had been friends. They are working people, and almost all of them are Βενζελικοί (Venzelikí), members of the liberal party. They have had neighbors who are communists, but they hadn't been acting the way they do now. During the occupation, however, someone brought a few EAM men to their area, and people split.

"Now, we find out that our friends have come to consider us enemies, since we haven't bought the EAM propaganda, as they have done. Because of that, some animosity exists between neighbors. And it seems to flare up not only when the girl comes to visit her mother, but also at times when hateful communists attack supporters of the girl, as it appears that it had occurred today."

One day, going to Alýki's from school, Uncle Yiánnis is sitting outside the British headquarters building. He asks me to stop and have a gazoza at a near kafenío. The place is full. We are sitting at an outside table. I tell him about the women's fight. He simply remarks that it's easy to start a fight in politics. When a group of partisans goes by, we hear the lady in the next table saying to the man sitting with her, "From listening to Badouvás and his men, I don't understand how come there had been any Germans left to gather in Haniá."

Uncle Yiánnis looks at me and smiles. Just the Sunday before, he and I had been discussing the behavior, claims, and counterclaims by the Badouvas and Petrakoyiórgis partisans. At this point, it appears to us that, according to them, only the nationalist partisans are the heroes of the resistance. And the biggest heroes are the Petrakoyiórgis and Badouvás partisans.

CHAPTER 42

Heroes and Antiheroes

Being an unwelcome boarder

The following Saturday afternoon, Uncle Yiánnis comes to the house. He will take me for vólta and supper, he tells Alýki. A vólta consists of a leisurely walking and sightseeing interlude, while visiting. We do our vólta, but this time at the harbor and around the harbor, especially on its long breakwater arm, enjoying looking at the ships in the modern harbor, and then the fishing boats in the smaller old fishing harbor, which had been built by the Venetians when they were masters of Crete.

In the evening we stop at a fish tavérna (tavern). My uncle finds a corner table where we sit; he always goes for corner tables, especially in estiatória (restaurants) and tavérnas. He orders a bottle of retsína wine, and we start a leisurely dinner. I have fried marides (smelt), and he has barboúnia (red-mullet)—his choice is terrific but much more expensive than mine.

After we finish dinner, we both order galatoboúreko (a delicious custard-type dessert) and coffee. As we are eating the dessert, he tells me that "ήρωας" in the English language is "hero." After coming from Egypt, my uncle, here and there, introduces me to English words that he likes or to make a point. He always has a reason for doing that, so I wonder what he has in mind.

As if he has guessed my thoughts, he doesn't disappoint me. Looking at me he asks, "What do we mean when we call a person hero, Mihalákis?"

Even though I now know what hero means and I have used its corresponding Greek word freely, I never have stopped to ask myself what is really the meaning of it. I suspect my good uncle is playing games with me, and I'm lost for a few moments, to the delight of my uncle. I notice his faint smile and I decide to jump at an easy answer. "A hero is someone who has done an extraordinary act under very trying or dangerous circumstances that most of us don't dare or want to do."

"Then, what do you think an antihero is?"

That really surprises me, and now I realize that my introduction to "hero" is because my uncle wants to introduce the concept of "antihero." The question surprises me, as I have heard the word "hero" among the British but never "antihero." I have some vague idea about what it might mean, as the term "anti" comes from the Greek language and takes its meaning depending how one uses it in a sentence—it could mean "instead," "instead of," "in the place of," "opposite of," or "against." My uncle, I find out later, has picked up that concept in Egypt while mixing up with British officers. After some hurried thinking, I want to say someone who doesn't want, care, or is afraid to be a hero. Then I choose what I think is a safer answer.

"The person perceived to be devoid of the traditional heroic qualities." But my uncle isn't satisfied with that answer. So he proposes to look at the present situation in Iráklio. By this time, we have finished the dessert and the coffee. We want to stay longer, so we debate what to order next, and we settle on another bottle of wine.

We begin talking about what is going on in Iráklio with the new order of things and the claims and counterclaims of the various partisan bodies. We differ in some labeling of events and people, but before we leave, I have some idea about antiheroes.

When Uncle Yiánnis asks me to name some current heroes, I oblige: "Uncle Kóstas, Dunbabin, Leigh Fermor." Then I add Petrakoyiórgis,

Badouvás and their men, the ones who joined them early on and stayed with them for the duration.

"That's fine, Mihalákis, but I didn't hear your mother's name."

"My mother's name?"

"Yes, your mother. Why didn't you include her?"

"I love my mother, but why should I include her?" I ask myself, so I ask my uncle, "I thought we are talking about war?"

"It's partly my mistake, Mihalákis. The question should have been about the concept of heroism. Heroism isn't just a war phenomenon. It happens every day in most walks of life. Still, your mother showed her heroism before the war and in this war.

"She is a heroine—a female hero.

"Look at your mother, my nephew. Let me tell you why she is a heroine," and then he moves on. "Your father, my brother, has never appreciated her high intelligence and beauty. Instead, he has chased other women who are inferior to your mother in both looks and intelligence. And in that process, your father keeps you, your siblings and your mother, living below the standards your properties are able to sustain, while he has a good time in the cities. Your mother stays in, suffering in silence and producing five fine children, which she has raised single-handedly. At the same time, she is criticized by ignorant priests and the villagers for her religion. Still your mother stays with her children and your father. That's heroic, my nephew."

"I never thought of it that way, Uncle Yiánnis."

"Wait, Mihalákis. I'm not through yet.

"And in all this my brother, your father, pretends that he is a responsible and caring family man. He is an antihero.

"Then war comes. Your uncle and I become soldiers. We go to Albania, we fight and return, and in spite of your mother's religion, she welcomes us back and takes care of us. This, in spite of the criticism she receives from her Jehovah's siblings in Aghios Ioánnis about catering to soldiers who are instruments of the Devil.

"But that isn't all. The Germans come. I leave early for Egypt, but your uncle Kóstas becomes an important member of the British intelligence team. Your mother doesn't stop him and your father, who also had joined the spy group, from coming to your house, no matter that they are bringing Colonel Dunbabin, a big instrument of the Devil, according to her religion and to the anger of her Jehovah's siblings.

"Still, the most dangerous encounter she ever faced and the most heroic war act she performed had been when the SS visits you. She not only had saved you and your siblings, but she also had saved the husband she despised, as she had known where your father was. That's heroic, my nephew."

We sit for a while, without talking.

Then my uncle adds. "Think, Mihális, that the world is a theater, and that we all have a role to play in it. When we play roles which include qualities that other people possess, or actions we haven't done ourselves, we are antiheroes. Judging from that, your mother is a hero, and my brother is an antihero."

After all this talk about my father, Uncle Yiánnis understands that what we have discussed doesn't affect my relationship with my father, as I let him know that, from the time I was in elementary school, I had realized the pain my father's misadventures had been giving to my mother. And then my uncle continues.

"Listen, my nephew, heroism comes in many forms, in many walks of life, but in this war Vyzári has been full of antiheroes—young and not-so-young men who played the role of heroes but they never had done a heroic act. Your mother acted heroically all her life in Vyzári, but in this war she had been among the three genuine war heroes our village produced. The other two are Dr. Iákovos, and your uncle Kóstas."

Yiánnis stops for a while and then continues, "The raw fact is that no partisan army, left or right of the political spectrum, inflicted significant damage to the Germans. The various skirmishes with the Germans had done nothing to lessen the power of the Germans on the island. That includes the highly touted battle of Potamous that took place in order to promote EAM and its ideology. That's why the participants ran away rather than face the German anger, leaving the Amári Valley villages at the mercy of the angry Germans.

"The heroes, my nephew, in that event are Lítinas, Dr. Iákovos, and the other men who faced the angry German officers at Fotiní. The antiheroes are the men who played heroism by setting the trap and then running away in order to do the heroic act of murdering, in cold blood, their hapless prisoners, while leaving the Amári villages at the mercy of the angry Germans. These men played the role of heroes, but they are antiheroes."

My uncle continues.

"The ashes of the Kéndros villages are still warm, and hundreds of bodies of men are rotting in their graves. But that isn't because of an action of Badouvás or Petrakoyiórgis. It is because a man, who simply loves the excitement dangerous actions bring, decides to abduct a general, no matter what a misery it will bring to innocent folk of the island. If that action had a valid purpose in our war against the Germans, this man would be a hero. But in this case, no such valid purpose exists, so he played the role of hero, but he is an antihero."

My uncle moves to another vein of the war in Crete.

"Look, Mihalákis, at what has happened here. The only group that significantly hurt the German operations on the island is Advance Force 133 through the information they gathered and passed on to the British intelligence in Cairo. That information enabled the British to seriously cripple the Germans' ability to move troops and supplies in the eastern Mediterranean, especially between Crete and Libya, and thus eliminate the possibility of Crete being of much help to Rommel in Libya.

"Yet, Dunbabin and your uncle Kóstas don't parade around as the partisans do, and more bizarre yet, the leftists look at them as if they are the enemies. The leftists, who didn't do anything substantive against the Germans on Crete during the occupation until they are sure Nazi Germany is dying, are so vehemently critical of the ones who did the most, if not all.

"Who are the heroes, and who are the antiheroes, Mihalákis?"

Uncle Yiánnis doesn't stop there. He continues.

"The real heroes are the farmers and monks, in villages and monasteries, as Sáta, Aghios Ioánnis and Préveli, who know that they face certain death and destruction of their homes and monasteries for forming safe havens for the wandering Anzac soldiers and the villagers who are helping the Anzac to reach those safe havens. The real heroes are in villages such as Aghía Paraskeví and Apodoúlou who had helped hide the abducted General Kreipe, when hundreds of German soldiers were roaming the streets of their villages and their fields.

"The real heroes are the patriots who sheltered commando teams, stayed silent about the whereabouts of the intelligence headquarters, the young women who had become lovers of important German officers in order to collect sensitive information from the German hierarchy, and the men and women working in German installations passing information to the spy ring.

"The real heroes are the men who abandoned their homes and families, in order to serve in the partisan resistance armies up on the mountains of the island. And doing so at the beginning of occupation and not after it's obvious that Germany is going down in defeat. Those men fought the raids of the German armies and have suffered untold miseries from hunger, cold, and armies of body lice. They are the heroes."

My uncle would have continued, but the place is closing, and we have to leave.

One morning, about a week later, Uncle Yiánnis tells me to go to the British delegation after school. Both of my uncles are there. My father, I'm told, is chauffeuring new British officers around—I mentally translate "diplomats." A prewar Buick sedan, which had been used by German officers, is now used by the British big shots to travel between Iraklio and Haniá, through Réthymno and elsewhere on the island.

That evening my two uncles and I go to a restaurant for dinner. During dinner, Uncle Kóstas reports that the city officials have assigned the three of us to a household whose members had been friendly with the Germans. We are moving there on Sunday. When I ask how they could afford to take free boarders, Uncle Yiánnis tells me, that he understands that all those households are well-to-do.

The house we move to is owned by a family that is supposed to be affluent. The couple have two children—a daughter and a son. The father must be in his late fifties, while the good-looking mother is in her early forties, the gorgeous girl is in her late teens, and the boy is in his middle teens. Uncle Yiánnis also reports that according to the local group he is associated with, it appears that the friendship with the Germans had been with the two women of the house rather than with the father.

When we move in, I'm wondering how they would treat us. After all, we are three interlopers forced upon them. But the father accepts us warmly. The wife isn't as friendly, but she is perfectly correct in her behavior. The boy, Byron, and I become friends immediately. His sister can't help of showing her distaste for us, especially for my uncles. I catch her once in a while looking at them with apparent revulsion—"Well," I think, "she is right; they aren't robust and good-looking as her friends, the German officers." Once in a while, I feel that I see the same expression on her mother's face.

Even though their family is being punished for their association with German officers, the two young siblings mingle socially with the young of other affluent households in the city. In time, Byron begins taking me to their parties. Even though I'm older and the only one wearing a military uniform, I feel that I'm readily accepted by his friends, most especially by girls, and politely tolerated by their parents.

Observing how well her son and I are getting along, his mother proposes to my uncles that I move to the spare bed in her son's bedroom. They move a table and a chair to my small bedroom, and it becomes my private study room; and I basically lock myself there in studying. The pretty girl is aloof but almost pleasant with me, even smiling at times, but as long as we are there, she shows a rather cool and dismissive disinterest toward us.

She is barely tolerant of our presence. Most of her time is spent outside their home. She doesn't help her mother with the housework. Instead she is deeply involved in the local nationalist youth organization and apparently spends her time in their activities, and that gave me my very first brush with political opportunism.

The leftist youth organization in the city is much larger, more active, and much more creative than the nationalist youth organization, as her father reports one evening at dinner. A few days later, I overhear a conversation between the girl and her father. She refers to her father's statement about the leftist youth group. She has visited it, and indeed her father is right. Now, she is inclined to drop the nationalist group and switch to the leftist group. Her argument is that the leftist group will be more challenging to her intelligence and offers the opportunity to use her talents more creatively.

Her father, however, doesn't approve. He agrees with her that it will be more challenging and possibly more fun. Still, he tells her that she can't do it. He reminds her that because of her and her mother, along with their friends, cozying up and mingling with German officers, they are now in this situation of having us in their home and having lost a good number of their friends. Under the present circumstances, she has to keep the agreement they have, so she must stay with the nationalist group.

That bothers me. Why would her father demand that she stay with an organization that she doesn't like? But, of course, I know the reason. Among many of the city's citizens, the political Left is more popular than the political Right. But the management of the city and of the whole prefecture is in nationalist hands. And the nationalists have the power of passing judgment on people who worked for or socialized with the Germans.

Our addition to the household of our hosts has added a significant burden on the two women of the house, the daughter claims, even though I have never seen her helping her mother. To lessen the mother's burden, Uncle Kóstas proposes and Uncle Yiánnis agrees, to bring Antiópe to Iráklio and have her stay with us. Antiópe is their first cousin and a spinster. Our hosts don't object.

Antiópe does the laundry, takes over the kitchen, and cleans the house—she also plays nurse to me when I get the measles. Now, the house mistress likes the new arrangement and visibly becomes comfortable with us. It gives her the freedom of hobnobbing with the wives of their social friends who still associate with them, but the daughter is still unhappy with us.

Although, our stay there becomes almost pleasant, the annoyed glances of the girl and the rare but biting casual comments of the mistress of the house seem to indicate that we don't measure up to their German friends and their former social network, some of which have dropped them, probably because of our presence. I come to a point of starting to feel uncomfortable, if not guilty, for staying there.

It becomes serious enough for me that one day when Uncle Yiánnis and I are alone I visit with him about my feelings. My uncle tells me that he has felt the same way. Still, the three of us need a place to stay, and this is really very little repayment for the miserable life we had lived during the occupation, while our present hosts had fun and games with the German officers. He further stresses that the father is actually relieved that the only official punishment they have to face for cozying up to the Germans is to host the three of us. Besides, he adds, Antiópe does almost all of the housekeeping. From then on, I enjoy my stay there, and I no more feel as much guilt as before for being an unwelcome guest in that house.

A young classmate of mine, Pýndaros Dialynás, my junior by five years, lives in the largest house in our neighborhood. It is a grand house. I'm advised that Pýndaros' family is one of the oldest, richest and most important in the city. He also is the best student in my class. He notices my problem with classical Greek literature and invites me to study with him.

Pýndaros is an intelligent, studious, and properly friendly young lad. His parents were able to have him start school at a younger age than normal. His parents also decided that he would study medicine in Europe, if I remember correctly. Because of that, they have employed tutors for him from the time he is a toddler. Those tutors teach him foreign languages and additional material in the main subjects of his studies.

That young man is, pretty much, instrumental in my being able to pass, barely I imagine, two years of classical Greek literature in about five months.

CHAPTER 43

Extreme Justice

Lawlessness

Because of the pressure of my studies, my social life is just the rare party my young friend, Byron, takes me to, and nothing else. I also have given up my visits to the British headquarters. Antiópe brings my food to the table I'm studying at in my small study room. Besides my rare association with the young man, I haven't had any lengthy social contacts with the other members of the host family, except when once in a while and when both of my uncles are here and they ask me to stop studying and eat supper with them and the family.

Actually, as the weeks pass by, my contact with my uncles becomes more and more limited. Uncle Kóstas is with Dunbabin, most often in the Haniá area, and Uncle Yiánnis hobnobs during the day with people in the British compound and with friends he had made while working in Iráklio before the war. He spends most evenings with Dr. Yiamalákis and his group, which Uncle Kóstas also joins when in town and free. Dr. Yiamalákis is an old friend of theirs. And I'm going to school most of the day, and then I'm closed in my room studying until I go to bed. When we see each other now, it is mostly fleeting encounters.

In the process, I become almost oblivious to the happenings in the city, the island, the country, and the world. The only news I hear is from what my young classmates talk about, and even that is what their fathers bring to the evening family meal. Almost all of my classmates are from the city, and it is obvious that their families are affluent. Their fathers are reporting to their mothers, at the dinner table, the events of each day. Pýndaros, however, doesn't seem to know much about what is going on, or maybe he doesn't care repeating in school or to me whatever happens in his home—or, possibly, his parents don't discuss politics or news at dinnertime.

One day, Uncle Kóstas opens my study-room door. That surprises me, as my uncles, knowing how pressed I'm in my studies, don't bother me when they come home. This time, however, my uncle tells me that Dunbabin wants to see me. The next day, I take the time, after school, to go to the British building.

Dunbabin takes me by the hand to one of the offices and closes the door. After we sit down, he asks me about my schoolwork and the reason I have stopped my frequent visits to the British headquarters. My answer involves the pressure of my studies, and as it turns out, he isn't aware of the "two-year in five months" agreement between Petrákis and my father. Then he tells me the reason he has called for me.

"Mihális, the intelligence service and the Greek police have located the Gestapo officer who beat you up in Sáta, and then continued trying to apprehend you," he begins.

"Really? Already?"

"Yes. He isn't a German, Mihális. He's a Greek."

I'm surprised, so after few moments I say, "He fooled me then. He spoke German exactly as the German officers. If he is Greek, why was he a member of the Gestapo?"

"You know about the Fifth Column, don't you?"

"Yes. That's the people from other countries than Germany, who secretly have sympathized with the Nazi ideology and when the opportunity arises, they have supported Germany and Nazism."

"Your tormentor had been among the young Greeks who had studied in German universities before the war. He had been recruited by his Nazi professors and had been trained as a Nazi youth recruiter of foreign students. When he returned to Greece, he became an active member of the Fifth Column cell in the Athens area.

"When the Nazi armies arrived in Athens, he was inducted as an officer to the Gestapo. That had been an anomaly, as only Germans were normally recruited for the SS ranks."

"Since he is Greek, I imagine the colonel who questioned my mother in Vyzári is Greek too."

"No, he's German. We had traced him in the prewar staff of the German consulate in Thessaloníki and the German Embassy in Athens. But, I have also talked to him in Haniá, where they are now waiting to be evacuated."

"How have you found this man?"

"Another collaborator who had been questioned by the police in Athens had given his name. Both of them are from Piraeus, and that's where the police had picked him up. They brought him here, and he is in jail."

"That's amazing."

"As I have told you before, that man has personally executed all the men of several families. And in doing that, he forced their women and children to watch him do it. He also has sent many men and women to jail, and eventually these people have either been executed, as your Sáta friend George Tyrákis, or they and their families had been sent to concentration work camps in Germany."

"When had he been brought here?"

"Three weeks ago. Your uncle and I hadn't been here. I'm told that he has a good number of visitors."

"Why?"

"Family members and friends of his victims, at times their whole villages, have come to see him in jail."

"Why?"

"They have a chance to see him now as a captive and not as tormentor and executioner. Most want to make sure that he has seen them. I believe that they want him to see that they are alive and free; that they have a future, but he doesn't have one."

"How does he react to this?"

"He is apathetic. No emotion—just cold stares at the visitors. A couple of times he has allowed some anger to surface, according to our men who are monitoring his visitors."

"When has that happened?"

"When men, like you, who have been questioned and tortured but they had been able to survive without breaking down, have told him that they had known the answers to his questions but they had fooled him."

The Colonel looks at me for a few seconds before continuing.

"Mihális, I have arranged with the police for the two of us to go to jail after visiting hours."

"I don't want to see him."

"It will be just us and him, Mihalákis, and you can tell him that you too fooled him."

"Kýrie (Mister) Yiánnis (I still addressed him by is wartime name), I don't think I had fooled him."

"Why?"

"I had watched his face carefully while he had been working on me; it had been full of raw hate. When the major watching us had told him to stop counting before he is to shoot me, I see his disappointment that he hadn't been allowed to kill me.

"Then the major spoke to him again. I imagine he had asked him to tell me that they will take me with them, and I see a thin, mean smile surfacing on his face.

"Maybe the rest of the Gestapo officers had thought that I hadn't known the answers to his questions, but he suspected that I did—especially after my stumbling in the Souris question. And I also believe the major had suspected that too. And that had been the reason the major saved me then. Instead, he decided to take me to Míres."

"A possibly good analysis, Mihalákis. Let me hear it."

"I believe an informer had advised the Míres Gestapo station about Papadoyiánnis and his family being in Aghios Ioánnis. Papadoyiánnis is a huge target for them, so that operation is for catching him. Most likely, the same informer had also given the names of Giórgis, me, and the fellows in Vathiakó and Níthavris as persons of interest to them. Since they have to go all the way to Aghios Ioánnis and all of us are on their route, they plan to pick us up too or to just question us."

"Okay."

"But they made two mistakes. The first and basic mistake is to set their hopes too high. They seem to have decided to get more information than what they already have, and to get it though Giórgis and me first and then from others in Vathiakó and Níthavris.

"Their second mistake is that in planning their excursion they don't allow adequate time for their trip. They probably have figured that Giórgis, with a pregnant wife, and I, just a kid, will break down easily and give them what they want. So they fail to figure the possibility of spending a lot more time in Sáta than they had allotted in their plan. For some reason they left from Míres much later than they should have.

"When much more than an hour passes and I'm still standing up, time becomes a problem for the major. They still have Giórgis to work on and then move toward their other targets and finally arrive in Aghios Ioánnis before or at daybreak and grab Papadoyiánnis.

"When we crossed sights, I imagine the major had seen something that tells him that his second lieutenant wouldn't be successful in breaking me down. So instead of spending more time on me or allowing the lieutenant to kill me, the major decides to take me to their headquarters for a systematic questioning. The same scenario occurs with Giórgis, but because of the time they had spent on me, they don't spend as much time with him.

"When they found out that not only I had escaped but I also warned Papadoyiánnis, they must have become angry. Besides that, they now know for sure that I tried to fool them. And since I know where Papadoyiánnis is, I must also know a lot about the resistance and possibly the spy ring. And that's why the major continues to persist in trying to capture me."

"It is a good analysis, Mihális; both your uncle and I have suspected something like that."

I have gone through this, in my mind, several times, always wondering if my suspicions are correct. To hear that both Uncle Kóstas and Dunbabin have similar thoughts reassures my own curiosity. So, I thank him for allowing me to present my analysis to him. But Dunbabin still looks at me as like he expects more.

"Kýrie Yiánnis, to see him now would serve no purpose for me. You see, he and the major must have realized that I became aware that they knew that I tried to fool them, and that's why they attempted several times to apprehend me again. And since they fail every time, they must feel that I have been taking the necessary precautions—which hadn't been the case. I had, of course, stolen his chance to execute me, but he probably blames his commanding officer for that."

Dunbabin just sits there smiling while looking at me.

Eventually, the regular process of justice seems to have begun in the city, as the deep inebriation from the liberation yields to a sober present reality, and the influence and therefore the abuses of the partisans retreat. The police forces begin asserting their power, and special courts are formed with official and tested jurists.

It seems to me, however, that there still exists a basic subdued anarchy, even though it appears to be an orderly flow of events in the city. But one can simply guess what is going on from incidents which are public enough to be brought to the school by the pupils. Two of those incidents stayed in my mind—one because of its cruelty and gruesomeness, and the other one because I personally know the man on trial.

One case disturbs the parents of one of my fellow pupils because it is barbaric, as he quotes his parents saying. After he describes what he has heard, I agree with his parents. It is the trial of a mother and her two daughters. According to the case against them, the mother has been a paid Gestapo informant while her city daughters have been lovers of

German officers and had channeled to the Gestapo the information their mother has been gathering. The three women are accused of betraying several patriots from their village and the villages around their own, and most of their victims had been executed and their families had been sent to concentration work camps in Germany.

The courtroom in which the trial of the women is being held is on the upper floor of the courthouse. During one trial session, a group of armed former partisans walks in. This isn't unusual because all former partisans are still armed. What is unusual is how many of them there are. The two unarmed policemen standing by the door allow the partisans to enter. The armed men don't sit down. They calmly and steadily walk toward the judge's podium, close to which are the three women on trial. The women know the men, and sensing imminent danger, they instinctively move back. The three most powerful of the group grab the women by the hair. The women cry and ask for help, but it is in vain. No one from the audience moves, and the policemen stand motionless—they don't dare challenge the partisans.

The armed partisans have formed a shield around their three men and the women. Even if anyone in the room attempts to help the women, he can't do so. The suspicion is that no one wants to provide any help to them—as most likely all the people sitting in the courtroom have been relatives or friends of the victims of those women. The three men, moving without haste, taking their time leisurely, withdraw from their sheaths the large Cretan-made knives they have under their belts. By now it has become clear to the women what punishment awaits them. This makes them hysterical.

The men taking their time start with the youngest daughter and end with the mother. Without haste, one at a time, they cut the throat, sever the head of each woman. They move to the open window and throw the head down onto the street below. The street's name is Δικαιοσύνη Οδός—Justice Street. It is one of the busiest streets in the city. By the time they finish many of the people in the room have left in horror. Afterward, the blood-covered men calmly walk out of the building.

Even though it resembles the punishment of some traitors during the occupation, which didn't particularly bother me then, it bothers me now. Those years, I felt it had been necessary, or appeared so to us. But now there is no such enemy that demands such uncivilized punishments of traitors, while we have police and judicial systems operating, even though they are still shaken up by the occupation.

Both of my uncles had been gone out from the city. Uncle Kóstas in the Haniá area and Uncle Yiánnis had gone to Sáta for some problem with our properties there. I wanted to talk with them about this action of the partisans, especially with Uncle Yiánnis on the ethical aspects of the action of the partisans but also that, as it appears to me, there is no acknowledgement of cases like these in news media.

The city moves fast to clean up the courtroom and the street. The police institute security measures for the trials of accused collaborators. They forbid armed partisans, or anyone carrying a gun or a knife, from entering the court building, and no large groups of men may enter the courtrooms. They also place armed policemen in the hallways of the court building and at the doors of the courtrooms.

🔲　🔲　🔲

Several weeks later is the trial of my tormentor, the Greek Gestapo lieutenant. At that time, the measures set down are even stricter. While most long trials last just a few days, his trial is scheduled to possibly last a week or longer. The reason for all this is the volume of his case, the notoriety of his actions, and the number of people who have volunteered or are called upon to testify by the special prosecuting attorney. Since I had known the man, I asked questions later. This is what I found.

The fourth day of his trial, one of the scheduled witnesses is a young man. When this young man had been in his middle teens, the lieutenant had tied up his grandfather, his father and his three uncles, and had forced his mother, grandmother and aunts, as well as their children to watch, while he takes his time shooting the men in the head, one at a time.

The Cretan mountain villagers wear styvánia (knee-high boots), which are made to order by the village's bootmaker, as are the new boots of this young witness. Because of the witness' youth, the policeman who searches him fails to carefully check the young man's new boots and lets him enter.

For more than an hour before the trial is to start, groups of two and three men and women begin entering the courtroom. Some of them sit in the center of the room and others close to the judge's station, close to the area that the defendant is to stand. Even though they sit close together, the people coming in show no interest in one another, so the policemen at the door ignore them all. When the young man comes in, the room is almost full.

He heads to the center of the room and takes the only vacant chair among the people sitting in several full rows of chairs in front of and behind him. People continue coming in, and once all chairs are taken, the policemen make the mistake of calling other policemen to bring more chairs. And still there are several dozens of people waiting in other rooms and the hallways. The policemen are aware of the notoriety of the defendant and don't think that it is strange that they have such an extra large crowd wanting to attend the trial.

The young man is to testify close to noon, before the one o'clock lunch intermission. During the trial, as the attention of the people is on the proceedings, the young man, with some help from his friends and relatives around him, takes off one of his boots. His village's shoemaker had constructed the boots in such a way that a small new Cretan-made sharp knife could be hidden in it. The young man retrieves the knife and places it in the pocket of his pants, purposely padded for the knife.

As some of his friends who scouted the trial in the previous days, the young man notices that the accused wears flimsy jail clothes and each witness has the freedom to move from his stand closer to the defendant in order to make a point, without the judge objecting.

The young man is telling the judge what he had seen the day that the lieutenant executed his family's males, and he moves close to the lieutenant in order to indicate the way the lieutenant behaved then. He looks around; the policemen are outside the courtroom.

In quick motions he pulls the knife from his pocket, forcefully pushes it into the groin of the standing lieutenant and then with all the strength he could muster thrusts the knife upward.

The young man has spent days, with the help of his fellow villagers, practicing this action scene. He has mastered it so well that even the former Gestapo lieutenant is so surprised that he hadn't had time to react before the knife begins moving upward.

There is an involuntary gasp from people in the room who hadn't been privy to the plan for this action. That brings the policemen in the hallway to the door. The judge orders the policemen to arrest the young man. Dozens of men and women have already formed a thick human shield between the policemen and their bloodied young friend.

The crowd of men and women loitering in the hallways moves en masse, pushing the policemen between them and the people in the courtroom. The policemen don't expect this and they hesitate, while the judge, seeing what is happening, ceases urging them to apprehend the young man. With the police in the room giving up in apprehending the young man, he and his friends around him walk out. Hundreds of villagers continue escorting them to a half a dozen taxis waiting for them.

I'm not happy. I do feel that the lieutenant should be executed, but only after the trial. I think that staying in jail waiting for his execution would be his punishment, instead of the execution itself. I feel that sitting on the floor of his cell, day after day, waiting for the day and time of his execution, he might realize how his victims felt, like my friend Giórgis Tyrákis. The way he died is too sudden, too quick—much too easy for him. There is no time for him to deeply agonize about the future he will not have.

The government hasn't prosecuted the young man, Uncle Yiánnis tells me few months later.

CHAPTER 44

Spoils of War

An uneven landscape

After the British evacuated the Germans from the Haniá area, the Cretan operatives of the British intelligence service return to the lives and jobs they had before the war or they seek new horizons. Actually, most of them had done so, except a few attached to Dunbabin and Leigh Fermor.

A lot of rumors fly around about some Amariótes having profited from their association with the British spy ring. From the Paradisanós brothers, my father becomes the owner of the prewar Buick sedan, in which he drove around the British agents for a few months. The British had taken it over after the Germans abandoned it. He used that sedan to start a taxi operation. Yiánnis spent, off and on, three years in British military hospitals in Cairo, and is again working for a bank in Iráklio. My Uncle Kóstas is the operative who is best positioned to gain significant monetary or other rewards. Not only is he the wartime Greek government's representative to the management of Advance Force 133, but he also had placed the family's house in Sáta at the control of the spy ring, which used it as its headquarters for months. That's enough stable and secure time for Dunbabin to put together his operation in the eastern part of the island. During the time Dunbabin is in Sáta, Uncle Kóstas not only feeds and shelters the spy ring's operatives, but he is also exposed to a terrible danger not only to himself and our whole family, but also all the villagers of the hamlet.

Both Aristédis Paradisanós and Giórgis Tyrákis benefit from their British "experience." Aristédis is placed in a good position with Shell Oil Company-Greece and eventually reaches the company's vice presidency before retiring. Giórgis is moved to and well-placed in South Africa. And both of them tell me that Uncle Kóstas has a number of choices. He can have a choice job in Athens or elsewhere in Greece, with an international outfit, or he may be helped to move and be set in business in one of the countries of the British Commonwealth of Nations. In such a case, he could have moved to Australia, Canada, New Zealand, or South Africa. Even the United States is a possibility, as it happens for George Tzitzikas.

Uncle Kóstas, however, refuses to even consider any of those possibilities. He steadfastly sticks with the claim, "What I did, I did it for the Πατρίδα (Motherland), and not for personal gain." When Aristédis tells me that, I'm puzzled and then angry.

What has my uncle done? He has a chance to leave the drudgery and loneliness of Sáta and he refuses to do so. Is he afraid to undertake new challenges? Did he really believe that in the future "his country" will recognize his contributions?

Practically all Cretans who served the spy ring in some way or another had already received citations by mail for their services. The ones I had seen were written in Greek. During a visit to our house after the war, Dunbabin addresses me. "Mihális, my government would like for you to have these citations." With that he gives me a large envelope with two citations inside. And since they are in English, Dunbabin translates.

One of them has been signed by General Paget, Commander in Chief of the Middle East Allied Forces. It says that I "…faithfully served the Allied Cause and thereby contributed to the liberation of Europe." The other has been signed by Field Marshall Alexander, Supreme Allied Commander of the Mediterranean War Theatre. It says that it is given as "…a token of gratitude for and appreciation of the help given to the Sailors, Soldiers and Airmen of the British Commonwealth of Nations which enable them to escape from, or evade capture by the enemy."

Initially, the two citations please me. So, I treasure them. Years later and somewhat more sophisticated, unearthing them, I finally had given them a good look. I'm disappointed. Yes, disappointed—deeply disappointed. What they say is nice, but I have wondered how many thousands of men and women have received both or either one of those citations. If they really have been just for me, I reason, my name should have been part of the printed words. Instead, my name has been added, by hand, in the proper space left among the printed words.

When I begin writing this essay, however, I take the time to visit those two citations. Yes, they haven't been printed just for me. Still, whoever had given my name to the staffs of General Paget and Marshall Alexander must have thought enough of me to include my name in his list of people he considered deserving to be remembered.

After all, I did feed Anzac soldiers when I, myself, had been hungry and had sent them to safer areas, I served in a British spy ring, I was beaten and interrogated by the Gestapo, and after escaping, became an unending constant Gestapo target, avoiding traitors and capture by German patrols by working in our fields during the day and sleeping away from home on the ground in summers and winters and by luck. And all this between the ages of 14 and 17 (1941-44).

Now, I value the gesture of the British in including me in those lists of appreciation—albeit, I have mellowed, a lot, in my old age.

CHAPTER 45

The Last Meeting

And then they forgot about us

It must have been about a year and a half later, if not longer, when Dunbabin and Leigh Fermor, accompanied by my uncles, come to visit us in Vyzári. It's the first time that we have seen them after the war. It is a strange visit. I suspect it's the last time we will see them, and so I tell my father. It had been a visit for telling us, without verbalizing it, goodbye forever; and yes, we never have heard from them again after they left our house the third day of their visit.

But it also is to impress upon us that if we expect assistance from them now or in the future, we wouldn't get it. But the props for that are ridiculous. Both of them wear ill-fitting clothes of questionable quality and condition. Dunbabin's is much worse than Leigh Fermor's. A few holes and small tears in his clothes that haven't been mended. It seems to me that the tears and holes are purposely done. And that bothers me.

I see that he notices that I'm wondering about his appearance, and half-smiles. I do like that smile though—it always tells a story. This time, it tells me, "So you noticed! Did you guess why?" And, of course I have and it further bothers me—and he knows it. Why does he have to mess up his clothes in order to tell us that we shouldn't expect any material

344

or other assistance from him. I do feel offended, and I still feel that way, even after they leave.

The second day of their visit, Dr. Iákovos has dinner with us. After the meal, a conversation follows. It's centered about various things that happened during the occupation years, including the Asómatos and Potamoús episodes. It is that time the two men visit with Dr. Iákovos about his contribution to the safety of the Amári Valley villages and their villagers.

At some point in that conversation they switch to the present. Uncle Yiánnis asks why Churchill lost the recent British election. Leigh Fermor's answer is that the people chose to vote that way. Dunbabin, however, follows with the fact that the British economy has seriously suffered because it had been severely affected by the war expenses, as well as the reconstruction of the country—Britain had been almost broke.

That economic situation, Dunbabin states, has resulted in severe but necessary economic and monetary adjustments. Those adjustments had been unpopular with England's electorate. The people had suffered during the war years and now, after the war is over, they are told that they will continue suffering. So in the recent election the socialist Clement Atlee, leader of the Labor Party, defeats the conservatives under Churchill.

What surprises me is Paddy's simplistic answer to my uncle Yiánnis' question. Dunbabin's explanation goes along with my thought that they use their attire as props, in order to discourage their wartime villager friends from asking for any assistance that now is beyond their influence, power, and authority. Their attire, Dunbabin's massacred clothes, and Leigh Fermor's simplistic answer to Uncle Yiánnis question scandalize me. "After all those years they had spent with us," the thought occurs to me, "haven't these guys realized yet that we aren't morons?"

After a few weeks, however, Uncle Kóstas somewhat mitigates my resentment. He had accompanied the two men in some of their "goodbye" sessions in a few villages of the éparchies of Aghios Vasílis, Amári, and Mylopótamos. He had witnessed cases where villagers appear, or verbalize it later, to have plans to ask for help, but they either stop doing so, or accept the statement that the two of them don't have the funds or the power and influence to assist them.

That is the last time that I saw or had contact with Dunbabin, who died in his middle-forties from cancer. It is also the last time I see Leigh Fermor, but I have had one contact through the mail with him a few years back, before he died in his late nineties.

The War Ends
But Not the Suffering

Tragic years for Greece

66 "T he reason for the fight is the problems war brings, even after there is no longer a war," Alýki, the plain, grade school-educated wise housewife from Aghios Ioánnis tells me, when I ask why her neighbor women are so viciously fighting in the little square just outside her Iráklio courtyard.

And so suffer the Eastern European countries after World War II. Roosevelt and Churchill allow Stalin to saddle the people of those countries with the communist yoke, which they shake off only after Stalin's death, a few decades hence. Thanks to Churchill, the only Eastern European country avoiding that yoke is Greece.

But this doesn't sit well with the members of EAM. Blinded by pure ideology, its members had set their vision and hearts on an alignment with the Soviet Union. And, of course, if such political alignment had taken place, the leaders of EAM would have taken over the government of the country, and since EAM's leadership had been controlled by the communists, Greece would have fallen by default into a communist state.

At the end of World War II, the political left, as managed by the communists through EAM, has the upper hand on the mainland. It has the largest army of partisans, it has scored more points in fighting the

German occupiers than the political right has, and it has potent support from a cadre of intellectuals and a large section of the population, especially among the destitute poor masses in the cities. But that's not all. Churchill's decision to interfere in the internal politics of the country by supporting the return of King George is not acceptable to the largest part of the population, a development that internally strengthens EAM's political hand.

Still, when the Greek government returns to Athens from exile in Cairo during the occupation, it becomes obvious to EAM that it will be a fringe entity in the management of the country. Churchill sees the seriousness of the situation and spends Christmas 1945 in Greece, attempting to find a solution. He fails. The EAM leaders, having all those thousands of armed partisans of ELAS, decide to revolt. They don't want to wait until, through the democratic process, they could come to power.

ELAS, which controls much of the countryside on the mainland, is now rebranded as the Democratic Army of Greece and goes back to the mountains, but instead of fighting the Germans, they now are fighting their own brothers, the Greek army. All wars are ugly, but civil wars are the ugliest. And so it is with the civil war that follows in Greece. Atrocities are inflicted, and people in the middle suffer worse now than when the Germans occupied the country. It is an especially torturous time—a tragedy.

Meanwhile, England, operating under dire economic conditions at the end of the war, asks President Truman to help Greece. Truman, seeing the finger of Stalin in what is happening in Greece, decides to help the Greek government. Truman acts wisely. He fails to commit any military forces to fight along with the Greek army during the civil war. Instead of sending American troops to Greece, he sends General Van Fleet (who later succeeds General MacArthur in Asia), and a group of military advisers. They are to train the Greek army in fighting a guerrilla war.

Still, the civil war drags on for years. Finally, an unexpected event takes place. Marshal Josip Broz Tito, the communist dictator of Yugoslavia, breaks away from Stalin. Since Stalin had agreed for Greece to stay with the West, he has Tito doing his bidding in the Greek civil war.

Yugoslavia supports ELAS through supplies, weapons, and for attracting and training recruits (some of them women).

When Tito breaks away from Russia, his support to ELAS evaporates, and the Greek army defeats ELAS. The defeated partisans melt into the Soviet Union. Throughout the civil war, though, but especially in its closing months, the ELAS partisans had been abducting children, sending them to the Soviet Union countries to be raised as communists. As reported by Ron Soodalter in the journal Military History (Vol. 31, No. 6), by that time the ELAS has been driven out of the county, it has abducted as many as "30,000 children between 3 to 14 years old." Only when I have my own children, I realize the pain the parents of those children suffer.

During that civil war, mainland Greece suffers worse than it has under the Nazis occupation. Whole towns and villages are destroyed or are abandoned, over 100,000 people die, and over a million are uprooted and become homeless. In the late forties and the 1950s, thousands of those displaced persons (called DPs) come to America through special government legislation for helping families who had become homeless because of the civil war, as well as the German occupation.

Partly due of the British influence, but mostly because the mistake the EAM leaders had made by using ELAS to start a civil war, the conservatives have, pretty much, governed Greece after the war until the late 1960s. Meanwhile, EAM splits into two political parties, socialists and communists. The socialists become a strong political force, while the communists are a fringe political entity.

I have heard more than once from Cretan EAM members accusations against the nationalist republicans of Crete, indicating that the nationalists stole the chance of EAM to govern Greece. But this has happened on the mainland, but not on Crete, where EAM had put its efforts in proselytizing new members rather than supporting the resistance.

When in the late 1970s, the socialists have taken over the government for more than two decades, they drive Greece into a catastrophic financial mess.

Greece has significant, highly valuable, and compelling archeological sites, and it has been blessed with hundreds of beautiful and inviting islands. Those attract a healthy tourist trade for the country—reportedly, 20% of Greece's GDP comes from tourism. The country, however, has a limited number of other significant resources that could be tapped to provide adequate funding for the current and developing needs of its people. So whichever government is in power, it doesn't have much room to maneuver in enhancing current social programs or in establishing new ones. Also the suspected chronic corruption in those governments makes things worse.

But, also, during the early years the conservatives hadn't even shown, in earnest, a serious interest in the plight of the poor masses—the proletariat. It appears then to those masses and to many of the intellectuals that the conservatives don't care about the poor and destitute citizens of the country. So, eventually the socialists, under George Papandréou, take over the government. The army, still smarting from that terrible civil war, sees this as a communist ploy—the army officers equate socialists with the communists of EAM. In an ill-conceived and badly advised decision, the army takes over the government. But after a few years, during which they make some grave mistakes, democracy returns to Greece— the country that had invented democracy.

Papandréou has a son, Andréas. Andreas Papandréou is educated in the United States, has married an American girl and is raising his family in America, and has been teaching economics in prestigious American universities. In his travels to Greece he notices that the dissatisfaction with the conservatives runs deep and that a large segment of the population blames, judiciously so, the United States (CIA) for both the army revolt and the subsequent invasion of Cyprus by Turkey. He also sees that the call by some intellectuals and the leftists to throw out the American military bases (Greece is a member of NATO) in the country is gaining traction.

When just before 1980 his father, George, invites him to move to Greece and take over from him the leadership of the socialist party, he decides to do so, and moves his family to Athens. Campaigning,

Papandréou proves to be a gifted orator, if not an unprincipled demagogue. He preaches that the Devil in this world is the United States, says that he will close the American military bases in the country, and promises to institute a number of new social programs. With such promises, and often attacking the "arrogant" America, the socialists win the election. He then becomes prime minister and stays so for about two decades.

As he had said, he closes the American bases. The catch, however, is that he closes the high-profile bases but allows America to keep several, including one in Crete's Souda Bay. He begins establishing new projects and, as he has promised, new social programs and expanding old ones. Money isn't a problem, anymore. Most of the people are happy, so they keep re-electing him.

The availability of easy money also spurs an economic boom in the country. Business is great, wages are up, there is hardly any unemployment, universities spring up all over the country, construction is booming, for the first time foreign travel is affordable, cities grow, while the villages lose population. The poor villagers and many subsistence farmers move to the cities and tourist centers, where good jobs are available.

Papandreou's generously funded social programs and projects are apparently loosely supervised, if at all, making it nearly impossible to effectively police them. So the people learn how to cheat the governmental systems, and it appears, from what I'm told, that the government seems to tolerate that cheating anyway, as apparently a lot of bribery of officials is going on. A vivid indication of all that is what has been unearthed now about the colossal avoidance of paying income taxes by most people, including the professionals and businessmen.

An apropos example of loose social programs is the public retirement system. Instead of having a single governmental-sponsored and funded public retirement system, Papandréou establishes and funds several such public state-financed programs, for members of different professions and types of work. And here is where the widespread retirement cheating enters. From almost all the retirees I meet, and who are willing to talk, I find out that many retire in their fifties and that basically all retirees receive benefits from multiple retirement programs.

It appears that because of the number of public retirement programs, the foggy or lean qualifications for benefits from each of those programs, the ongoing bribing of officials, and the loose supervision and policing of all public programs, a retiree may qualify to receive benefits from several programs. And each one of those retirees receives benefits that are generous enough to make some comparable beneficiaries of the American Social Security program blush.

Besides the generous retirement programs, the government establishes a program called "Efápax." It wasn't clear to me how that program was funded. According to what I was told, at retirement, a person receives a single payment from that program. The amount of that single payment in such relatively short time surprises me. During one of my visits to Greece, a friend of mine in his fifties, who had just retired from a government job, tells me that he has used that single efápax payment to buy a nice condo apartment in Athens for his single daughter.

This loose and wasteful way of governing is also seen in the reportedly myriad projects that are funded by the government. Apparently, local socialist leaders and their parliament deputies establish projects, even if they aren't needed. This, of course, pleases most people in the locations the projects are established and maintained, and helps the local socialist deputy to get re-elected to the parliament.

An example of that is a project that has to do with the Potamoús skirmish. Apparently, the area's socialist deputies in the Parliament had the government fund a rather elaborate, by local standards, memorial structure at the location of the ELAS incident with the German troop transports. But they don't stop there.

The government bestows a government special income to EAM members who "claim" to have taken part in the Potamoús incident, and that income is above any other income they may receive from the government. The socialists in my own village receive that allotment. This, when there are reports questioning if any of them had even made it to the site of the altercation at the actual time the armed conflict took place.

This, after one of them has the honesty to publicly acknowledge that he hadn't made it all the way to Potamoús at the time of the altercation, but wouldn't say anything about the others. He got the allotment anyway. One wonders how many men from the dozens of villages around Potamoús had been receiving that allotment and, worse yet, how many similar cases had happened throughout the whole country. It appears that the only qualification for receiving that allotment is the word of the local socialist leader to his Parliament deputy.

The country's infrastructure begs for a lot of major projects that would potentially contribute to future development of the economy of Greece and provide new resources for the country. With the billions upon billions of euros that Papandreou and his successors were able to get, they could have done that—the limited number of projects that they had done proved to be too few for seriously advancing the economic base of the country. Instead, they chose to spend those billions mainly in social programs and pet projects so they may be re-elected over and over again. And according to rumors, the graft within the government, and among the rich and powerful, and even among the common folk, goes wild.

Money is plenty, but where is it coming from? Apparently the people are so inebriated by the good life that they don't care to ask. And Andreas and his successors don't volunteer any explanations. When at some point the conservatives take over the government, they act no better than the socialists. Instead of letting the people know from where all that money comes, they keep quiet, and spend money and have a good time just as the socialists do. Such silence and behavior make them conspirators with, and no better than, the socialists.

It is no surprise then, that the mores and the work ethic of the population are adversely and dramatically affected—especially among the young. People don't seem to work as hard as when I lived in Greece. Men and women from other Balkan countries and elsewhere do the menial jobs. Socially, in my trips there, I see a totally different country than the one I had left when I came to America for college studies.

Anyplace I go in Crete, Athens, or elsewhere in the country, coffee shops, restaurants, taverns, centers of entertainment, are full of men and women of all ages. Obviously most people, if not all, have money, and apparently much of it. "These people here," I tell myself, "must have it much better than the hardworking people in America, including me."

But, how do they do it?

I have been puzzled. I have been a college mathematics professor, college president, and a university chancellor in America, and I haven't been able to afford such a posh lifestyle as I generally see happening in Greece. My wife, a teacher, works, my children aren't allowed to spend long late evenings out of the house, don't eat out in restaurants or attend entertainment centers on their own, as I see young people, even of high school pupils, doing in Greece, and doing so habitually, I'm told. Instead, my children have part-time jobs, delivering newspapers in the very early morning or working in fast-food restaurants after school, while attending high school and college.

What I see now brings back the memories when I'm growing up on Crete. My parents have enough income to live fairly comfortably, but never had enough extra money to give it to me for spending it on restaurants, taverns, or entertainment centers.

What I see now in Greece is actually the life of the economic segment of our American society which includes the very well-to-do, the rich people—which doesn't include me and the great majority of the working Americans. My family lives comfortably, but we all work. Any extra funds my wife and I might have are kept for emergencies and an occasional trip to Greece.

Still there is some explanation to all that, as I have read a few months ago. The money supporting all those programs and projects and in turn contributing the good life of the people came from funds Papandreou and the rest of the Greek governments after him borrowed from international lending sources.

And that is fine, but what isn't fine is the size of the loans to fund unsustainable social programs, and that Papandréou and his successors don't tell the people where the money comes from and, more critical yet, that Greece is obligated to pay that money back, including accumulated interest.

The borrowing went unnoticed until the 2008 global financial crisis, when the young Giórgis Papandréou, the son of Andréas, had become prime minister. He finally takes the honest road and tells the European Union leaders what is financially happening in his country. All those programs, all those projects, all those funds financing a plush and easy life is borrowed money. The Greek governments, I'm told, are able to avoid the European fiscal rules by "cooking" their financial books.

The citizens of Greece have had all that fun from those huge amounts of money that had been borrowed for more than twenty-five years! It is something that both the socialist and the rest of the politicians hadn't had the decency to inform the people of Greece. So, now all hell breaks loose in the country. Suddenly, draconian financial austerity comes to the country in order to stop the waste and to begin repaying all those loans, something that unfortunately many of my fellow Greeks don't, or refuse to, understand.

Programs and jobs disappear, plush salaries and generous retirement benefits either cease to exist or are severely downsized. Stores are closed, companies go bankrupt, people commit suicide. Radical political groups, both on the extreme left and the extreme right make their ugly appearance. Some people go into the streets rioting and destroying things, making a bad situation even worse.

The hapless common and mostly innocent people become angry and scared. They don't know what has happened. Most of them don't understand or don't want to understand. Led by vocal opportunist leftist leaders and a few intellectuals, the people refuse to accept the real cause of their problems. Instead they blame specific governments, the stock market, the endemic corruption and graft in Greek governments, and an international conspiracy to destroy Greece.

The lenders, especially the IMF, the European Central Bank, and Germany haven't handled the situation well. Fearing that other Euro-zone countries might follow the example of Greece, they take measures that seem to be in punishing the Greek people in a manner that smells more as revenge than a well-thought-out plan in helping the country to regroup and eventually become able to pay back the lenders. But when it comes down to hard facts, however, the lenders don't trust Greece,

And, actually, it does appear to be a mission impossible project for such a little country, which doesn't have natural resources commensurable with the weight of that huge debt, and then saddled with the Sisyphean financial task of demanding repaying the debt, but not giving the country the means for becoming able to do so.

Still, the root of the financial illness of Greece goes back to the Greek-American professor of economics who had started the whole thing. That professor had realized that by hoodwinking the Greek people with easy borrowed money and lots of social programs, he can stay in power for a long time, and he had done so—for almost twenty years.

Now the pain is terrible, as my friends there tell me. It is a disheartening situation, and the only hope is that some accommodation might be reached that would lighten the load on the people.

You see, at the end of the day, it isn't the people's fault. Their leaders, mostly of the leftist political and social persuasion but also the conservatives, have failed them. The people may have not bothered asking questions, but it really is the blunder of their leaders. It is the malevolent behavior of their prime ministers, ministers, and parliament deputies in leading the people into a dream.

And that dream had been that all of a sudden Greece has become not just a rich country, but a very rich one.

Select World War II References

There is an immense number of books on the Second World War. Many of them include the involvement of Greece in that conflict. A few volumes, written mostly by European and Anzac writers, are devoted to extensive treatment of the involvement of Greece in that struggle, and fewer yet mention at much length of Crete.

Antill, Peter, *Crete 1941: Classic Battles—Germany's Lightning Airborne Assault*, University Park, IL, Osprey Publishing Ltd, 200

Beevor, Anthony, *Crete: The Battle and the Resistance,* Britain, John Murray, 1991

Blytas, George, *The First Victory: Greece in the Second World War*, River Vale, NJ, Cosmos Publishing, 2009

Buckley, Christopher, *Greece and Crete 1941*, London, HMSO, 1952

Churchill, Winston, *The Gathering Storm*, New York, Bantam Books, 1948

_____ *The Hinge of Fate*, New York, Bantam Books, 1974

_____ *Their Finest Hour*, New York, Bantam Books, 1974

_____ *Triumph and Tragedy*, New York, Bantam Books, 1953

Clark, Alan, *The Fall of Crete*, Efstathiadis Group, Athens, 2004

Cooper, Artemis, *Patrick Leigh Fermor*, New York, New York Review of Books, 2015

Damer, Sean & Frazer, Ian, *On the Run: Anzac Escape and Evasion in Enemy-occupied Crete*, Penguin, 2006

Dunbabin, Tom, Editor, *Tom J. Dunbabin, An Archaeologist at War*, Iraklio, Crete, Society of Cretan Historical Studies, 2015

Ever, Peter, *Forgotten Anzacs: The Campaign in Greece*, 1941, Scribe, 2008

Forty, George, *The Battle of Crete*, Hersham, 2001

Gilbert, Martin, *The Second World War: A Complete History*, New York, Holt Paperbacks, 1989

Hadjipateras, Costas & Faflios, Maria, *Crete 1941 Eyewitnessed*, Athens, Efseathiadis Group, 1989

Harokopos, G., *The Abduction of General Kreipe*, Iraklio, Crete, Kouvidis-Manouras, 2003

Hastings, Max, *Inferno, The World at War*, Vintage Books, New York 2012

_____ *Winston's War*, Vintage Books, New York, 2010

Higham, Robin, *Diary of a Disaster: British Aid to Greece 1940-41*, University of Kentucky 1986

Iatrides, John (editor), *Ambassador MacVeagh Reports: Greece 1933-1947*, Princeton University Press, 1980

Keegan, John, *The Second World War*, Penguin Group, New York, 1990

Kiriakopoulos, G., *Ten Days to Destiny: The Battle for Crete 1941*, Brookline, MA, Hellenic College Press, 1997

Kokonas, K., *The Cretan Resistance, 1941-45*, Iraklio, Crete, Manouras-Tintakis, Co, 2004

Lind, Lew, *Flowers of Rethymno: Escape from Crete*, Kangaroo Press, Kenthurst NSW, 1991

MacDonald, Callum, *The Lost Battle: Crete 1941*, Macmillan, 1993

Moss, Stanley W., *Ill Met by Moonlight*, Athens, Eftaciadis Group, 2007

Panayiotákis, George, *The Battle of Crete*, 8th Edition, Γιώργιος Παναγιωτάκης Iráklio, Crete, 2007

Papagos, General Alexander, *The Battle of Greece 1940-1941*, Athens, Alpha Editions, 1949

Pettifer, James, *The Greeks: The land and people since the war*, New York, Penguin, 1994

Psychoudakis, George, *The Cretan Runner: His story of the German occupation*, Murray, 1955

Reegan, John, *The Second World War*, New York, Penguin Books, 1990

Shores, Christopher, and Brian Cull with Nicola Malizia, *Air War: Yugoslavia, Greece and Crete*, Grub Street, 1987

Simpson, Tony, *Operation Mercury: The Battle of Crete 1941*, Holder and Stoughton, 1981

Spencer, John, *Battle of Crete*, Heineman, 1962

Stephanidis, Theodor, *Climax in Crete*, Faber and Faber, 1946

Stewart, Ian Mcd, *The Struggle for Crete: 20 May-1 June*, Oxford University Press, 1966

Thompson, Peter, *Anzac Fury: The Bloody Battle of Crete 1941*, William Heinemann, Australia, 2010

Wason, Elizabeth, *Miracle in Hellas: The Greeks Fight On*, Museum Press, 1943

Willingham, Matthew, *Perilous Commitments: The Battle for Greece and Crete, 1940-1941*, Spellmount, 2005

Θεοδωράκης, Ασκλήπιος, *Η Εθνική Αντίστασης Κρήτης 1941-1945*, Τυπογραφιον Κοστή Φραγκουλή, Ιράκλιον Κρήτης, 1971

Λίτινας, Αντώνης, *Χρέος στην Ιστορία*, Αθήνα, Εύα Λίτινα, 2005

Παντινάκης, Μανόλις, *Νικητές στο απόσπασμα-Το Αμάρι Στις Φλόγες, Ρέθυμνο*, Κρήτης Καλαιτζάκις Εκδοτικές Επιχειρήσεις, Α. Ε., 2008

Σταυρακάκης, Νικόλαος, *Η Πληροφόρηση στην Κατοχή*, Γραφικές Τέχνες Μιτρόπολις Α. Ε., 2008

Τζίτζικας, Γιώργης, *Ελευθερία και Δόξα, Ηράκλιον, Κρήτης*, Εταιρία Κρητικών Μελετών, 2011

Crete is a beautiful island, with picturesque villages tucked into the sides of majestic mountains and brilliant blue water lapping at its shorelines. The terrain that adds to its beauty, however, also makes life harder for those who live there.

I grew up in the village of Vyzári in the Amári Valley. *Photo by Terry Moyemont*

My father, Emmanuel, right, and my uncles (Kostás, left, and Yiánnis, center) were all involved in the Cretan resistance.

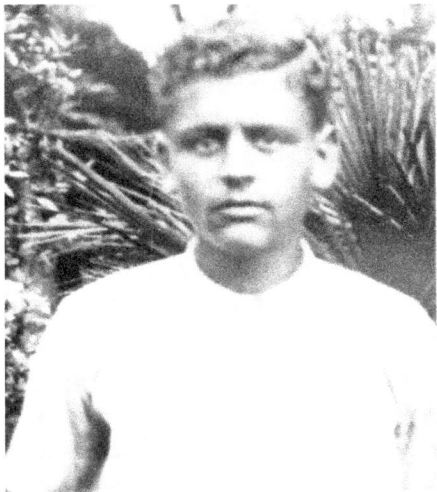

Michael Paradisanos: before the war, left, and after, right.

The Paradisanos family in 1947. In the back row: Ounania (sister), Michael, Titos (brother), Pelagia (sister); seated: Emmanuel (father) and Maria (mother); and kneeling, George (brother).

This image, taken in more recent years, shows my family's farmhouse in the hamlet of Sata. I was tortured by the Gestapo in the kitchen of this house. I escaped through the stables where the animals were kept, out the door of the stable area, shown on the left.

This is the second story of the Paradisanos family home in Vyzári. This home is where the SS barged in with the intent of taking my family away to a concentration camp, but my mother convinced them that we should be spared.

The bottom photo shows the road leading to the house; the red door leads to the courtyard inside.

CERTIFICATE OF SERVICE

This is to certify that PARADEISANOS Michael .... has during the period October 1942 to October 1944 .... faithfully and loyally served the allied Cause and thereby has contributed to the liberation of EUROPE

No. W/2
Date June 1945.

Commander-in-Chief

I received these certificates after the war from the British government.

Below: Michael Paradisanos as a Greek Air Force cadet.

This certificate is awarded to

Michael Emm. Paradesanos

as a token of gratitude for and appreciation of the help given to the Sailors, Soldiers and Airmen of the British Commonwealth of Nations, which enabled them to escape from, or evade capture by the enemy.

H.R. Alexander

Field-Marshal,
Supreme Allied Commander,
Mediterranean Theatre

1939-1945

The olive trees around Vyzári are ancient. Villagers are very proud of them.
Photo by Terry Moyemont.

I left Greece as a young man, but many parts of my life story are still there. Here, I am visiting the grave of my mother.

After leaving Greece, I made a good life for myself in the United States.

Seated around me in the photo below is my family: Clockwise from the top left, my son, George, daughter, Maria; my wife, Ann; and my son, Andrew.